HARD TIME

HARD TIME

A BRIT IN AMERICA'S TOUGHEST JAIL

SHAUN ATTWOOD

MAINSTREAM
PUBLISHING

EDINBURGH AND LONDON

First published in Great Britain in 2010 by
MAINSTREAM PUBLISHING COMPANY
(EDINBURGH) LTD
7 Albany Street
Edinburgh EH1 3UG

ISBN 9781845966515

This book is a work of non-fiction based on the life, experiences
and recollections of the author. In some cases, names of people, places,
dates, sequences or the detail of events have been changed to protect
the privacy of others. The author has stated to the publishers that,
except in such respects, not affecting the substantial accuracy
of the work, the contents of this book are true

A catalogue record for this book is available
from the British Library

Typeset in Champion and Concorde

Printed in Great Britain by
Clays Ltd, St Ives plc

3 5 7 9 10 8 6 4 2

*For my parents, sister, and all those who didn't
make it out of Sheriff Joe's jail alive.*

AUTHOR'S NOTE

Joe Arpaio of Maricopa County, Arizona, boasts he is 'America's toughest sheriff' and the most famous sheriff in the world. He feeds his inmates green baloney and dresses them in pink underwear. But he's also the most sued sheriff in America. His jail system is subject to investigation by human-rights organisations including Amnesty International and the American Civil Liberties Union because of medical negligence, violence and the extraordinary death rate. Victims include Charles Agster, a mentally disabled 33 year old arrested for loitering. He was hog-tied, jumped on, punched and strapped into a restraint chair, where he stopped breathing. And Brian Crenshaw, a partially blind shoplifter the guards pulverised for failing to produce his ID. He was found comatose with a broken neck, toes and severe internal injuries. The list goes on, earning Arpaio the nickname the 'Angel of Death'.

Most inmates housed in Arpaio's jail system are unsentenced. They're supposed to be presumed innocent until found guilty, yet the conditions in the jail system are far worse than those in the prison system where sentenced inmates are housed.

Despite all of the adverse publicity and investigations, Arpaio is still in charge. He's had two books published and starred in the TV shows *Smile . . . You're Under Arrest!* and *Inmate Idol*.

> 'It costs more to feed our police dogs than our inmates. The dogs never committed a crime and they're working for a living.'
>
> – Sheriff Joe Arpaio

7

1

....

16 May 2002

'Tempe Police Department! We have a warrant! Open the door!'

The stock quotes flickering on the computer screen lost all importance as I rushed to the peephole. It was blacked out. Boots thudded up the outdoor stairs to our Scottsdale apartment.

Bang, bang, bang, bang!

Wearing only boxer shorts, I ran to the bedroom. 'Claudia, wake up! It's the cops!'

'Tempe Police Department! Open the door!'

Claudia scrambled from the California king. 'What should we do?' she asked, anxiously fixing her pink pyjamas.

Bang, bang, bang, bang, bang, bang, bang!

'Open the door!'

We searched each other's faces.

'Better open it,' I said, but before I could make it to the door – *boom!* – it leapt off its hinges.

Big men in black fatigues and ballistic armour blitzed through the doorframe, aiming guns at us. Afraid of being shot, I froze. I gaped as they proceeded to convert my living room into a scene from a war movie.

'Tempe Police Department! Get on the fucking ground now!'

'Police! Police! On your bellies now!'

'Hands above your heads!'

'Don't fucking move!'

As I dropped to the floor they fell upon me. There was a beating in my chest as if I had more than one heart. Crushed by hands, elbows, knees and boots, I could barely breathe. Cold steel snapped around my wrists. I was hoisted like a puppet onto my feet. As they yanked Claudia up by the cuffs, she pinched her eyes shut; when she opened them, tears spilled out.

'I'm Detective Reid,' said a tall burly man with thick dark hair and an intimidating presence. 'English Shaun, you're a big name from the rave scene. I'm sure this raid will vindicate the charges.' There was a self-satisfied edge in his voice, as if he were savouring a moment of triumph.

Dazed by shock, I fumbled around for an appropriate response. 'There's nothing illegal in here.'

He smirked knowingly, then read my Miranda and consular rights.

I wanted to put my arms around Claudia to stop her trembling. 'Don't worry, love. Everything's going to be all right,' I said, trying to hide my fear.

'Don't fucking talk to her! You're going outside!' Detective Reid took a dirty T-shirt from the hamper and slapped it on my shoulder. 'Take this with you!'

'I'm exercising my right to remain silent, love!' I kept yelling as they pushed me out of the apartment.

'Shut the fuck up!' Detective Reid growled.

'We told you not to fucking talk to her!'

Yelling over each other, they shoved me down the stairs. They briefly removed my cuffs, so I could slip the T-shirt on.

'Stand by the stairs and keep fucking quiet!' Detective Reid left me guarded by a policeman.

The heat of the sun rising over the Sonoran Desert soon engulfed me. Detective Reid escorted Claudia out and locked her in the back of a white Crown Victoria. It sped off with my girlfriend of one and a half years. Police in state uniforms, federal uniforms and plain clothes swarmed our place. Every so often, Detective Reid and a short bespectacled lady conferred. Neighbours assembled, fascinated. Sweat trickled from my armpits and crotch. I thought about Claudia. What will they do to her? Will she be charged?

Detective Reid stomped down the stairs, scowling. 'Tell us where the drugs are, Attwood. It'll make things much easier for you in the long run. They in the safe?'

'In the safe's just a coin collection and stuff like my birth certificate.'

'You're full of shit, Attwood! Where's the key for the safe? You might as well just give the drugs up at this point.'

'The key's on my key chain, but it needs a combination as well as a key.'

'What drugs are in it?'

'None.'

'Don't play games with us, Attwood. Don't force me to call a locksmith.'

'I'm telling the truth.'

'We'll soon see about that.' He sounded desperate.

I was about to volunteer the combination, but he pulled out a cell phone and dialled a locksmith.

'Get in the back of that car over there,' said an officer in a dark-blue uniform, 40-something, with a rugged face. He looked the type who liked to take a detour on the way to the police station to teach certain criminals a lesson. New to manoeuvring in handcuffs, I fell sideways onto the back seat. I straightened myself up, and he threw a pair of jeans on my lap. He got in the car, mouthed a stick of gum and turned on 98 KUPD Arizona's Real Rock. He bobbed his head to the music as he drove. Every now and then he looked over his shoulder, and I saw two tiny distorted images of me on the lenses of his reflective aviator sunglasses.

'Looks like we're gonna be waiting outside,' he said, parking by Tempe police station.

Sealed in the Crown Victoria, I knew my life would never be the same after today. Cuffed, cramped, sweaty, I asked myself, *How did I end up here?*

Drugs start out fun at first. That's why I did them. I have no excuses. No sob story to tell. I was raised by good parents in a loving home. Other than having to eat Brussels sprouts with my Sunday dinner, I suffered no abuse as a child. I excelled at school, and dated some of the most popular girls at college. Even when my mother launched her shoes at me for teasing my sister or my father showed my girlfriends naked pictures of me scampering around as a baby, I never had an urge to run away from home. In fact, I enjoyed living there so much I chose the nearest university, Liverpool, so I wouldn't have to move out.

When raving began in England, I went to a club in Manchester called the Thunderdome and tried Ecstasy and speed for the first time. Before drugs, I didn't dance, but on Ecstasy and speed I couldn't stop dancing, smiling and hugging people I didn't know. Studying hard on the weekdays, I lived to rave every weekend with a friend from my hometown, Wild Man. Every time I took drugs, I told myself, *I can quit whenever I want. I can party and still function. I'll never get addicted.* I was oblivious to the downside.

Even though I sat some of my finals coming down off Ecstasy – with techno beeps and beats resounding in my brain – I scored a 2:1 with

11

honours. Wearing a mortarboard cap over my short Mohawk and a ceremonial robe with what looked like a superhero's cape, I strutted into the Philharmonic Hall in Liverpool. Receiving my BA in Business Studies, I – the first in my family to go to university – soaked up the admiration from my parents: an insurance salesman and teacher from a chemical-manufacturing town called Widnes.

Long before my graduation, I set my career sights on finance. I'd been following the stock market since age 14 and at 16 had doubled my grandmother's money in British Telecom. I read hundreds of books on the subject. Historical accounts of legendary stock-market operators made the hair on my arms stand up, made my spirit feel at one with the likes of Jesse 'the Boy Plunger' Livermore and promoted visions of my own future financial greatness. After university, I applied to be an investment analyst in London. Convinced I'd be hired on the spot because of my passion for the stock market, I ended up going through months of gruelling interviews. Each job rejection crushed my optimism.

Casting around for work elsewhere, I thought of my aunt Sue in America. She lived in Phoenix, Arizona, where she'd earned a reputation for being one of the toughest insurance adjusters in the Wild West. She said Phoenix was booming, and from previous visits during my teens – that involved her slightly altering the date of birth in my passport so I was allowed in bars, and her introducing me to people in said bars as Paul McCartney's nephew – I knew I could go a long way there with just my English accent. My parents supported my decision to emigrate, and in 1991 my mum waved me off from Runcorn train station. 'My whole life is in that case,' I told her. I was sad to leave but excited by the prospect of conquering Wall Street. I planned to make my first million within five years.

I touched down in Phoenix with a six-month traveller's visa and only student credit cards to survive on. My aunt Sue showed me how to obtain a Social Security number and forge an H-1B work visa using a simple printing set from an office-products store. 'It's fuck or be fucked in the business world,' she said, and coached me on what to say to prospective employers. I felt nervous bluffing about my status in the country at job interviews, but getting a job as a commission-only stockbroker was all the proof I needed that it paid to bend the rules.

For the first few months, I cold-called from 6 a.m. to 9 p.m. for no pay, walked to work and lived off cheese on toast and bananas. When my credit cards reached their limits, I feared I'd have to return to

England. Seeing I was getting nowhere, the three hardy stockbrokers I shared a table with schooled me in the art of poaching other brokers' clients. Things started to improve.

Stretching their advice beyond its intended limits, I had the idea to dumpster dive for sales leads. In Fashion Square Mall's busy parking lot, I sat in the car of another rookie stockbroker, reconnoitring the dumpster used by our rival, First American Biltmore Securities. When no one was looking, we hurried to the dumpster. Wearing rubber gloves and armed with box cutters, we extracted bags of garbage. Each bag we sliced open assaulted us with the odour of coffee-soaked paperwork and leftovers putrefying in the desert heat. We examined the contents, found nothing and threw back bag after bag. We almost gave up. But then we found a bag full of client account statements and correspondence. We took the bag back to my apartment and split the leads. Starting with those investors who'd written letters of complaint, we opened new accounts. One transferred his six-figure portfolio to me.

After breaking the record for the most new accounts opened, my commissions started to climb. Convinced the meaning of life was making money, I had become a piranha among the sharks.

Five years later, I was the top producer in the office, grossing more than $500,000 a year. I had my own secretary and cold callers. I won awards and was sent to luxury hotels and skiing in Colorado. But I'd worked so hard I had what the stockbrokers called BOBS: Burnt Out Broker Syndrome. To counter my stress, I returned to partying on the weekends like I'd done at university.

The first time I took Ecstasy in America was at the Silver Dollar Club, a gay bar frequented by ravers in Phoenix's run-down warehouse district. Hovering around the bar, I waited for my high to arrive. It took about 30 minutes for my knees to buckle. The sides of my head tingled as a warmth inched in. The warmth swept my face, the nape of my neck and travelled down my spine. My diaphragm and chest moved in harmony as my breathing slowed down. Each exhale released more tension. I grew hot but relaxed. Unable to stop smiling, I drifted over to the dance floor in the dark room. The dancers on a platform grabbed my arms and pulled me up. Inhibitions gone, I moved effortlessly to the music. I closed my eyes, and allowed the music to move me. I seemed to float. Rush after rush swept my body like electricity. *Are you ready?* came the vocals. *Jump everybody jump everybody jump . . .* I leapt from platform to platform. When DJ Sandra Collins played Prodigy's 'Charly', I thought I was at an English rave. I danced my way to the front of the main stage, dripping sweat, hands in the air, eyeballs rolling towards heaven, hugging the strangers around me, grinning at the throng of freaks below. I felt right at home.

Tired of being a worker ant, I salted money away into tech stocks, and retired from stockbroking in 1997. With no office to attend or boss to answer to, I thought I could make a living out of partying. It began with house parties that went on for days, fuelled by drugs I bought for all of my friends.

I still remember how nervous I felt the first time I bought 20 Ecstasy pills in America. I had to wait in my parked car outside an apartment in Tempe while a Native American high on Special K went inside with my $400. Stuck to the seat by my sweat, I was sure Drug Enforcement Administration (DEA) agents were about to jump out of nowhere with guns and surround my vehicle. I was also worried about the Native American running off with my money, or the people he was dealing with pulling a gun on him. Even when he returned with 20 Eurodollar Ecstasy pills, I drove away terrified, convinced I'd be pulled over at any moment. But when I didn't get robbed or caught or run into any of the other scenarios I'd seen in *Miami Vice*, I started to believe I could get away with anything.

I wanted my American friends to enjoy the rave atmosphere I'd experienced in England, so we mostly did Ecstasy. My number of friends increased fast – as it does when you're giving drugs away for free. When the local dealers could no longer supply my needs, I found out who their main supplier was in LA – a surfer gangster called Sol – and arranged to buy 500 hits from him.

Two carloads of us took the I-10 to a house in West Hollywood. Annoyingly, Sol wasn't home at the prearranged time. From a vantage point in a side street, we sat in our cars and waited. Our stress rising. Carrying a surfboard, Sol showed up hours later.

'I'll go in now,' I said to Wild Man. 'If I'm not back out in 15 minutes, come and rescue me.'

Wild Man was my raving partner from England who'd grown into a goliath. Two years younger than me, I'd looked out for him when he was just a chubby boy his older brother used to beat up. In his later teens, he honed his fighting skills on nightclub bouncers.

'I'd like to wrap that fucking surfboard around his head,' Wild Man said, 'seeing as he's kept us waiting this fucking long. Why don't I just kick his door down and take his shit?'

'That's not good business,' I said.

'It's not good business him keeping us waiting out here for two hours either!'

'If you rob him, then who're we going to go through?' Turning to Wild Man's cousin, Hammy, I said, 'Keep the Wild Man under control, would you?'

'That's like trying to keep a bull from a red rag,' Hammy said. 'I'll do me best.'

I got out, and knocked on Sol's door.

'Come in,' Sol said.

'I've been here a while.' Entering his house, not quite knowing what I was getting into, I feared someone might jump out and rob me.

'I lost track of time,' he said with an indifference that irked me right away. 'I have your 500 Mitsubishis. I'll be right back.' He went into another room. For a few seconds, I half expected him to reappear with a gun. But my heartbeat slowed down when he brought out a Ziploc bag with more pills than I'd ever seen.

'How much MDMA's in them?' I asked, feasting my eyes on the quantity.

'125 milligrams. From Holland. I don't sell any Made-in-America bunk. Besides, I'm told you can afford a lot more than 500. I'm sick of Arizona ravers coming to my house and buying a hundred here and there. I'd rather sell bulk to one person. It'd be safer for all of us. And the product will be good like these.'

'Can I taste one?' I asked.

'Taste one?' he said, surprised.

'I always chew them. They have a distinct taste,' I said, studying his face for hints of deceit.

'Want a chaser?'

'Water, please.'

I examined a pill. More dirty white than beige. Speckled like a bird's egg. A press of three diamonds: the Mitsubishi logo. Chewing it, I recognised the sharp chemical taste that precedes an Ecstasy high. 'It's a good pill. Here's seven gees. If you want me to buy more, I expect a much better price next time.'

The Ecstasy my friends and I didn't eat, we dealt to the local dealers in Arizona. Making money from the dealers enabled me to increase the scale of things. I began throwing raves for thousands of people, generating enough profits to give away hundreds of Ecstasy pills every weekend and to squander thousands on lavish after-parties and other drugs like Special K, GHB and speed. The more I fed my friends with drugs, the more they pampered me. I was buying popularity, especially with the glitter girls who spoiled me at the after-parties. Due to all of the drugs and sexual attention, I was beginning to lose touch with reality. But I was enjoying every second of it without thinking I'd ever get caught.

The ravers nicknamed me 'English Shaun' and 'The Bank of England'. I was considered one of the wealthiest people in Arizona's rave scene. So as not to get robbed in a scene that attracted all sorts, I formed my own security team. One of my security guards, G Dog – a tall Mexican-American with long hair and prison-tattooed arms – urged me to meet his brother, Raul. He said if Raul and his associates had my back, I wouldn't have too many problems in Arizona.

The grenade launcher on top of the biggest TV I'd ever seen belonged to Raul, who was watching a much smaller CCTV screen showing the comings and goings on the street crowded with lowriders outside his home in Tempe.

'This is the English guy I want you to meet,' G Dog said.

Raul, short and plump, tilted his head back. 'Wattup, homey,' he said without smiling.

'Pleased to meet you,' I said, shaking his hand. 'I like your TV.'

'Damn, you talk funny – like an accent – I guess you are from England, homey. Come through to the kitchen. Meet my homies.'

Raul introduced me to a gang of gargantuan Mexican Americans. Heavily tattooed, they were standing around a table laden with slabs of crystal meth, cocaine and various weighing scales. They eyed me suspiciously. The biggest swung a spoon with cocaine towards my face. 'Snort it.' There was danger in his wide and alert eyes.

Concerned, I looked to G Dog for help, but he just nodded back with a serious expression. G Dog hadn't told me these men were members of the New Mexican Mafia, the most powerful criminal organisation in Arizona at that time. Or that the man with the spoon was a hit man on a killing spree. Sensing the gravity of the situation, I rolled a hundred-dollar bill, pushed one nostril flat and snorted the cocaine through the other.

The man with the spoon nodded and shook my hand. But he didn't smile. None of them smiled.

'Shaun, let's go talk business,' Raul said, leading me into a bedroom. 'G Dog tells me you can get this Ecstasy shit and that it's all good.'

'I can get it,' I said, my throat gagging on the numbing aftertaste of the cocaine.

'None of us have ever done that shit. The only thing I do is smoke good weed – know what I'm saying? – hydro, kind bud. I'm having a party at the weekend, some women are coming over, and we wanna check your Ecstasy out.'

I was present when they all took Ecstasy for the first time. Not only did they smile, it reduced them to overgrown teddy bears who wouldn't stop hugging me. That's how I earned the protection of the New Mexican Mafia. It was a relationship that probably saved my life later on, when, for reasons of their own, they killed some rival gangsters who were about to shoot and rob me.

In the run up to the dot.com bubble, I started day trading and became a millionaire. Now I had enough money to really expand my operation. My new main supplier in LA, Mike Hotwheelz, was arrested, and the other LA suppliers like Sol couldn't fill my increasingly large orders, so I imported bulk Ecstasy. At the peak of things, I had my own rave clothing/music store and LSD chemist. I married one of the most glamorous glitter girls in the rave scene, Amy – a political science student at the University of Arizona who was also a bisexual topless dancer – at a chapel on the Las Vegas Strip, and we moved into a million-dollar mountainside home in Sin Vacas, Tucson. I had run-ins with gangsters such as Sammy the Bull Gravano, my main competitor.

The first time I discussed business with members of Sammy the Bull's crew, I brought along one of the notorious Rossetti Brothers, who also worked security for me. Outside the meeting place, Heart 5 in Tucson, I drank some GHB, which had the effect of making me fearless. I said to Rossetti, 'While I talk to Spaniard, make sure you're always somewhere you can pull your gun in case they try to kidnap me. I'm not going to start any shit, but who knows how big a crew he's with or what might happen.'

'No problem. If they try anything, I'll open up on the mother-fuckers.'

I was at the bar when a six and a half foot man with dark spiky hair and biceps as broad as my neck tapped me on the shoulder. 'I'm Mark, Spaniard's partner. He wants to see you in the VIP area.'

'OK, Mark.' I shook his hand and followed him.

'Glad you came, English Shaun,' said Spaniard, a well-groomed Hispanic. 'Mark, clear that sofa so we can all sit down.'

Mark yelled, 'You need to move, so we can sit down!' The people on the sofa jumped up.

To the side of us, Rossetti slipped into the VIP area.

As I sat down between the two of them, the GHB jolted my brain. It made me playful and crazy. Like my grandfather used to do to me, I squeezed their legs just above the knee and said, 'So what's this all about?'

They were taken aback for a few seconds, then Spaniard laughed, and said in a friendly voice, 'Look, we know you're doing your own thing. You've got a lotta people working for you. As do we. It would be best if we worked together rather than be enemies.'

'What're you proposing?' There are not many things in the world more reckless than an Englishman on GHB, yet I could always negotiate business shrewdly no matter how high I was.

'We're getting a lotta pills, and we figure we can give you a better price than what you're paying.'

'You don't know what I'm paying. I'm familiar with your pills, and I don't think the quality is there. I'm getting European pills. None of the coloured pills you guys are getting.'

'Who the fuck do you think you are, talking shit about our pills?' Mark yelled.

Because of the GHB, Mark didn't scare me. I viewed him as a monster but a funny one with a little brain.

'Hey, Mark, calm down,' Spaniard said.

'Do you have any idea who Jimmy Moran is?' Mark said, still fuming.

'No,' I said.

'Sammy the Bull,' Mark said. 'That's who we work for. One call to him and we can have you taken out to the desert.'

I was aware of Sammy the Bull from the news. He'd been a hit man for the Gambino Crime Family run by John Gotti, aka 'the Teflon Don'. Later on, he became an FBI informant, confessed to killing 19 people, and helped the Feds put the Teflon Don away for life. Still, looking at those two in their shiny animal-print polyester shirts, I assumed they didn't have as much power in Arizona as my associates in the New Mexican Mafia. I glanced at Rossetti. The look on his face said, *Should I shoot that lunkhead or what?*

Almost imperceptibly, I shook my head at Rossetti.

'There's no need to say all that,' Spaniard said. 'Forgive Mark, Shaun. He gets upset real easy. He's a bit of a hothead.'

'I have no problems with you guys. But I really don't care who you work for. You just moved in. Over the years, I've made friends with a lot of locals,' I said, playing it like a gangster.

'I hear you,' Spaniard said, implying he knew of my connections. 'But what if we can get you a better price on pills, would you be interested?'

'I appreciate the offer, guys, but no thanks. And here's why: before you guys moved into Ecstasy, the police pretty much ignored us. Now your runners are going around bragging they're the biggest Ecstasy barons in the world. That's brought considerable heat to the scene. And I'm not saying this to put you guys down but to give you a heads-up on what's happening. Every weekend at the raves, we've got undercover cops and vehicles hanging around. We've got undercover vehicles taping who's going in and out of the raves and driving through the parking lots taping licence plates. It's no coincidence that the police moved in shortly after you guys. It's not each other's crews we need to beware of, it's the cops.'

'What about your security team?' Spaniard asked.

'What about it?' I asked.

'Will our runners have problems with your security guys jacking their pills?'

'I don't want to start a war with you guys. If my security grab someone and we find out they're part of your crew, we'll let them go. Ecstasy's so hard to get and the demand so high, there's enough of a market for us to coexist. But if I tell my security not to jack your runners, I don't expect any problems from you guys for my runners in the Scottsdale scene.'

'Sounds like a good agreement,' Spaniard said, and shook my hand.

Years later, when I became friends with Sammy the Bull's son, Gerard Gravano, he said he'd headed a crew dispatched to kidnap me from The Crowbar in Phoenix. Wild Man and his girlfriend had fought that night, so we had left the club in a hurry. That's why the Bull's crew just missed us.

The meltdown of my business interests came on fast. The NASDAQ, where I'd invested most of my money, crashed in the latter half of 2000. Some of my smugglers were arrested at airports in America and Europe. Most of my crew were doing so many drugs they were growing paranoid and scheming against each other – my top salesman tried to rob my LSD chemist, resulting in a shootout that made headline news. I could no longer afford my mountainside home and the $20,000-plus a month I was paying in bills for that home and multiple cars and apartments. My wife, Amy, was arrested in a grocery store, high on drugs, walking around barefoot, babbling to herself, with shotgun shells in her handbag. Later on, she bought a one-way ticket to Egypt to commit suicide. She ended up overdosing on prescription pills and slitting her wrists in her hotel room, where she was rescued by staff. With us both too messed up to sustain our relationship, it fell apart – like everything else in our lives.

Drugs had scrambled my mind. I reacted to the disasters by trying to numb myself with even more drugs, accelerating my own downfall. Through bad choices, I lost almost everything. All of the fun, glitz and glamour were gone. I was no longer swanning into raves with my entourage, getting hugged and thanked left and right by partiers high on my Ecstasy. I was hiding out in an apartment in Tucson, fearing the police or rival criminals were coming to get me, having to take Xanax to fall asleep. The meltdown put an end to my large-scale criminal activity, but I feared the name I'd made over the years as English Shaun would eventually lead to my arrest.

Towards the end of it all, an attorney I used whenever one of my crew was arrested called me into his office.

'How're you doing, Ray?' I asked, shaking his hand.

'I'm good. It's you I'm worried about.'

'Why?' I asked, growing alarmed.

'My sources at the DEA tell me it's time for you to get the hell out of Arizona.'

'Since the stock market crashed, I've not been doing much anyway.'

'You shouldn't be doing anything at all! You've had a good run. Now's the time to get out. You're an intelligent guy. You've got your whole life ahead of you. If you continue on, there's only one way this is going to end.'

I knew he was right, but I still couldn't stop my personal use. The woman who encouraged me to sober up was Claudia. I met her at a friend's apartment. She mocked me for being a raver – which I couldn't help but admire, not to mention the desire it kindled – so I asked her out. She said no – further inflaming my desire – so I obtained her number and pursued her for months. It paid off. I won the heart of one of the most caring people I'd ever met. Thanks to her, I'd mostly quit partying, returned to online stock trading, enrolled in Scottsdale Community College to study Spanish and put the English Shaun persona behind me. She didn't approve of my raver friends, so I didn't let them know where we lived. As my mind started to clear, I grew more afraid of the consequences of hanging out with the people I used to lead. Knowing the police were onto me, I mostly stayed at home on my computer. We were saving up to start new lives in LA, where she wanted to be an actress and I planned to do a Masters in finance. But there was no chance of any of that happening now.

'Bring him in,' someone radioed.

The driver parked by a mobile police unit. He uncuffed me, told me to put my jeans on and escorted me to a man sat at a desk.

'Fill this out.'

NAME, DATE OF BIRTH, SOCIAL SECURITY NUMBER, HOME ADDRESS, OCCUPATION, WORK ADDRESS . . .

'I'm exercising my right to remain silent,' I said.

'You must fill this out or else we'll book you in as a John Doe, and you don't want that.'

I complied and was escorted into the police station. 'What about my right to make a call?' I asked, desperate to notify Ray the attorney.

'Not now. Straight to a cell.'

He deposited me in a small cell. Clean and air-conditioned. It had two bunks and a stainless-steel toilet with a built-on water fountain. The smell of bleach rose from the recently mopped floor.

The police put Cody, the head of my security team, in the cell opposite. Close to average height and weight, he wasn't intimidating. I'd put him in charge due to his knack for staying sober while the rest of us were high. I'd initially disliked this quirky character who sported a blond crew cut and preppy clothes. But he proved to be trustworthy and a methodical smuggler. That's how he became my right-hand man.

I rushed to the front of the cell. We exchanged nervous smiles, like children caught smoking.

'Where they get you?' Cody asked.

'Knocked my door down. And you?' I asked.

'You gotta hear this.'

'What?'

'I was out and about, taking care of bills and shit, driving from place to place, and I noticed a helicopter above me. I watched it for a while and it didn't go away. So I drove to the other side of town, and there it was, still above me. I thought I was losing my mind. I thought of *Goodfellas*, how the helicopter was above him every time he looked out of his car. No matter where I went, it stayed with me, but I still wasn't 100 per cent sure. So, to see if I was just sketching, I decided to speed back over to the other side of town. I get on the freeway and head east. I'm in the fast lane. I notice the helicopter's still above me, to the side. I'm cruising along wishing the helicopter would go off in another direction, and I notice a bunch of cop motorcycles in the traffic behind me. I slowed down, expecting them to overtake me, but they surrounded my car – four of them! – and signalled for me to get off the freeway. There was nothing I could do. I pulled off, parked and they arrested me.'

'Helicopters and biker cops! My God! At least my arrest wasn't as dramatic as yours. SWAT knocked our door down, yelled and pointed big guns at us. Tell you what, they sure spent some money on these arrests. Not a good sign. They catch you with anything?'

'Nothing for them to catch me with.'

'Same here. They tore my pad apart looking for drugs. Took my computer and everything. We should be able to get bonded out when they don't find anything,' I said, hoping it to be true.

The sound of jingling keys and approaching footsteps halted our conversation. My cell door clinked open, and in came DJ Spinelli. A short man with a round, friendly face who'd played techno at my raves.

'You too!' I said. 'How'd they get you?'

'I was ambushed!' he said.

'What?' Cody said.

'I had to get a real job to pay the bills. Today was my first day at work raising money for the Republican Party.'

'Republican Party!' I said, and we all laughed.

'So I'm at work, and I receive a call from a cop saying my place has been burglarised and I need to return home immediately. I explained the situation to my new boss, and he gave me permission to leave. I'm driving home, and the same cop calls my cell phone: "Where you at? You heading home?" I told him I was and hung up. Then he called two more times. He was antsy. I should have known something was wrong. When I got home, I was arrested.'

'Crafty bastards,' Cody said.

* * *

'Come out, Attwood!' A young policeman escorted me to a room full of electronic equipment.

'Mug shot. Get against that wall,' he said.

'Is this good?' I was in no mood to smile at a camera.

'Where's that accent from?'

'England.'

'I'm from England, too. Which part?'

'Widnes, Cheshire.'

'Rugby-league town, eh?'

'Yes.'

'How'd you end up in here?'

'They knocked my door down.'

'If they knocked your door down, you must be in a lot of trouble. Stay still right there.' He took my photograph. 'Well, nice to have met you. Good luck with your charges. Maybe they'll ship you back to England.'

If only, I thought.

'Get in the strip-search room,' said a large African American.

The room was tiny, cold, bare.

'Take everything off.'

I undressed. The day's events had retracted my penis, which I shielded with my hands to minimise my embarrassment.

'Now raise your arms. Good. Open your mouth. Raise your tongue. Good. Lift your nutsack. Good. Pull your foreskin back.'

'What?'

'Pull your foreskin back. You could have drugs in there.'

The request was too much for my penis. It wanted to hide inside my body and die of shame. Reluctantly, I drew back my foreskin.

'Good. Now turn around. Bend over and spread 'em.'

Spreading, I felt humiliated and vulnerable. I told myself it was no different from the mooning I'd done as a child. Just when I thought the worst was over, he said, 'Spread 'em wider.' It was beyond mooning now. More of a visual raping. 'Good. Let me see the bottoms of your feet.'

Relieved the strip search was over, I was escorted back to my cell and served a hot meal. Salisbury steak. Mash. Gravy.

It was night-time when two transportation officers carrying boxes of steel restraints extracted us from our cells to take us to Sheriff Joe Arpaio's jail system, where new arrestees were housed. They cuffed my hands and tethered the cuffs to my torso with a belly chain. The heavy leg cuffs cut into my ankles, and I could only shuffle out of the jail.

'Watch your heads getting into the van!'

I bundled myself into the van, surprised to see more of my party friends, including Wild Man, Misty, Melissa, Boo and Wild Woman. Galvanised by the day's events, everyone tried to talk at once.

'Where's Claudia?' I asked.

'They let her go,' said Wild Woman – who had emigrated from my hometown to be with Wild Man. She was in her 40s, blonde and tiny, but tougher than most men. Armed with a bar stool during a pub fight, she'd put multiple people in hospital. We'd nicknamed her and Wild Man the Wild Ones.

'Thank God for that,' I said.

'I was outside the room they were questioning her in,' Wild Man said. 'She was crying 'cause they said they'd found some prescription pills without prescriptions in your apartment, and she was facing some very serious charges. So I yelled, "Serious fucking charges my arse," and they tried getting crazy with me. Daft pig bastards.'

'What's gonna happen to us?' asked Melissa.

'Our attorney friend probably knows we've been arrested by now,' I said, hoping he had. 'He'll be doing all he can to find out what's going on. Any of you get caught with drugs?'

They all answered no except for Melissa.

'If they didn't find any drugs,' I said, 'I don't see how they can hold us for very long.'

'Where they taking us?' Cody asked.

'The Horseshoe,' Wild Man said. 'We'll be stuck in filthy holding cells for days while they process us.'

'Why they call it The Horseshoe?' Cody asked.

''Cause you go in at one end and work your way round the cells in a horseshoe shape,' Wild Man said. 'They kept me in there for almost a week one time 'cause I wouldn't tell them me name.'

The van parked in a subterranean lot. A transportation officer allowed the women out first. The 30 or so male arrestees waiting to go inside the jail stopped heckling the prostitutes in the line and focused on my female friends.

'Ooh, babies!'

'Nice ass!'

'Show us your titties!'

'Come and play with the bad boys!'

'This way, honey!'

'With those boobs, I'm surprised you ain't got two black eyes!'

Shuffling towards the men, the women cowered. The last woman out of the van was Wild Woman.

From inside the van, Wild Man watched his fiancée. Other than an eyebrow reacting – one shot up and stayed up, while the other didn't budge – he seemed unperturbed. But I knew that particular eyebrow formation meant he was about to do something in character with his name.

In a Liverpudlian brogue that sounded as if she were hawking phlegm, Wild Woman scolded the men, who responded by turning up the volume of their chant, 'Show us yer boobs!'

'Get out of the van!' a transportation officer yelled.

Wild Man stooped out, stopped on the top step and unfurled the physique of a bear. He cocked his head back, targeting the men over his Viking's beard. 'If you don't pack it in and leave my woman alone, I'll have any of you when we get inside those cells.' He nodded at The Horseshoe and grinned. 'If you think I won't, just keep it up and see what happens.' Wild Man laughed in a way that said he really knew how to hurt someone. That shut up most of the men.

2

....

'Any pain, bleeding, fever, skin problems, lice, scabies, open sores?'

'No,' I said into the speak holes of a Plexiglas window in the crowded pre-intake room at the Madison Street jail.

The old lady fired more screening questions and grimaced at my answers as if my voice pained her. The Tempe transportation officers removed our chains and left us in the custody of Sheriff Joe Arpaio's deputies.

'Take your shoes off, put your hands up against the wall and spread your legs!' yelled a drill sergeant of a guard in the admissions' hallway.

Guards patted us down, examined our shoes and confiscated our shoelaces.

'Step through there,' yelled a female, pointing at a walk-through metal detector.

On both sides of the corridor, the inmates in the intake holding cells were banging on the Plexiglas windows. Outside the cells, the guards were shouting surnames, slamming doors and cursing the inmates.

'You, this way!' a guard yelled at me.

I walked by a Mexican woman in a black restraint chair. Limbs shackled. Chest strapped. The drool string dangling from her chin swung like a pendulum as she wriggled in the tilted-back seat. When a guard hid her head in a spit hood, she howled like a cat on fire.

'I'm Attwood.'

'Get in there!' The guard pointed at one of the first holding cells in The Horseshoe.

My heart pistoned as I entered a cell containing dozens of men, most of them huddled on the floor in a variety of uncomfortable positions. Swastikas and gang graffiti – South Side Posse Bloods, Aryan Brotherhood, South Side Phoeniquera – loomed down from the walls. I gagged on the plague-like fug.

'Excuse me,' I said, pushing through the men clustered around the door yelling at the guards. At either side of the room, rows of men on steel double bunks formed shelves of humans. Manoeuvring over the patchwork of limbs and bodies, I found a space with a urinous odour by the toilet. Resting against the filthy back wall, I slid down. I was congratulating myself on finding a place to sit until I noticed insects shaped like almonds darting on the floor. Cockroaches! I flicked one off my sneaker and rose fast. I brushed the surrounding ranks of them away with my feet. Some of them scaled the ankles of a hobo sleeping under the nearest bunk and disappeared into his trousers. I'd never been surrounded by so many people and felt so lonely. Everyone looked agitated, and I soon lapsed into the same state. Every five minutes or so, the cell door swung open and a guard ordered someone in or out. Desperate for relief from the suffocating atmosphere, I hoped my name would be called next.

'Fuck you! Get up!' said an old hobo, rising unsteadily. His face belonged on a shrunken head in a jar. He slurred a string of insults, the top of his grimy beard sinking into his mouth as he spoke.

Grumbling, his rival rose. The cell hushed, as if the curtains had opened for a violent comedy show. His rival swung, missed and fell on a gang member.

'Don't fucking fall on me, you drunk-ass motherfucker,' the gangbanger said, pushing one hobo into the other.

Ranting, the hobos fell as one, tied together by their own bluster until they twisted apart.

The disappointment in the lack of bloodshed was palpable until a black man roused by the antics of the hobos yelled, 'Why you look at me?' at the man sitting next to him.

'What're you talking about?' the man said, sidling away.

'He's a crazy Cuban,' someone said.

On his feet now, the Cuban ranged the room like a time bomb. Watching him confront people, I feared I'd be the one he'd explode on. He was gravitating towards me when the door opened.

'Attwood, get out here! Stand over there!' a guard yelled, pointing at a ledge down the corridor.

'Sign here,' said a woman behind a Plexiglas window.

'What am I signing for?'

'Charges.'

'Good. It's about time I found out my charges.' I signed and she slid me a form:

CONSPIRACY BOND 750000.00 CASH ONLY
LEAD/ASSIST CRIM SYN
ILL CONT OF ENTER-EM
USE ELEC COM DRG TRN
ILL CONT OF ENTERPR . . .

'What's all this mean?' I asked, stunned by the size of the bond.

'You need to go up there,' she snapped.

'Where?'

'See the guard at that cell?'

'Hold on. I've no clue what any of this means.'

'What?'

'These charges, and it says my bond's $750,000 cash only.'

'Lemme see.'

I gave it to her.

'Must be a computer error,' she said. 'It can't be that high. It's probably seventy-five thousand.'

'I hope so,' I said, easing up a bit but still dazed by the big number.

'Go over there. The next cell.'

Sweat and grime gnawed my skin as I urinated. I perched myself on the end of a top bunk. The cell filled quickly. The shock and bewilderment on the faces of the new arrivals abated as they shared arrest and crime stories heavy on police brutality.

A tiny Mexican entered, his dilated eyes darting haphazardly. Yelling, he banged on the Plexiglas at such a rate the other bangers stopped to admire his ability. Hyperventilating, he cupped his left pectoral and looked over his shoulder as if expecting an attack from the rear. He must have swallowed his drugs when the cops came, I thought.

A big bald man in a black T-shirt swaggered in, addressing the cell as if he knew us all. 'I was on my way to Disneyland with my little daughter. They pulled me over for speeding. But giving me a speeding ticket woulda been too easy for this motherfucker. He ran my name, and a warrant came up. Thank fucking God I called her mom. He arrests me in front of my kid – now that's fucking child abuse if you ask me! I'm supposed to be at my other kid's birthday this weekend. I'll be pissed if I miss her fucking birthday party. I hope this only takes two days. Awww fuck! I love my kids. Awww fuck!'

Then an even bigger man, whose beard lent him the aura of a pirate, came in and said to the bald man, 'Hey, Chad, they're gonna try and ship me back to New Mexico. They've got a body, but they can't link me to it. They've got nothing on me. Motherfuckers!'

Much to my relief, Cody arrived. I climbed down and we hugged. We discussed our bonds.

Chad interrupted our conversation. 'You've gotta cool accent, man. Did you say you've gotta $750,000 cash-only bond?'

'Yes, but they said it's a mistake,' I said, turning to Cody for support.

'Lemme see your paperwork.'

'Here you go.'

'That ain't no mistake, buddy,' Chad said.

'What do you mean it's not? She just told me it is.' I went dizzy.

'Conspiracy. Crime syndicate. Were you guys whacking people or what?' Chad asked.

'No. They raided my apartment. There were no drugs found or anything.'

'Well, you've got drug charges.'

I'd been involved in drugs for so long, identifying which transactions they'd charged me for was as likely as raising $750,000.

From outside, Wild Man banged on the Plexiglas and mouthed, 'What's your bond?'

'It says three-quarters of a mill! What's yours?' I yelled.

'Half a fucking mill!'

His response torpedoed my plan to bond out. 'Aw shit!' I said, agonising over having to tell my parents. I knew the news would devastate them 5,000 miles away in England.

'Get in this cell! Do you hear me?' A guard grabbed Wild Man.

'I've got it,' Chad said. 'You're part of Sammy the Bull's crew.'

'I'm nothing to do with him,' I said, not wanting to admit any criminal relationships. 'I did throw raves years ago, though.'

'That's it then. Raves. Ecstasy,' Chad said. 'With a bond like that, you might be on the news tonight.'

'I hope not,' I said, fearing members of my family in Arizona would see me.

A guard slid a large plastic bag into the doorway. 'Who's hungry?' The prisoners all shifted towards him at once, like ducks on a pond to someone with bread. He threw brown paper bags at them.

'They're Ladmo bags,' Chad said. 'Green-baloney sandwiches.'

Things such as food were far from my mind. Curious, I looked in the Ladmo bag. A grapefruit. Bread dotted with blue mould. Slices of processed cheese leaking an orange oil. Green baloney – slimy cuts of meat, iridescent but with an underlying greenish shine.

Baloney consists of various low-grade meats, fat, flavourings, preservatives and colourants. Sheriff Joe Arpaio introduced it in an attempt to get the cost of feeding each inmate down to 40 cents a day. Green baloney is unfit for commercial sale due to oxidation, and it was often delivered to the jail in bags labelled 'Not For Human Consumption'. Stolen by inmates, some of these bags surfaced in the offices of attorneys suing Arpaio. The term Ladmo bag came from the children's television programme *The Wallace and Ladmo Show*. Ladmo distributed paper bags to children with food and toy gifts. The bags had a surprise element and became skimpier over time, hence the analogy.

In a hurry to distance myself from the rank smell, I off-loaded my Ladmo bag on the men casting around for leftovers. Attempting to refresh my mouth, I ate the grapefruit.

'Attwood! Come on! Hurry up!' yelled a female guard.

'Right here!' I scrambled to my feet, relieved to be on the move again.

'Go and see her in that room in the corner.'

The room was full of electronic equipment, like a photocopy store.

'Who're you?' a woman asked.

'Attwood.'

'Wash your hands and come here.' I resented her talking to me as if I were a piece of property. She grabbed my arm, spread my fingers onto a scanner and rolled each finger. Each print surfaced on a screen with the words: PRINT SUCCESSFUL. She printed the various sections of my hand. 'You're done with me. See her.'

'Put this ink on your hands!' yelled another female. 'Good. Now gimme your hand.' She grabbed my hand, separated and pressed my fingers down. 'Relax! Relax! What's wrong with you?' Her attitude made me seethe inside. She pushed my hand onto the inkpad and then my palm onto the print card.

'Wipe the ink off your hands with this.' At arm's length, she gave me a paper towel. It disintegrated immediately, so I had to wipe my hands on my jeans. 'See him next,' she said.

'Stand on that line. Look up at the camera. OK. Good.'

The camera flashed.

'Put your head in there,' he said, pointing at a metal box.

I didn't like the look of the metal box. 'I'm not going to get radiation from this, am I?'

'No. It just takes a picture. Put your eye up against that part.' He pushed a button and my retina appeared on a screen.

In the next cell, I again perched on the end of a top bunk. I felt safer up there, above the mass of testy men, cockroaches and drunken hobos. An ache soon spread throughout my body. It must have been the small hours because I was exhausted from sleep deprivation – almost a day since my arrest.

'Everyone pee who needs to pee! You're going to court!' a female yelled.

The sleepy group rose and formed a line for the toilet. Men aired their hopes of getting their bonds reduced, raising mine.

The guard yelled names to the tune of urine splashing, water flushing and bursts of flatulence.

'Attwood!'

Thirsting for fresh air, I stepped into the corridor.

'Go sit in that booth, Attwood!'

A lady in a booth slid out a form. The young woman hovering behind her was the one who had conferred with Detective Reid outside my Scottsdale apartment on the day of the raid. She had timid mousy features and curly brown hair.

On the form, I put the Tucson address where I had lived with my ex-wife Amy, as I was using this for my green-card application. Sensing something underhand, I listed the Scottsdale apartment as a second home. I explained I had two addresses, and the lady insisted a note had been made on the computer. The woman behind her snickered, and walked away. I felt uneasy.

'Finished? Go through that door into the courtroom!' a guard yelled.

Joining the fatigued captives on rows of plastic chairs in the large white courtroom, I gulped down the cool air. Over to my right, sitting at a desk by the bar, was the familiar woman from the raid. Her presence gave me a bad feeling. Everyone was waiting for the judge. I clung to the possibility of him reducing my bond.

The clerk of the court was sat at a desk next to the judge's bench. She stood up, cleared her throat and said, 'When your name is called, line up at this desk, and the judge will call you one at a time. He will ask you some questions, and when he is finished with you, you will step to the desk at the other side of the judge's bench where you will sign your court papers. You will then proceed back to your seat. Does everybody understand?'

There were a few murmurs of assent. The judge entered.

'All rise. Judge Powischer's court is now in session.'

Judge Powischer trundled to his bench like an overweight clergyman. His face was grotesquely impassive, as if he were under the influence of a dental anaesthetic heavy on cocaine.

'Garcia! Watkins! Snyder! Vasquez! Castillo! Johnston! Lynch!' the clerk yelled.

The first group of defendants jumped up like a team of firefighters responding to an emergency call. In an apathetic voice, Judge Powischer chastised them, one after the other, for committing petty crimes.

'Walker! Ramirez! Brooks! Wright! Lopez! Washington! Attwood!'

Judge Powischer read my charges. When he quoted my bond, the crowd gasped.

'Do you have anything to say on your own behalf?' he asked, his slitty brown eyes radiating impatience.

'Your Honour, I was arrested yesterday morning, told the raid would vindicate the charges, but no drugs were found. I trade stocks for a living and have an investment in a clothing store, but there's no way I can pay this bond. I'm–'

'Enough!' Judge Powischer's head swivelled towards the familiar woman.

She rose, her face becoming animated around large glasses as she launched into her statement. 'Judge, I'm Gloria Olivia Davis, prosecutor for the Organised Crime Division of the Attorney General's Office. About six years ago, Tempe Police Department began receiving reports of an Englishman involved in throwing raves and distributing drugs in and around the Phoenix and Tempe area. Surveillance was set up, but the Englishman moved around a lot, eluding earlier investigations. He used numerous aliases: so many we couldn't even list them all in his indictment. Detectives only discovered Mr Attwood's real name this year and were finally able to capture him. It is the allegation of the state that Mr Attwood is the head of a drug organisation and that he has been operating a continuous criminal enterprise in Arizona for at least six years. The Attwood Organisation specialises in the distribution of club drugs, including the drug he is most well known for: Ecstasy. Mr Attwood is not a citizen of this country. He is a citizen of England. He thus poses a considerable flight risk if he were to be bonded out. Mr Attwood is also a liar, Judge. He lied to your own staff here today, stating that he lives in Tucson when he in fact lives in Scottsdale. He also put that he works at a store, in sales – maybe he meant drug sales? The state requests his bond remains the same.'

'Bond remains the same. Next!'

His words were like a kick to the testes. I wanted to throw up. I had to steady my hands to sign the court papers. Back in my seat, I brooded on the impossibility of bonding out and having to tell my parents. I wondered how much longer I could stay awake before I broke down.

'Everyone who has seen the judge,' the bailiff yelled, 'go through that door and get back into the jail right now!'

Apprehensively, I returned to The Horseshoe: an apprehension that turned into dread when I saw the number of men sardined in the next cell. I wedged myself in past the tiny Mexican from earlier, who was still hyperventilating. I spotted another familiar face and sighed. It was the Cuban. He was standing next to the Mexican, staring blankly, like a wind-up toy waiting for someone to turn the key in his back.

I worked my way to the toilet and unbuttoned my pants. Urinating, I winced at the smell. I cupped water from the sink in my hand and leant forward. My eyes slammed shut as I splashed my face. The water cooled my skin and washed away some of the grime and tiredness. Removing my T-shirt released the odour of stale sweat and yesterday's deodorant. I wetted the T-shirt and wiped my face and armpits. I put the T-shirt back on. It clung to my body, cooling it down. My mouth tasted foul. Gargling water failed to stop the burning in my throat. I picked the coating of white scum off my lips in tiny clumps and strings. Sitting down against a wall, I could feel the filth in the air reattaching itself to my skin. A headache set in. I drifted in and out of consciousness, and my worries took on surreal dimensions. Every time I felt too itchy, I revisited the sink and repeated my bathing ritual.

Except for the Mexican and Cuban, everyone looked exhausted. The Cuban had been staring at the wall for a while, his eyeballs bulging slightly more than the Mexican's. Every ten minutes or so, he reanimated and yelled at someone. Inevitably, my turn came.

'Why you look at me?' He stared at me hard.

I was tense enough, yet he managed to elevate my tension. 'I wasn't looking at you. My friend, are you OK?' Try to calm him down, I thought. Do a good deed.

'You fuckin' no-no look at me!' he yelled louder, his head convulsing as if demons were trying to burst through his crown chakra.

Maintaining eye contact, I rose. I felt my stress surge into anger at him. I knew this was wrong. But some force was pushing me to fight him. Expecting to be the one he'd finally attack, I steeled myself. Raising my arms, I shifted my left side towards him.

'Take no notice,' an old Mexican American said. 'He's crazy.'

Shouldn't be fighting a crazy, I thought. No backing down either. With everyone watching to see how I'd react, I didn't want to show any weakness.

'Why you look at me? Why you fuckin' look at me?'

Figuring he was testing me, I responded the way I'd heard many of the others respond: 'Shut the fuck up!' I was immediately taken aback by the severity in my voice.

The Cuban shuffled away, pivoted like a robot and headed for the tiny Mexican. He stopped next to the Mexican and stared out of the window. The expectation of a confrontation was palpable. Even men who'd been nodding off fixated on the twosome. But the Cuban settled back into a trance. Just when the spectators were losing interest, the Cuban started muttering and trembling.

'Who look at me no-no look at me!' he yelled at the Plexiglas, as if imaginary people in the corridor were eyeballing him.

Hearing this, the Mexican jumped like a startled animal and then thundered on the Plexiglas with both fists.

The Cuban whirled towards the Mexican. 'Why you fuckin' look at me?'

Still pounding on the Plexiglas, the Mexican yelled for someone to save him from '*el diablo*'.

'You fuckin' look at me! No-no look at me!' the Cuban yelled, wagging his finger in the Mexican's face.

They fed off each other's hysteria until a hillbilly guard the size of a buffalo swung the door open and said in a bumpkin voice, 'What in the Sam Hill's goin' on in here?'

When the Cuban yelled 'Why you fuckin' look at me?' at the guard, the Mexican ducked under the guard's arm and sprinted down the corridor.

'Hell's bells!' The guard slammed the door and radioed for backup.

I couldn't resist vying for viewing room at the Plexiglas. Side by side, two guards were marching towards the Mexican, driving him back towards the hillbilly, who was blocking the corridor like a rugby forward eager to squash a winger. The Mexican feinted to the left, and the hillbilly lurched in that direction. The Mexican veered to the right and zigzagged around the guard.

'This little fella's quicker than a bob cat!' the hillbilly yelled.

Keys jingling and a staccato of radio interference announced the arrival of groups of guards at both ends of the corridor – big guards snapping on rubber gloves, marching with menace in their stride. The Mexican skidded into a U-turn and headed back towards the hillbilly. But within seconds he had nowhere to go. He swivelled his head wildly, appraising the situation like an animal aware of its imminent slaughter. Boots squealed as the guards fell upon him. He resisted briefly, kicking and yelping, but then curled into a ball. He was pinned down, picked up and thrown into a restraint chair. As they strapped him in, his tiny body panted as if his chest were about to explode. As they slid the chair down the corridor, his screams faded out of earshot.

The hillbilly extracted the Cuban and placed him in a cell opposite. We watched the Cuban shout at a man. Then a large figure rose from the floor at the back of the cell as if roused from sleep. Approaching the Cuban, the figure knocked people out of the way. It was Wild Man. He came up behind the Cuban and applied a chokehold. The Cuban's arms windmilled then flopped down. Wild Man dropped the Cuban to the floor like a sack of potatoes, grinned at us and lay back down.

Other than the heat rising and falling, I had no sense of night and day. The heat was up again when a guard extracted me to see a nurse at a desk in the corridor. I was well into my second day now. The nurse mocked my accent and took my blood pressure. She stuck a needle in my arm.

'I fucking hate needles. I'm refusing this shit,' Wild Man said, sitting down next to me opposite another nurse. 'How're you, la'?' he asked, addressing me in the Liverpudlian slang for lad.

'Shattered. I need sleep. Hungry. I can't eat green baloney.'

'You ready?' the nurse asked Wild Man.

'I told you, I'm refusing.'

'It's for your own good.'

'I'm fucking refusing,' Wild Man laughed.

'How can you refuse?' I asked.

'I just did.'

'I didn't know that,' I said.

'They got you good, didn't they?'

'I guess.'

'If you're refusing, get back to your cell!'

'Tara, la,' Wild Man said.

'Tara, la,' I said.

As the nurse applied a band-aid to my arm, Wild Woman and my female friends arrived. Prisoners leered and banged on the Plexiglas.

'How're you doing?' I asked.

'It's terrible,' Melissa said.

'But Wild Woman's taking care of us,' Misty said.

'What do you mean?' I asked.

'I already twatted one fucking daft bitch for picking on Misty 'cause she's Asian,' Wild Woman said.

'She headbutted some chick and boxed her down,' Boo said.

'They know better than to fuck with me now,' Wild Woman said. 'I'm in no fucking mood. I hope another daft cunt talks some shit. I'm looking for some fucker to take my fucking anger out on.'

'You! Stop talking to the females! In fact, come with me!' A guard led me to a cell on the third corridor.

'It's the $750,000-bond man!' Chad yelled.

'What's up, brother!' Cody said, and explained he'd been discussing our prospects with Chad and Tony, the pirate-looking murderer.

'If you haven't got any priors,' Tony said, 'the worst they can give you is five years on a Class 2 felony.'

'What's priors?' I asked.

'Prior felony convictions.'

'I've got no prior felonies. I've got a misdemeanour from years ago.'

'Misdemeanours don't count,' Tony said. 'You're looking at five years max.'

'Five years!' It seemed like the rest of my life.

'That's the worst you're looking at,' Tony said. 'Five's a walk in the park. You're also eligible for probation.'

'I'd sign for probation right now just to get out of here,' I said.

'If you're a first-time non-dangerous drug offender, you're eligible for probation. Take no notice of that bond. It's just a scare tactic and so you can't bond out and prepare a good defence. Just make sure your crew keep their mouths shut when they try to scare them into snitching. "Cooperate or you'll never see the light of day,"' Tony said in a mock voice. 'It's all bullshit. If no drugs or money were found, then they fucked up. You're gonna have to be careful 'cause they spent a lot of money on this case, so they're gonna be looking to justify it. Get a real good defence attorney, and you'll be all right. Don't sign the first plea bargain they offer you unless it's for less than five years.'

The door swung open, and the hillbilly tossed Ladmo bags at us. 'It's like feeding a pack of javelinas. Y'all smell about the same.'

Hunched over their Ladmo bags, the men bartered items of food as volubly as traders on the New York Stock Exchange. A line formed for the toilet. The stench of bowel movements soon dominated the other odours our bodies were letting loose. Chad and Tony amused themselves by throwing grapefruit peel at anyone who dared, accidentally or otherwise, to fall asleep.

The door swung open. 'Attwood, come with me!'

I arrived at a massive cell at the end of The Horseshoe. It had multiple bunk beds on two opposite walls and a toilet at the back. Some of the inmates were in street clothes, others in jail attire. Black-and-white bee-striped pyjamas. Pink boxer shorts. Orange shower sandals.

As this was the last intake holding cell, I thought I'd better ask my aunt Ann (my aunt Sue's older sister) to notify my parents before I ended up who knows where. On the wall by the cell door was a collect-call phone. To dial, I had to stoop – to prevent suicides all of the phones in the jail had been designed with short cords. I was so disgusted with what I was about to do that hanging myself seemed an easier option. I half hoped no one would answer, but Ann did. Surprised by the news, she reassured me she'd tell my parents as gently as possible. I hung up the phone feeling sick. I'd just sent a bomb over the Atlantic Ocean aimed at my parents' home. I sat on my own for a bit, imagining their reactions, the devastation I'd surely caused such gentle and caring people.

The door opened every few hours, and a guard yelled the names of the inmates being transported to one of Arpaio's local jails.

Wild Man introduced me to Maximum Ted, an old-timer who'd killed his wife in Florida and had been classified to the Madison Street jail's maximum-security quarters. He'd been shipped from a Florida prison to face charges of stealing a Renaissance-era painting from a wealthy Arizonan. With all of my male co-defendants present, I asked Maximum Ted for advice.

'What they'll do next is try to play you all off against one another, so they can build cases against whoever they want to portray as the big players. They'll assign you all scumbag attorneys who are on the payroll of the state, and the attorneys will try to frighten everyone into signing plea bargains so they don't have to do any real work, like defending you at trial. The sooner you sign a plea bargain, the sooner they get their fee and move on to their next victim.'

'No shit!' Cody said.

'Yes. Your best bet is to form a united front. Have a highly paid attorney act as the lead attorney for the whole case. The prosecutor is relying on the domino theory in a case like this. If one of you falls, you all will.'

Good advice, I thought.

In tones of solidarity, we pledged a united front. If the police had no drugs, no evidence, there was no case, and no need for anyone to cooperate. Or so I thought.

Hours later, my name was called. A guard escorted a group of us to a changing-room. We were instructed to strip naked, deposit our clothes in a bin liner and put on the jail uniform. I returned to the cell dressed like a chain-gang con from a black-and-white movie.

After the next delivery of Ladmo bags, I scoured the area for fruit and ate a few oranges and grapefruits. My eyes stung as I watched men nod off, fall on their neighbours, wake up and repeat the cycle. But I was beyond tired and entering a kind of madness. I desperately needed to do something for my skin – it felt as if lice were burrowing into it – so I marched to the water fountain with some grapefruit peel, ripped my top off and splashed water on my upper body. Attempting to reduce the onion stink in my armpits, I squeezed grapefruit peel below them.

'Does that work?' a skinhead yelled. 'Gimme a piece!'

I threw him some. Smelling my left armpit, I watched the skinhead squeeze the grapefruit peel. The onion smell had gone, replaced by the stink of a chemistry-class experiment gone wrong. I splashed more water onto my armpits. Pacing the cell, I felt the rush of a trapped animal. My mind started to slide. Thoughts of never being free again were rising, hovering, flitting, as if I had a skull full of hummingbirds.

I wanted to explode, thump a wall, project my anger onto something. Anything. I felt a primeval rage.

I was distracted by an inmate at the front of the cell announcing the names on the new batch of IDs on the guard's desk: 'Attwood, your ID's white. Medium security. You're off to Towers jail.' My journey through The Horseshoe was almost over. Now that I'd been booked in and seen by a judge, I was to be housed in one of Arpaio's jails in accordance with my security classification. Wild Man and I had been classified as medium-security inmates. The rest of my co-defendants were minimum security, so they would be housed at Durango jail.

A guard called my name but not Wild Man's. Disappointed that Wild Man was not being transported with me, I was chained to four other inmates. A hippy. A lanky African American. A middle-aged bespectacled man. Someone who resembled a homeless version of Jack Nicholson. Gripped by anxiety, I yelled goodbye to my co-defendants. I prayed my next destination would be softer on my soul than The Horseshoe.

3

··········

Sunlight bore down on my head and glistened off the transportation guard's Terminator sunglasses as we waited outside Towers jail – a complex of beige buildings, including six identical towers, surrounded by chain-link fences, razor wire and a few palm trees, on the outskirts of Central Phoenix. With only 20-odd officers guarding close to 1,000 unsentenced prisoners, the jail was dangerously overcrowded and understaffed.

The entrance door buzzed open. 'Everyone get inside. Wait for the interior door to open!'

Chained together, we shuffled into a bare room.

A young guard unlocked the interior door. 'Line up in the corridor!' He had spiky hair and was wearing the standard beige uniform with black boots and a utility belt.

Inmates in the holding cells rapped on the Plexiglas and heckled us.

'Turn and face the wall! First in line, raise one leg and lift your foot toward me!' The transportation guard removed our cuffs and chains. 'This lot are all yours now. I'm outta here.'

'Wassup, Kohlbeck!' the Jack Nicholson-looking inmate said to the young guard.

'Not you again!' Officer Kohlbeck said, frowning.

''Fraid so.'

'What's your name?'

'Boyd.'

'Smoking crack again, were we, Boyd?'

Boyd smiled, displaying what was left of his teeth. 'Any chance of Ladmo bags? We haven't eaten all day,' he said in the tone of entitlement used by those who know how to work the system.

'Any Ladmo bags left?' Officer Kohlbeck shouted.

At the reception station, a guard sighed, slammed down *The Arizona Republic*, opened the refrigerator, grabbed some Ladmo bags and chucked them at us.

Making green-baloney sandwiches, my companions showered the floor with breadcrumbs.

'I need you all in this cell. Show me your IDs as you enter!' Officer Kohlbeck said.

The empty cell had three sets of double bunks and a toilet in the corner with no privacy divide. It wasn't as filthy as the cells in The Horseshoe. I sat on a bottom bunk. The bespectacled prisoner sat aloof from the other three, who chatted like regulars at a social club.

'I gotta take a crap,' Boyd said.

'Me too, dawg. But you called it first,' the hippy said.

'This chow always sends me straight to the shitter,' the African American said.

There was no privacy, yet they went about their business as casually as young children pick their noses. The toilet flushed louder than on a plane, and I wondered why they pushed the button as soon as they sat down and kept flushing.

For days, all I'd eaten was fruit. Desperate to freshen my mouth, I unpeeled an orange and ate some slices. The juice soothed my mouth. But a few minutes later, I felt stomach cramps that spread to my bowels. I'd reached such a low in my life it was now necessary to go to the toilet in front of four strangers. That three of them had gone before me offered little comfort. Searching for something appropriate to say, I played around with sentences like, 'Hey, guys, I need to take a dump.' But I couldn't get the words out. Instead, I adopted a diversion strategy: I gave them my Ladmo bag. As they argued over the food, I rushed to the toilet, pushed my pants and boxers down and tried my best to act like someone who'd been going on the toilet in front of strangers all of his life. The seatless steel toilet chilled my behind. Straining in vain, I regretted ever attempting the toilet. Convinced I needed to go, but was just too nervous, I took some deep breaths. Eventually, something happened. But not much.

My deposit was barely underwater when Boyd said, 'Goddam, put some water on that to kill the smell, dawg!'

It dawned as to why they'd flushed so much. Blushing, I pressed the button. The toilet flushed, splashing water upon my backside like some out of control bidet. I wanted to get off the toilet, but I had to wipe. I picked up the institutional toilet paper. Coarse and thin. I wondered what the subtlest method of wiping was. I didn't want to stand up and indecently expose myself. How had they done it? Seated with one buttock raised. I copied their method. All done, I ran water over my hands, dried them on my pants and returned to the bunk. I was aching all over, and the metal surface added to my discomfort. In the foetal position, I drifted in and out of consciousness for hours.

I was roused by Officer Kohlbeck's voice. 'Line up in the corridor!'

We shuffled out of the cell.

'I need to pat you down! Turn around, put your hands against the wall and spread your legs! I hope for your sakes none of you have any weapons or drugs keystered!' I was unaware that keystered meant drugs stored in your rectal cavity, that most inmates were involved in keystering tobacco, drugs and paraphernalia.

Kohlbeck patted me down. I was beginning to lose count of the number of men in uniform who'd karate-chopped my crotch in recent days. Officer Kohlbeck donned wraparound sunglasses and escorted us down a series of corridors. 'Right! Stop there!'

A hibernating bear of a Mexican lay curled up and snoring on the floor of an adjoining corridor.

'Wake the hell up, trusty!'

The trusty blinked a few times. A pained look came on his face. Reluctantly, he rose.

'They need mattresses and bedding!'

The trusty fetched us blankets, sheets and towels. We helped ourselves to torn thin mattresses leaking a toxic-looking black soot. My companions coiled their mattresses around their belongings, so I copied them.

'All right. Keep walking! We're going to Tower 2!'

Shouldering our mattresses, we exited into a breezeway with an expanded-metal roof. We passed two recreation pens surrounded by chain-link fences and razor wire. Due to the weight of my belongings and the heat, sweat was running into my eyes by the time Kohlbeck buzzed us into Tower 2.

As we walked down the cement-block corridor, tattooed men wearing bee stripes banged on the Plexiglas at either side of us: zoo animals yearning to attack their visitors. Unnerved by the rows of hard faces, I wanted to look straight ahead, but my eyes instinctively jumped to the sources of the loudest banging. Some of them mimed smoking: their way of asking if any of us had smuggled in cigarettes.

'Stop below the bubble,' Officer Kohlbeck said.

We stopped in the middle of the building – all Plexiglas, metal and concrete. In the centre were spiral stairs leading up to the control tower – a giant fishbowl in the air giving the guards a view of the four identical pods lettered A, B, C and D. Separated by cement-block walkways with Plexiglas windows, each pod took up almost a quarter of the space below the control tower and had its own electronically activated sliding door. Walking in a circle in the control tower was a guard struggling to keep an eye on the almost 45 men in each pod. The other guard was watching surveillance screens. He occasionally pressed a button on the control panel to open one of the sliding doors to allow an inmate in or out of a pod. At the back of each pod were two storeys of cells facing the day room and the control tower. Each pod had stairs running from the middle of the upper tier down to about six feet before the sliding door at the front of the pod. The stairs were metal grid, so the guards could see through them. Most of the inmates in the pods were sizing us up. I steeled myself to join the overcrowded population of sweaty, hungry, violent men. A guard descended the control-tower stairs and ordered us to wait further down the corridor. Officer Kohlbeck disappeared. We sat on our rolled-up mattresses. The men in the pods talked to us in sign language.

'He's swindowing you,' Boyd said, pointing at a skinhead with a swastika and skulls on his chest.

'Swindowing?' I asked.

'Talking through the windows,' Boyd said.

'What's he want?'

'To know if you're affiliated.'

'Affiliated?'

'With the gangs. Probably 'cause your head's shaved.'

'I'm not. Can you tell him this is my first time?'

'Sure.' Boyd raised his right arm to almost head height, hand horizontal, palm down, and then shook his head and hand in sync.

'Thanks,' I said.

The skinhead waved his arms around.

'Now he wants to know if you're bringing any dope in.'

'No dope, no smokes.'

The inmates kept harassing us for contraband. I was starting to regret not being a smoker. I wished I had something to throw to the wolves other than just myself.

A guard descended from the control tower and directed the African American and the hippy to D pod, the rest of us to cell 12 in A pod.

The sliding door burred open, unleashing the stink of smoke and body odour. As I entered the pod, the heavy atmosphere weighed on my lungs. In the day room were four steel tables bolted to the floor: two at either side of the metal-grid stairs. The inmates at the tables stopped playing cards and watching the small TV fixed on a wall to check us out. I felt their eyes follow me up the stairs and along the balcony.

Boyd bolted ahead to A12 and claimed the bottom bunk. David, the quiet bespectacled man, quickly put his mattress on the middle bunk, leaving me the top, the smallest slab of sleeping space. The cell was the size of a bus-stop shelter. The floor was concrete, greasy black with grime. The walls were stained brown. On one side of the cell were our three bunks separated from a steel combination toilet and sink by a thin wall. The other side consisted of just enough floor space to do push-ups on and a tiny steel table and stool bolted to the wall. The toilet at the front of the cell reeked of sewage. The front wall was metal grid – the guards and prisoners outside could see right in – so there was no privacy for the toilet. At the far end of the cell, a tiny barred window granted a view of the desert, chain-link fences and razor wire. On the top bunk, there was hardly enough room to raise my head without it hitting the ceiling, which it did as I arranged my mattress and bedding.

'I can't believe they put three people in these,' I said.

'They were originally designed for one man,' Boyd said. 'Rather than build more cells, they double-bunked them. Then, when they got away with that, they triple-bunked them. So now you've got 45 men living in a pod designed for 15.'

'When're they going to start putting four in a cell?' I asked.

'They already do,' Boyd said. 'There's just enough floor space for a mattress, so the fourth guy sleeps on the floor.'

My cellmates both urinated. They were soon snoring, shrouded in white sheets like corpses awaiting burial.

For a few hours, I tried to sleep, but my heart refused to settle down, and my mind was all over the place. Afflicted by the shock of the newly incarcerated, I began hallucinating. I heard my name whispered in the day room – *English Shaun. Yeah, him. English Shaun. That's him. Let's get him.* I saw men line up on the balcony, preparing to give me a heart check.

I knew about heart checks from Rossetti – one of the few members of my security team who'd been to prison. He'd told me gang members usually attack new arrivals to see if they show heart by fighting back.

Fighting back earns respect. Those who don't fight back are considered weak and open to getting extorted and punked (raped).

I knew I had to fight back or, better yet, attack them first to show heart. I visualised some of the moves I'd learned in kickboxing. I saw myself punching, kicking, mowing my attackers down like Kwai Chang Caine in *Kung Fu*. No problem. In theory. I was psyched up until my mind swerved to concern for my teeth. I had invested a lot in American dentistry. Fighting multiple assailants would expose my investment to unnecessary risk. I might even have to write off a tooth or two. But if I didn't fight now, I would lose more teeth in the long run fending off extortionists and rapists.

'If you don't stand up for yourself during a heart check, everyone'll punk you,' Rossetti had said.

Teeth be damned! I jumped off the top bunk and charged from the cell. 'Come on, motherfuckers!' I was slapped in the face by silence. There was no one on the balcony. I almost laughed out loud.

The day room had emptied except for four African Americans slamming dominoes down on a table with excessive force. They frowned at me in a way that said, *Just another crazy white boy wigging out on drugs again.*

Out of the cell now, I figured I'd best do something appropriate. Radiating purpose, I marched down the stairs. I tried one of the phones bolted to the wall, but it didn't accept telephone numbers. I needed instructions on how to work it. The African Americans were really hurting their dominoes, and I had to think twice before interrupting their game. 'Any of you guys know how these phones work?'

One of them took me to one side, and said, 'Are you on drugs, man?'

'No,' I said.

'You look paranoid.'

'I've been up for days in The Horseshoe.'

'Where you from, man?'

'England.'

'No shit. That's cool. Look, man, I'll give you a heads-up 'cause you're new here. You be running round all paranoid and shit, motherfuckers'll be thinking you got something to hide, and you'll get your ass smashed double quick. Get some sleep, man, and settle down.'

'I will after I make a call.'

He picked up the phone. 'Look, tell me the number. I'll put you through.'

I thanked him, and gave him my aunt Ann's number. He dialled it, spoke his name into the phone a few times and passed it to me. Desperate to hear how my parents had reacted to the news of my arrest, I listened to her phone ring. When she answered it, a computerised female voice told her it was a collect call from the jail and asked her to press 0 to accept the charges.

'Shaun, are you OK?' Ann said.

'Yes. Did you get through to England?'

'I spoke to your mum. As you can imagine, she's pretty devastated. Your dad was at work. Fortunately, Karen was there with your mum,' she said, referring to my 28-year-old sister, a trainee journalist living with my parents. 'I think she was in a state of shock 'cause after I told her, she started talking to me as if nothing had happened. She said "How're your lot?", which I thought was strange.'

Oh my God, I thought. What have I done to my mum?

'She said for you to call them as soon as you can, any time day or night.'

'I'd better do it right away. Look, I don't know how much these calls are costing, so I'm going to hang up and try to call England.'

'OK. They'll be glad to hear your voice.'

Trembling, I put the phone down. The African American put me through to England. Ashamed of where I was, I prayed they'd be supportive. Karen answered and accepted the collect call.

'Shaun's on the phone!' Karen yelled, then in a lower voice said, 'What have you done? Mum and Dad are in a proper state. They're worried sick.'

'Look, it's not as bad as it sounds,' I said.

'God, I hope not. For Mum and Dad's sake. They don't deserve this, Shaun.'

'You'd better let me speak to them,' I said, bracing myself.

'Anyway, I hope you're OK in there. It must be a nightmare. Here's Dad. Bye! Love you.'

'Love you too.' Speaking to Karen reinforced my guilt. She was right. My parents didn't deserve any of this.

'Are you OK?' Dad asked.

Hearing the strain in his voice, I felt awful. I imagined my mum taking it the worst. 'I'm in trouble, but I'm fine,' I said, trying to sound reassuring.

'Well, we'll do whatever it takes to help you.'

I was relieved. 'They've given me a list of charges, but I haven't a clue what they mean. My bond's $750,000, and I know none of us has that kind of money.'

'I know about the bond. I rang the jail.'

'What did you find out?'

'It sounds pretty serious. I was on that daft automated line for about 45 minutes, going around in a loop – press 1, press 2, press 3 – putting your booking number in at different stages, and all of a sudden a voice popped up. I explained the situation to her. As soon as I said, "I'm calling from England about my son who has been arrested," she immediately wanted to help me. The English accent has its advantages.'

'It does. It's helping me in here. What did she say?'

'I said, "I can't understand what's happened. I can't believe what's going on or why he's been arrested." She said, "Give me his booking number, and I'll find out what I can for you." She gave me the charges – which I didn't really understand – and then she said, "The bond is $750,000. This looks pretty serious."'

I felt panic setting in again. 'Oh dear. I'm so sorry. Mum must be worried sick.'

'She's bearing up.'

'I'd better speak to her then.'

'OK, here she is.'

'Shaun, are you safe in there?' Mum was crying.

I felt ill. 'Yes, I'm all right, Mum,' I said, not wanting to add to her worries.

'What's all this about?'

'I can't really say much on these phones, Mum. I was raided, but no drugs were found. My bond's so big, it doesn't look like I'll be going anywhere anytime soon.'

'I can't believe this has happened,' she said.

'I know. I'm so sorry. I've got money in some accounts, and I'm going to have to get a lawyer.' I didn't know it at the time, but the police had hacked my computer with a NetBus Trojan horse and were in the process of seizing the stock-market investments I'd made in the names of British citizens I'd flown over.

Her voice calmed somewhat as she told me firmly, 'We'll do what we can to help you.' I knew then my parents would be there for me no matter what. 'Is Claudia OK?'

'She was arrested, but they released her. You should give her a call.'

The female computerised voice said, 'You have 30 seconds remaining.'

'It's going to hang up, Mum.'

'We love you very, very much. We'll do what we can.'

'Love you too. So sorry about all–'

The line went dead. They were later billed £50 for the call – part of the collect-call exploitation of prisoners' families.

As soon as I hung up, the African American started asking me questions about England. I sat with him at a vacant table, but the hurt I'd caused my family made it hard for me to concentrate on answering him.

About five minutes later, the African American grew uneasy and said in a loud voice, 'You'd better go talk to your people.'

'What do you mean?' I asked, wondering what was going on.

'You stick with your own kind in here,' he said. 'Your people might not like you talking to me. Now go on now.' He nodded at a corner of the pod, stood up and walked away.

Lingering in the doorway of the corner cell were three skinheads. Young. Tattooed. Waiting.

Forcing a smile they failed to return, I joined them. 'I just got here,' I said, conscious of the fear in my voice.

'You need to come inside the cell, dawg, so we can have a little chat.'

'OK,' I said.

'Go in there, dawg.'

I walked into the cell, stopped by the window and turned around. Looking at them, I could feel my left eyelid twitching. One of them blocked the doorway. Another leaned an arm adorned with a Valknut – three interconnected triangles found in early-medieval Germanic inscriptions – against the wall, forming a barrier.

'Where you from, dawg?'

'England.'

'What the fuck you doing out here?'

'I was a stockbroker, then I threw raves.'

'So what they arrest you doing, dawg?'

'I'm not quite sure. They didn't actually arrest me doing anything. I was just–'

Raising his forearms, the biggest skinhead stepped forward, fists clenched. 'What the fuck you mean, you're not quite sure?'

I braced to be attacked.

'How the fuck don't you know what your charges are?'

I'll try to push my way through them and escape.

'I do but–'

'Every motherfucker knows his charges! Whatchoo hiding from us?'

Got to push through them. If I fight against the wall, they'll just close in on me.

'He's bullshitting us!' The third closed the door but not so it was locked.

I'm screwed. Charge and hope for the best.

'If you got sex offences, you'd better tell us now 'cause we will find out!'

'I don't have sex offences. What I mean is, I don't understand my charges: conspiracy, crime syndicate. I'm new to this. The cops just raided me, and nobody's explained what evidence they have. I thought they'd let me go when they didn't find any drugs at my apartment. I don't know what's going on.'

'Where's your paperwork at?'

'Right here,' I said, fishing it out of my top pocket.

'Lemme see.' The biggest skinhead snatched the charge sheet. Reading it, he said, 'Goddam, dawg! $750,000 cash-only bond! You some kinda Mafia dude or what?'

'No. I threw raves. We did drugs. Everyone had a good time.' I wondered if my charges were acceptable to them.

'I shot someone in the chest at a rave,' the mid-sized one said in a scary matter-of-fact tone. 'He was on GHB. I'm getting 10 for attempted murder.'

A raver, or doesn't like ravers?

'I'm here for drugs too, dawg. Name's Rob,' the biggest one said. 'Stand up and hold your fist out, man.'

Heart check? I thought. I raised both fists, dropped my chin and tried to squint like Lee Van Cleef.

They laughed at me. 'Not like that! Just hold a fist out like this, dawg.' Rob held his right fist out as if he'd just lost at the card game raps. I copied him, and he bumped his fist into mine. 'That's how we shake hands in here, dawg.'

I laughed, and they joined in. My tension fell like a firework returning to earth.

'It's to avoid catching diseases from people's fingers. There's a lotta sick motherfuckers up in this joint.'

'My mouth's killing me. How do I get a toothbrush?' I asked.

'I'll grab you one, dawg,' Rob said. 'I'm the head of the whites for this pod. Used to be in the Marines.' He held out a tiny toothbrush. Splayed and stained.

'Thanks, Rob. Why's the toothbrush so small?'

'So we can't make shanks out of them.'

'Shanks?'

'Jailhouse knives. You've gotta lot to learn, dawg.'

'Got any toothpaste?'

'Here you go.' Rob smeared the toothbrush with AmerFresh, a brand made in China that Sheriff Joe Arpaio provided the inmates – five years later, the FDA found AmerFresh to be contaminated with diethylene glycol (DEG), a toxic chemical used in antifreeze and as a solvent.

'Do you mind if I brush my teeth at your sink?'

'Nah, go ahead, dawg,' Rob said.

I shuffled past them to the sink. The AmerFresh put out the fire in my mouth.

'You need to take a shower, too,' Rob said.

I thought of all the shower scenes I'd seen in prison movies.

'Everyone coming from The Horseshoe fucking stinks. You're making our race look bad going around smelling like that. We don't wanna have to smash you for bad hygiene.'

'No problem. Where's the showers at?' I asked, still brushing my teeth.

'In the corner, next to this cell,' Rob said, pointing at the wall.

'Better get in there before they call lockdown,' the mid-sized one said.

'What time's that at?' I asked.

'Ten-thirty.'

'All right, I'm off to the shower then.' I cupped water in my hand a few times to rinse my mouth with, then stepped towards the door.

Rob blocked me. I flinched. 'Not so fast. We ain't finished with you yet.'

His last sentence crushed me. 'What is it?' I asked, afraid of what he might say.

Rob cocked his head back, narrowed his eyes. 'What do you know about your cellies?' Accusation had returned to his voice.

'Cellies?'

'Cellmates.'

'Not much. I guess Boyd's here a lot, but the other one, David, has barely spoken a word.'

'Yeah, we know all about crackhead Boyd. What about the other one? Any idea what his charges are?'

Rob trained such a gaze on me, I gulped. 'No idea.'

'We think he's a mo.'

'Mo?'

'A chomo. A child molester.'

'Uh oh.'

'You can get smashed in here for having a celly who's a chomo.'

My tension escalated again. 'What should I do?'

'Usually, we'd tell you to tell him to roll up, but we're gonna handle it for you.'

'OK. Thanks,' I said, unsure why I'd thanked them. 'I'd better go and get my shower then.'

'You do that. And don't go in the shower barefoot. Towers' foot rot ain't nuthin' nice, dawg.'

I returned to A12 for my towel. In the day room, I stripped to my boxers, and placed my clothes on one of the vacant tables. I was relieved the shower area was tiny and not one of those big communal affairs. Out of the two showers barely separated by a small divide I chose the one furthest in, as it provided more reaction time if I were attacked. Tiny black flies bothered my face as I balanced my boxers and towel on the showerhead. I stepped into a puddle of scum and pubic hair that swirled around my shower sandals when I turned the water on. I found a piece of soap in the puddle, rinsed it off and applied it to my armpits and genitals. Feeling vulnerable, I showered fast and got dressed in the day room.

Figuring the skinheads had told David to leave by now, I was surprised to see I still had two cellmates. I climbed up to my bunk, mindful not to bump my head. There were no pillows, and the thin mattress was uncomfortable. Trying to sleep with my head so close to the ceiling and my nose to the wall was like being in a coffin. My body ached, and rotating through various sleep positions only relieved it temporarily. My pulse remained fast, but I eventually passed out from exhaustion.

* * *

High-pitched static ringing in my ears roused me from a nightmare. I felt something rough itching my skin: an old blanket. *Where am I?* Inches from my face was a cement-block wall. Raising myself in a hurry, I hit my head on the ceiling. *Ouch!* Sweeping my vision across the room, the shock of the environment hit me all over again. My heart was beating so fast I doubted it had ever slowed down. There was a roar as toilets flushed all over the place.

More static assaulted my ears, followed by a voice crackling out of the public address system: 'Chow's in the house! Line up at the slider! Fully dressed with your IDs!'

Boyd sprung from his bunk, urinated, threw his clothes on, dashed out.

'It's breakfast time,' David said, putting on his bee stripes.

'Not more green baloney,' I said, dreading going another day without food.

About 40 men were out for chow. Yawning. Rubbing their eyes. Cursing the place. Apprehensively, I trod down the metal-grid stairs and joined the queue. The sliding door opened, and Officer Kohlbeck, holding a clipboard, checked IDs while a trusty doled out Ladmo bags and small cartons of milk. As each inmate took a Ladmo bag, he yelled what he'd like to trade.

'Meat for peanut butter!'

'Jellies for cheese!'

'Who said meat for peanut butter?'

'Over here, dawg!'

'I've got cheese. Who's got jelly?'

'I've got jelly!'

'Over here!'

'No! Take mine, dawg!'

'Milk for tonight's dinner juice!'

'I'll take it, dawg!'

Each race occupied one of the octagonal-shaped steel tables. The blacks called themselves kinfolk. The whites: woods. The Mexican Americans: Chicanos. The Mexicans: paisas. In the scramble for table space, the senior members of each race quickly took ownership of the four stools bolted to each table. Some prisoners took their Ladmo bags back to their cells.

I returned to A12. David was on the stool, Boyd the bottom bunk.

'Park your ass there,' Boyd said, nodding at the toilet. 'The best seat in the house.'

Looking at the toilet, I shook my head.

'Here, put this over it.' Boyd threw me an old towel. 'It'll reduce the smell.'

Using the towel, I sat down on the toilet. Inspecting the contents of my Ladmo bag, I regretted not having had the nerve to yell what I wanted to trade. I found some crackers and devoured them.

'I'm lactose intolerant. Anyone want another milk?' David said.

I was on the letter Y of the word yes when Boyd's arm struck out like a rattlesnake.

'I'll break bread, dawg,' Boyd said, smiling at me.

'Break bread?' I said

'Split the milk with you.'

I didn't fancy sharing Boyd's germs. 'You're all right. Keep it.'

Wolfing his down, Boyd eyed my food. 'You gonna eat that, dawg?'

'I can't eat this crap,' I said.

'I'll handle it for you.'

'Mouldy bread! How can you eat it?' I asked.

'You just scratch the mould off. You'll be doing it soon enough. Eating green baloney just like the rest of us.'

'Here you go,' I said, handing it to Boyd.

'Good lookin' out, dawg!'

I sipped my milk. A12 was towards the middle of the upper tier. There was an iron-railing balcony in front of it and the top of the stairs to one side. My view was almost as good as that from the control tower. I sat there intrigued by the inmates downstairs using sign language to communicate with those in adjacent pods. When the guards weren't watching, the trusties passed items from pod to pod by pushing them under the sliding doors. There was no way two guards could monitor all four pods at once, so contraband was passed unnoticed.

'What're they passing?' I asked.

'Dope. Tobacco,' Boyd said. 'There's usually only one syringe in each tower, so everyone has to share.'

'What about catching diseases from sharing?' I asked.

'Most of them have hep C anyway. Why'd you reckon that guy's yelling at the guard for bleach?'

'To clean his cell?' I asked.

'Nope. So the fellas can bleach the needle before shooting up.'

'So after green baloney everyone just moves on to doing drugs?' I asked.

'Pretty much. There's more drugs in here than anywhere in the world.'
His answer surprised me.

David grabbed his towel, and started to walk out of the cell.

'Where're you going?' Boyd asked with accusation.

'Take a shower,' David said and left.

'Boyd, can you show me how to use the phones? I must call my girlfriend.'

'Sure thing, dawg,' Boyd said.

Downstairs, I followed Boyd's instructions. I entered my booking number and repeated my name multiple times for the PIN-LOCK Speaker Verification Service. Claudia answered. My spirits surged to her voice. 'You OK, love?'

'I miss you,' Claudia said.

'I miss you loads,' I said, pressing the phone to my ear to make her presence closer.

'I sleep at my mom's or on the floor in the sweaty T-shirt you wore for kickboxing, with my foot touching the door 'cause I'm afraid someone's gonna bust it in again.'

'I'm so sorry, love. I just . . . I wish I was there with you.'

'I'm gonna visit you–'

'Yes, visit me! Please visit me! I must see you. This place is–'

'It must be horrible. You OK?'

'I'm fine so far. Well, kind of. Just stressed. It's crazy in here. I don't know where to begin.' Not wanting to burden her, I changed the subject. 'When are you visiting?'

'Tomorrow.'

'Great! Oh God, you don't understand how much I really need to see you right now.' Remembering her plight, I asked, 'What happened to you with the cops?'

'That Detective Reid told me I was going to jail for a long time, and that you're never getting out, and–'

'Never getting out! Why?' I asked, squeezing the phone handle as if it were a stress ball.

''Cause you've got so many charges. He said, "It's OK to talk about him 'cause he's never getting out." He really tried to threaten me to turn and talk. That time we went to your dentist in Tucson, he said we didn't go to the dentist, we picked up drugs.'

'That's crazy!' I said, hoping he was only trying to bluff her and not out to put me away for ever. 'How long were you there?'

'Close to dinner time. Ten to twelve hours. They kept telling me my mom was calling the jail asking if they'd fed me my vegetarian food.'

'That's funny,' I said, smiling sadly.

'She sent my brother to pick me up with bean burritos from Taco Bell. What's gonna happen, Shaun?'

'Don't worry, love. They didn't find any drugs, so they shouldn't be able to hold me too much longer. The problem is my bond.'

Cries for help and thuds stopped the chatter in the day room.

'Hold on,' I said, craning my neck.

The commotion was in the shower area, about 15 feet behind me. Skinheads were attacking a naked figure on the floor. Inmates stopped what they were doing, gravitated towards the shower area and formed a sinister audience.

'What is it?' Claudia asked.

'Looks like . . . er . . . some kind of disturbance.'

'What? What's wrong? You all right?' she said, her voice starting to crack.

'Sure . . . er . . . I'm fine. It doesn't involve me,' I said, distracted by the violence and proximity of the growing crowd.

The naked man raised his head, and I recognised David. There was a plea for help in his eyes as they briefly met mine – a look that froze me against the wall.

'Er . . . I might need to get off the phone here soon.'

'Die, you sick chomo fuck!' Rob yelled, dropping his heel on David's temple.

'*Arghhhhhhhhhhhhhhh . . .* '

'What's going on? Are you OK?' Claudia asked, her voice hitting some high notes.

The skinheads vied for stomping room. David arched his back in agony.

'Yes. I'm fine,' I said, struggling not to relay my fear. 'It just gets crazy in these places, that's all.'

The blows silenced David. Blood streamed from his nose.

'I have to go now. I love you,' I said, not wanting to worry her any further.

'Love you too. Every time I go to my mom's house, I take your sweaty T-shirt and Floppy.' Floppy was a Build-A-Bear creation that played my voice saying, 'Happy Valentine's Day. I love you, Bungle Bee.'

One of the skinheads jumped up and down on David. I thought I heard his ribs snap.

'I can't wait to see you tomorrow. Bye, love.' I hung up.

The spectators had adopted the safety-in-numbers survival strategy of the wildebeest. None of them dared venture from the herd. Mesmerised by the violence, they watched from a safe distance. Gripped by the same instinct, I joined the back of the herd.

As if they'd exhausted their supply of aggression on David, the skinheads stopped the beating and marched away in unison. David was a whimpering heaving mound of flesh, blood pooling around his head.

What kind of world am I in? I thought. This stuff really happens. It could have been me last night. How will I survive?

Just when the violence seemed to be over, a rhinoceros of a man with spider webs tattooed on his thick neck approached the skinheads. 'How come we can still hear the little bitch?'

'We fucked the chomo up good, dawg,' Rob said.

'Not good enough.' The man went to the shower with the casual gait of someone going to the shop to buy a bottle of milk, grabbed David's neck, and started slamming David's skull against the concrete as if he were trying to break open a coconut. *Crack-crack-crack* . . .

I was revolted but compelled to watch. The big man had increased the stakes, and I didn't doubt the code of these people included killing anyone who interfered or flagged down a guard. Even walking away would be a show of disapproval, an invitation to be attacked next. I was terrified.

David's body convulsed. His eyes closed. Then stillness. Silence. He remained on the floor until a guard walked the pod ten minutes later.

'Everybody, lockdown! Lockdown right now!' the guard yelled.

Shouting at the guard, the inmates returned to their cells, slamming their doors behind them. Guards rushed into the day room. Pressing myself to the cell door, I watched them remove David on a stretcher. There was fluid other than blood leaking from his head. A yellowish fluid.

4

....

'Cells A5, A7, A12, roll up!' announced the guard in the control tower.

'What's he mean, roll up?' I asked.

'They're moving a bunch of us out,' Boyd said. 'Roll your mattress around your shit. We gotta go downstairs.'

'But we only just got here!' I was afraid and exasperated. I'd arrived at Towers jail hoping for relief from the mayhem, but seeing David get smashed had affected me more than the violence at The Horseshoe. Images of him on the stretcher, unconscious, possibly dead, were replaying in my mind.

'They roll people up all the time. They might think we had something to do with what happened to David 'cause he was our celly. We might be going to lockdown.'

Great, I thought. *I'm a suspect in a possible murder. And what the bloody hell's lockdown? Are there places worse than this?* Afraid of what Boyd might say, I didn't ask. I figured I'd just tough it out when I got there. I coiled my mattress around the bedding and carried my belongings onto the iron-railing balcony.

'Where ya moving us to?' yelled a black prisoner on the metal-grid stairs, windmilling his arms at the guards in the control tower. I stopped behind him, hoping he'd get out of my way. The guards ignored him. He waved again. His short sleeves fell back, exposing triceps protruding like thick horseshoes. When he gave up, I followed him down the stairs. I parked my rolled-up mattress by the sliding door that allowed us in and out of the pod.

'Where're you from?' I asked.

'Kingston,' he said, greeting me with a raised fist.

'I'm Shaun from England,' I said, bumping his fist.

'Just call me Kingston, Shaun,' he said in a friendly Caribbean voice, making me feel a bond with this fellow foreigner.

'How'd you end up in Arizona?' I asked.

'Got busted at Sky Harbor Airport. Shoulda never got off the plane. Was going from LA to New York. The plane stopped in Phoenix, so I figured I'd take a look around. They stopped me before I got back on the plane, found $100,000 cash in me carry-on. They took the money and arrested me.'

It seemed unjust. Was he telling the truth? He didn't look the criminal type. I believed him but decided against asking why he had so much money. Too personal. 'They robbed you,' I said, suspecting it was drug-related.

'Yeah, man. They ran my name, figured out I wasn't a citizen, took the money, and now they've started deportation proceedings against me, so I'll never be able to get the money back. It's kinda my fault for getting off the plane. I never knew Arizona was this bad. This state's the worst, Shaun. New York and LA don't fuck with you like that. I'm telling ya.'

'You won't be able to get your money back from the state?' I asked, thinking bringing drugs into Arizona wasn't one of my brightest ideas either.

'That's the thing: it's not my money,' he said, shaking his head.

'Oh no.' I pegged him as a smuggler for a yardie gang.

A pair of arms sleeved in white-supremacy tattoos threw a mattress next to mine. 'Wattup, wood!' They belonged to a stocky man with cropped ginger hair and an all-American square jaw. He was a few inches shorter than me, with a freckly face, a bulbous red nose and a collection of red marks on his forehead and cheeks that could have been acne or small lesions.

'I'm Shaun,' I said, bumping his fist. 'From England.'

'I'm Carter. Us woods gotta stick together in here.' He squinted at Kingston. 'Know what I'm saying, dawg?'

I didn't like being told who I could talk to, but I didn't want to make any enemies either. *Better play on my ignorance.* 'I'm new here,' I said, in a light-hearted way.

Carter leaned towards me, gazing without blinking. 'Well, learn fast if you don't wanna get smashed.'

Talking to Kingston had distracted me from the dangers of the environment, but Carter restored my stress. I didn't know what to say. Was he giving me advice or threatening me? I felt sweat trickle down the hairs in my armpits.

An announcement interrupted our conversation: 'Pill nurse in the house! Come to the sliding door with your IDs and a cup of water. Pill nurse in the house!'

The sick and mentally ill emerged from their cells bearing paper cups of water. They crowded our area, changing the dynamic of the day room. There was too much going on for Carter to bother me now.

A few seconds of static were followed by the guard's voice: 'Get away from the day-room door! Form one straight line!'

The sick lined up. The door slid open.

A Bulgarian shot-putter of a nurse stepped inside the day room and scowled at the men. 'Name?' she yelled at the first in line.

Holding up his ID, he replied, 'Washington.'

'Here's your lithium, your Prozac.' She watched him mouth the pills and drink water. 'I hope to God you swallowed them!'

'Yeah,' the man said, rubbing his left eye.

The nurse was furious. 'I don't believe you! Open your mouth. Raise your tongue. OK. Next!'

Each prisoner received the same treatment. Then as soon as she left, those who'd pretended to swallow their medication offered them for sale: 'Drugs for thugs!'

'Seroquel for one item!'

'Who wants Thorazine?'

'Gimme the Thorazine, dawg!'

'The best sleeping pills over here.'

The day room bustled like a marketplace. I was still admiring the barter, trying to decipher the terminology, when the control guard hit the button to activate the sliding door. I picked up my mattress and walked out. Being on the move again increased my anxiety.

A plump middle-aged guard with a blond flat-top streaked down the corridor. 'Pick your shit up! You're going to *my* tower – Tower 6!' he yelled, leaning into his stride as if he couldn't wait to take control of us. He spotted Boyd and smiled slyly. 'Oh no! Not you again!'

'Why Tower 6, Officer Alston? 'Cause that's where lockdown is?' Boyd asked.

Lockdown. David's dying. We're going to lockdown. I did nothing to save him. When he dies, I'll be charged with murder. It might even get pinned on me by the skinheads, and if I say it wasn't me they'll kill me too. Must stop thinking about David and the way he looked at me.

'None of your beeswax,' Officer Alston said. 'All that matters is you troublemakers behave in *my* tower. That includes not lying to me. Ever! I detest liars. So if you wanna stay off my shit list, don't lie to me. Now head down that corridor!'

Only just got here, I thought, and I'm lumped in with the troublemakers.

Or is this guard crazy? Some kind of military nut? Bracing to deal with a pod full of troublemakers, I shouldered my curled-up mattress and set off.

'Mordhorst still your shift partner?' Boyd asked.

'Yeah. I bet he just can't wait to see you again,' Officer Alston said.

Why's Boyd so cheerful? I thought. He knows where we're going. Maybe it's not so bad after all.

'Mordhorst ain't nuthin' nice,' Boyd announced. 'He just loves his job. He's the most grieved guard at Towers.'

'And he's proud of it,' Officer Alston said. 'He collects grievances. Wallpapers his home with them.'

As we walked down the cement-block corridor, the Tower 6 inmates mobbed the Plexiglas at either side of us. Afraid to stare directly at them, I flicked my eyes from left to right. Some of the whites nodded at Carter, which I took as a bad sign. In the control tower was Officer Mordhorst, a squat man with a round ruddy face, a bulldog eager to bite someone for no reason. I made a mental note to stay out of his way.

'C's lockdown. B's max security,' Boyd said, pointing at those pods. 'We must be going to D or A.'

Not lockdown? I thought. The relief distracted me momentarily. Until I realised I was about to be plunged into a new mob and who knew what danger. I had the jitters of a child stepping onto a roller-coaster for the first time. Would I be accepted? Would I be smashed? We stopped at the foot of the control tower. Tower 6 was identical to Tower 2, except in C pod the inmates were all locked down for violating jail rules. I noticed a group of prisoners in D pod looking at me. *What's going on? Have I lost it again or are they looking at me? Yes, they are. I must be a target.* One of them pointed at me. I felt my body heat rise. He was a buff hippy and looked familiar. Friend or someone I'd crossed?

Officer Alston read our cell assignments – mine was upstairs – and radioed Officer Mordhorst to activate D pod's sliding door. Taking some deep breaths, I planned to rush to my cell, and take it from there like yesterday. Hope for the best. Boyd dashed in first with a theatrical manner. Good old Boyd. My guinea pig.

'Look who it is, everyone!' someone yelled in the day room. 'Jack Nicholson's back!'

Boyd drew their attention. Good. He bowed and they laughed. Even better. That's exactly what I wanted to hear: laughter. Not the sound of someone getting smashed in the shower. *Keep them laughing, Boyd, at least for the ten seconds it'll take me to get to my cell.*

I stepped onto the metal-grid stairs. Seven seconds. Six. I was almost at the top, a mere three or four seconds away from my cell, when someone came up behind me. Fast. My back muscles clenched as I braced to be attacked.

'Shaun! English Shaun!'

I craned my neck, but kept going. It was the buff hippy. What did he want?

'It's Billy! Remember?'

'You look familiar, but I don't remember.' I tried to search my memories. Nothing registered. My mind was too congested with fear of the present to travel back to the past.

'I'm Billy,' he said, tapping his broad chest. 'I was in your limo with you outside the Icehouse that night you got Larry the Limo Driver so high he had to call out another limo driver. You stole my glitter girls, Samantha and Aubrey.'

I stopped at the top of the stairs. *Billy! Fellow raver!* My relief gushed. *I actually know someone in here. Surely this will help.* 'No shit! It is you. But you've doubled in size.' I wanted to hug him.

'Fellas, this is English Shaun!' he announced to the day room. 'I know him from the streets. He's a good fucking dude.'

Members of all four racial groups clustered around their separate tables looked over, and a few of them actually nodded and smiled. I couldn't believe it. *These men are smiling. They don't want to kill me.* I'd shown Billy a good time the night we'd partied and never expected to see him again. I walked along the balcony feeling a bit safer. He followed me into D10 and closed the door to almost-shut.

D10 was to the left of the top of the stairs, at the same height as the control tower it faced. It was a standard Towers' cell: six-by-nine foot, illegally triple-bunked. There was a mixture of unclean smells hanging in the hot air. The toilet stank as if tomcats had marked their territory on it. The short podgy man perched on the bottom bunk was giving off body odour with a vinegary tang to it. Scrutinising me with amused curiosity, he looked like a pocket-sized Henry VIII. He had Henry's features, but his long unkempt beard made him seem deranged. 'Wattup, dawg! I'm Troll. One of your new cellies.'

'I'm Shaun, Troll.' I placed my mattress down, and we bumped fists.

There was something endearing about this crazy-looking little guy. I was hoping to get more acquainted, but the door swung open and banged against the wall, making me jump.

A topless man with WHITE PRIDE tattooed across his midsection barged past Billy. Everything about him screamed king of the jungle. Size. Aura. Blond mane. 'Wattup, dawg! I'm Outlaw, the head of the whites.'

'I'm Shaun, a friend of Billy's.'

'Hey, dawg, you need any hygiene products, anything like stamps, envelopes?' Outlaw asked.

'I'll sort him out, dawg,' Troll said.

'Hey, you wanna go smoke, dude?' Billy asked.

'I don't smoke.' Being offered their kindness and saying no felt weird. I was tempted to start smoking just to bond.

'Everyone in here smokes,' Billy said. 'The more you get to smoke, the more important you are.'

Troll cackled like one of those fantasy-movie creatures who never causes any real harm. 'Good lookin' out on not smoking, dawg. We're trying to keep this a smoke-free cell. There's not many in here who don't smoke.'

I was relieved Troll didn't smoke.

'Are you sure you don't wanna jump in the car?' Billy said

'The car?' I asked, confused.

'Come smoke with us.'

'Thanks, but I'll pass.'

Billy and Outlaw darted out.

'I guess I'm on the top bunk,' I said.

Troll stood up. 'You start at the top and work your way down as your cellies leave,' he said, his frown exuding the authority of a teacher over a pupil. 'Look, I gotta go play spades. Catch you later, dawg.'

I was surprised he'd left so fast. Everyone seemed to be rushing to go somewhere in this place that went nowhere. Strange. After making my bed, I sat on the stool and tried to unwind. Impossible. I'd seen and been through so much, my nervous system wouldn't calm down. Although glad of the move to Tower 6 and Billy vouching for me, I still expected someone to attack me at any moment and couldn't take my eyes off the doorway. They'd let David settle in before pouncing on him. That could easily happen to me. I wondered if my heartbeat would ever return to normal.

I was happy to see Billy return. He sat on the toilet. 'So they finally caught up with you, eh?'

I told him about the raid and my charges. 'How about you?'

'I was on the news about six months ago. I reported a burglary at my house. The cops came out and got suspicious. A few days later, they sent SWAT to arrest me.'

'You called them out and they ended up arresting you?' A mosquito whined by my ear.

'I refused to be arrested. I was in a standoff for hours. It was all over the news. I've been here ever since. Haven't even done a crime.'

'That's outrageous! You shouldn't be here. I hope they let you out soon.' I thought about Kingston and decided Billy had suffered even more misfortune. I needed information: 'What's it like in here?' I hoped to make sense of the violence, so I wouldn't fall foul.

His expression darkened. 'You've gotta be very careful, Shaun. Watch what you say to people. Don't let anyone bulldog you, 'cause if anyone gets anything out of you, it opens the door for everyone else. If anyone calls you out – like says you're a punk-ass bitch – you gotta fight or else you automatically get smashed by your own race. Fights break out all the time over stupid shit. I've seen people get smashed over an orange or a brownie. I had nine fights in my first three months, so I quit doing meth, started working out, and I gained sixty pounds.'

Nine fights in three months! I need to get bigger. 'With this bloody rubbish food how can you possibly gain weight?'

'You gotta have your people put money on your books.'

Claudia. Must call her again.

'There's a store list you can shop from once a week. Had red death yet?'

'What's that?'

'The evening meal. Slop with mystery meat in it.'

'Oh no! Sounds worse than green baloney.' I was hungry for information on greater threats than food. 'I've got a question.'

'Go on.'

'What's all this head-of-the-race stuff about?'

'Each race has a head. Mexicans. Chicanos. Blacks and whites. Each head has torpedoes – usually youngsters looking to prove themselves – who smash people for their head, no questions asked. That's how they earn their tattoos. If the head of your race holds a meeting, you've gotta go or else you get smashed for failing to represent your race. The head of the whites is usually some Aryan Brotherhood dude here from prison. Outlaw is our head. So far we've not had a race riot under his rule. That's good. There's always someone getting smashed, but just try to stay away from the drugs, drama and politics and you'll be all right.'

'OK,' I said, worriedly trying to digest his advice.

'I'm glad I'm off meth. Now I just smoke weed and do these pills called Pac-Mans. Some guy who has seizures sells them to me. Hopefully, I'll be out of here soon and not have to deal with this bullshit. There's a lot of meth in the pod right now. Some of them have been up for days. So just be careful, 'cause when they've been up like this they start sketching out on each other and shit gets crazy. You'll be all right in this cell, though. Troll's a good celly, and so is Schwartz.'

'Schwartz?' I asked, imagining a neo-Nazi.

'Yeah, but don't be fooled by the name. Schwartz is a Chicano, a youngster, a cool little dude. And Troll spends a lot at the store every week. He's a rich kid from Cali. Anyway, man, you're trying to settle in, so I'll leave you alone. If you need anything just come down to D14.'

'Thanks, Billy,' I said, comforted by what he'd said about Troll and Schwartz.

I had to wait almost an hour in the day room before a phone became available to call Claudia.

'I'm glad you called again,' Claudia said. 'It sounded so crazy in there last time.'

'I'm much better. They moved me,' I said. 'I met someone I know, and it's much safer where I am now. How about you?'

'Not good,' she said, starting to cry.

'What's the matter?'

'What do you think's the matter? You've been arrested!'

'Look, I'm all right. You've got to be strong. We've both got to be strong.'

'I feel so scared for you in the jail, especially after that last call.'

'I'm OK. What happened didn't affect me.' Again, I saw the image of David on a stretcher, his head leaking fluid. 'How're you?'

'I can't sleep properly since they knocked our door down. One night, I was laying in my mom's bed with Floppy and – remember how I used to bother you to hold your hand while we were sleeping? – I did that to my mom. At first she thought it was OK 'cause she was half asleep, but then later on I held her hand so tight she jumped up and threw my arm away.'

I laughed. 'That's–'

'It really scared her. I don't know exactly what she said, but it was something along the lines of, "What the fuck are you doing? You're weird! Stop snuggling me!"'

Imagining her short, tough, beer-loving mum saying such things, I laughed hard, and Claudia joined in. 'What time are you coming to visit tomorrow?'

'I'm gonna try and get there for 9 a.m. 'cause that's when they open.'

'How'd you find all this out?'

'I called the phone number and went through all the different prompts, where you press different numbers. It gave the visitation schedule and all that stuff. What do you think I should wear?'

'Anything. I just need to see you.'

'I can't wear sexy clothes.'

We both laughed.

'It doesn't matter. I just need to see you. And please find out how to put money on my books before I starve to death.'

'Are we going to be able to hug each other, hold hands, kiss each other?'

'I don't know. I'll have to ask my cellmates. I hope so. I really need to hug and kiss you right now.'

After calling Claudia, I lay on my bunk, my mind bobbing around on the swirl of events. Staring at the ceiling a few inches from my head, I wondered how much of the brown splatter was blood and whose blood would be up there next. Every now and then I slapped away a mosquito with its landing gear out. Then the voices started again, rising from the chatter downstairs, insisting I get smashed. Other voices joined in, led by Billy's, defending me. Concluding it was a rerun of yesterday when I'd charged onto the balcony for no reason, I took no action. But I continued to hear voices, one minute getting frightened and convinced they were real, and the next, telling myself I was going crazy and shrugging them off.

Troll entered with a baby-faced Mexican American. 'Here's our other celly, Schwartz.'

Glad of Schwartz's warm eyes and smile, I leaned onto my side and dangled my fist for him to bump.

'Viddy well, little brother. Viddy well,' Schwartz said, imitating a working-class English accent. 'I heard you're from England.'

'That's a great *Clockwork Orange* impression,' I said, looking down at him from near the ceiling.

'We were all feeling a bit shagged and fagged and fashed, it being a night of no small expenditure.'

'That's the best I've ever heard an American do it,' I said. 'How the bloody hell did you learn all that?'

Schwartz sat on the stool. Troll took the bottom bunk, so I was looking down on the top of his head.

'I watch it all the time. It's one of my favourite movies. I practise Alex's lines at home.'

I was thankful for all things English that were novelties abroad. *Maybe my Englishness will continue to help me in here.*

'Aren't you wondering how you ended up in a cell with a Chicano called Schwartz?' Troll asked.

'Yes,' I said.

'Got a Mexican mom,' Schwartz said. 'Pop's American. His parents are German.'

'Then we're fellow Europeans,' I said.

We discussed our charges. Troll had Class 2 felonies, including fraudulent schemes and artifices; Schwartz, a petty drug possession.

Schwartz demanded I climb down from my bunk so he could demonstrate something. On the tiny steel table, he placed a black pawn on a chessboard. 'I'm getting bonded out soon, but I'll be right back. Compared to you two, I'm just this little guy.' He pointed at the pawn. 'In the real world, this is how people like me get pushed around.' He knocked the pawn over with a white castle and surrounded the castle with black pawns. 'The only way the little people like me can push back against the big people with power and money is when we gang up like this.' He moved the pawns closer to the castle. 'But when we push back, they call the big guns in, and we can never ever win.' He circled the black pawns with the larger white pieces and knocked the pawns down with a white knight and bishop.

I laughed at how well Schwartz had summarised a subject I'd struggled to understand in economics: Karl Marx's theory of class conflict.

'It's the same in jail. They'll do us dirty, and we'll take a stand, flood our cells and shit, but then they'll send the goon squad in.'

'The goon squad?' I asked.

'Sheriff Joe Arpaio's goons,' Schwartz said. 'They're massive dudes who come in, throw us around, make us get butt naked and blast us with Tasers and shotgun rounds.'

'Shotgun rounds!' I said, hoping he was joking.

'Non-lethal. You'll see them soon enough,' Troll said, chilling me more. 'You play chess?'

'Not for about 20 years,' I said.

'Let's play.' Troll started setting up the board.

Schwartz stood up. 'I'm outtie. Later, cellies.'

'Whoever draws white or wins a game gets to sit on the stool. The other stands.' Troll held out two fists. 'Pick one.'

'The left.'

He unclenched a black pawn. 'Unlucky, dawg.'

Troll listened to his tiny black radio via earplugs and sang during the opening stage of the game. I was rusty, and it showed. But my rustiness lowered his guard, and he made some careless moves. He turned the music off too late to stage a comeback. Heckling me into losing concentration didn't work. I won by a narrow margin. He said, 'Ain't that-about-a-bitch,' abandoned his radio and continued to talk trash, probing for chinks in my psyche as we started the next game. I complimented him on his chess ability, hoping to throw his game off. Playing Troll taught me a lot about his crafty side. We ended up tied 3–3.

'You've got game, dawg,' Troll said, returning to his bunk.

I stayed on the stool. 'You too. How did someone as intelligent as you get busted?'

Troll rested his elbows on his thighs and steepled his fingertips. 'I was going in banks with fake IDs and cashing cheques. I'd take out small amounts, get to know the bank staff, and when I felt comfortable, I'd withdraw a large sum. The crazy thing is, on the day I got busted the cops had already let me go.'

'What do you mean?'

'The bank called the cops. The cops came and questioned me, and I bullshitted my way out of it. I left the bank and was on my way to my car when the Feds stopped me. I tried to bullshit the Feds, but they were having none of it.' He pressed his palms together as if praying to erase his arrest. 'That was a year ago. I've been here fighting my case ever since.'

'I can't imagine what it must be like to be stuck in this hellhole for a year,' I said, clinging tighter to the hope I'd be released somehow. 'I'd go insane.'

'Last year, they offered me five years, and I refused to sign the plea bargain. I'm from Cali. You have to kill someone there to get five years. So what did they offer me the next time? Eighteen fucking years! This state's the worst to get caught in. Arizona ain't nuthin' nice, dawg.' He dropped his chin onto his palms and stared at the concrete as if at a funeral.

'So now what?'

His eyes met mine, and sparkled irrationally. 'I'm fighting back, dawg! I've filed a Rule 11.'

'Rule 11?'

'It means you're not competent to stand trial. If you file a Rule 11 and they determine you're crazy, they send you to the nuthouse and let you go after a few years.'

'A lot of people must be filing Rule 11s then.' I added, filing a Rule 11 to my list of legal options.

'They are. But not many get it. It can take them years to run all the tests while you sit rotting in here. I've got to act like I'm nuts every time I see the doctors. That's why I don't shave or take care of myself and I look like a troll. Some guys go in to see the doctors and eat their own shit. Would you eat your own shit if they'd let you go tomorrow?'

'I don't want to think about it.'

Troll grinned like a juvenile. 'If they said all you had to do was suck off the judge and he'd let you go, would you?'

'You are a Rule 11!'

Cackling, Troll slid a brown paper bag out from under his bunk. 'Hey, wanna candy bar or something?'

'I'm bloody starving,' I said, salivating.

'Snickers?'

'Hell, yeah!' I demolished the Snickers in record time, appreciating it more than anything I'd ever eaten.

'In here, he who controls the food, controls the prisoners. And I'm talking about store food, not state food like red death. I used to get $500 worth of store a week. They had to bring two trolleys with store on them: one for the rest of the pod and one just for me. Then they decided I must be getting extorted for the money on my books, so they changed the rules and now the limit you can spend on store is $100 a week.' His eyes latched onto the control tower. 'Looks like swing shift's here. The whole atmosphere changes when Mordhorst goes home. We've got Mendoza and Noble.'

'What're they like?'

'Mendoza's the Chicano with the glasses on. Stutters a lot. Seems friendly enough, but I've seen him slam motherfuckers to the ground. The youngster's Noble. Some kind of cage fighter. A military reservist, too. We've got way more play with these than the other two.'

'Play?'

'Yeah, we can get away with more shit.'

Hours later, I was on my bunk reading Troll's Spanish dictionary when Officer Mendoza announced. 'Chow's in the house! L . . . L . . . Line up at the slider! Fully dressed and with y . . . your IDs or you will not be s . . . s . . . served!'

Troll sprung up. 'Come on, let's get in line, so we don't have to wait around.'

We dashed downstairs. The men awaiting red death had the dissatisfied look of Russians in a bread queue. The first in line presented his ID to Officer Noble and took a tray from the trusty. Noble ticked each name off his clipboard, so no one could claim a second tray.

When Troll received his, he turned to me and said, 'I don't eat red death. I donate it.' He gave his tray to a gaunt man who'd been hovering to one side of us and hurried up the stairs.

A trusty handed me a large brown plastic tray. The slop – red death – looked like carroty vomit blended with blood. Meat and gristle in assorted shapes, shades and sizes were protruding from it. Gagging on the gamy smell, I placed the tray on the nearest table and sat down. Because I was one of the first to get served, the races hadn't mobbed the tables yet, so I'd forgotten about the segregation.

Seconds later, a cannonball of a Mexican tapped me on the shoulder. 'You can't sit here!' He had a shaved head, deep-set eyes and long eyelashes.

Dozens of men focused on us. I maintained eye contact.

The Mexican put his hands on his hips. Raising his voice, he said, 'This table paisas' table!'

Mexicans surrounded me. None smiling. I'd been a fool to think I was safe due to Billy's introduction. Maybe I was safe from the whites, but what about the other races? *Where are all of these Mexicans coming from? I've got to get out of here but not in a cowardly way.*

'No problem,' I said in a deep voice, trying to sound tough. Standing up, I looked around.

Troll flew down the stairs. 'England, you can't sit there!' Turning to the Mexican who'd tapped me on the shoulder, he said, 'Hey, Carlo, this is England, your new neighbour. England, say hello to Carlo, the head of the paisas.'

The atmosphere turned friendly as fast as it had soured. *I can't get over this place: the Mexicans aren't going to smash me now. We're all going to be friends.* I bumped fists with Carlo, greeting him with the limited Spanish I knew. He seemed to appreciate my effort.

'Come over here!' Billy yelled.

The whites were laughing at what I saw as a potentially life-threatening situation. Had I blown it out of proportion? I thought of Rob the skinhead's words in Tower 2: *You've gotta lot to learn, dawg.* It was standing room only at the whites' table.

'Give him some room on the corner,' Outlaw said.

The whites were shovelling down slop, chatting, gnawing on the mystery meat. Some of them eyeballed my tray.

With my stomach cramping as if it were trying to digest its own walls, I was in a hurry to eat. I dunked my plastic Spork into the red death, fished out a chunk of potato, and scraped most of the slop off. I raised my Spork – salivating in the way Englishmen are conditioned to do at the prospect of a good spud – and was just about to devour it when I spotted the lesions. Large. Brown. Deeply engrained. My Spork stopped short of my lower lip. Devastated, I returned the potato to the slop. Eating the two slices of bread that didn't have any mould on them dried my mouth up.

'Any of you guys want this food?' I asked.

All of their eyes crowded my tray at once.

'I'll take care of that. Not even gonna eat your donut, dawg?' Outlaw asked with disbelief.

I slid my tray to Outlaw. 'It's all yours.'

'Good lookin' out, dawg!' Outlaw snatched the donut, and divided the red death among the whites.

Now they'd classified me as a food source, they were slightly warmer towards me. I took advantage of the tiny elevation in their mood to excuse myself from the table. Depressed by hunger, I trudged home and found Troll munching commissary.

'A month from now, you'll be eating red death just like the rest of them.'

'I wouldn't eat red death if it was the last meal on earth, and I don't see you eating it either!'

Troll must have been a mind reader. 'I can give you another Snickers, dawg, but you're gonna have to get me back on store day.'

'No problema.'

I played chess with Troll until 10.30 when Officer Mendoza announced, 'Lockdown! Lockdown! Ki . . . Ki . . . Kiss each other good night and return to your cells!'

Whooping and yelling erupted in the day room.

'We ain't locking down!'

'Fuck you!'

'Come make us lockdown!'

Some of the prisoners pelted the Plexiglas with rotten grapefruits. The more hyperactive chased each other around, cackling like children on a playground. Reluctantly, they drifted back to their cells and slammed their doors. They taunted young Officer Noble, walking cell to cell with a headcount clipboard. When Noble left, the obscene banter grew louder. Mexicans sang in Spanish. Men chatted through the vent system. Others exchanged threats and swore they would fight when the doors reopened. Every now and then everyone hushed to listen to a dirty joke. It was hours before the only sounds left were snoring, the fan rattling on the day-room wall and water dripping from the shower as steadily as my life leaking away.

5

....

I was sitting on the toilet watching *Jerry Springer* through my doorway – cell D10 had one of the best views of the day-room TV – when the announcement came: 'D10, Attwood, you have a regular visit!'

I jumped up, giddy and excited, grabbed my anti-shank toothbrush, smeared it with AmerFresh and leaned over the sink – a steel basin above the toilet caked in toothpaste spit and chin shavings. Pushing a metal button made water dribble from the tiny faucet. Attempting to get rid of the foul breath caused by the vapours rising from my constantly empty stomach, I brushed until my gums bled.

'D10, Attwood, turn out for your visit!'

Prisoners in the day room parroted the announcement. Some came to my door.

'C'mon, dawg! You've gotta visit!'

'Get your ass out there, dawg!'

'I'm coming! I'm coming!' I yelled, applying state deodorant to my armpits. The previous layer had gone the way of my sweat. The deodorant bubbled and fizzed and settled into a foam with a cleaning-products smell. I didn't know the prisoners shunned the state deodorant, that most of them used the ladies' stick deodorant from the commissary. I threw my shirt on, attached my ID to the upper left side and rushed from the cell. I came bounding down the metal-grid stairs as joyful as a dog fetching its first stick of the day, harangued from both flanks by men yelling, 'Who's coming to see ya, dawg?'

'The missus!' I said proudly, and waved at the guard.

The control guard saw me right away and hit the button to open the sliding door. 'Do you know where the visitation room is?' he asked over the speaker system.

Looking up at him in the Plexiglas bubble, I shook my head.

'You!' He pointed at another prisoner in the corridor. 'Show him where the visitation room is!'

'Wassup, dawg!' the youngster said.

Beaming at the prospect of seeing Claudia, I said. 'All right, dawg!'

Starting with dawg, I'd been adding jail slang to my vocabulary in the hope of fitting in.

Smiling back, he said, 'Follow me, dawg.'

We exited the building. The sun blinded me for a few seconds. We took the short path down the breezeway and turned right into Visitation.

'Stay in there until the visitors are all seated.' Officer Green – the most obese guard I'd seen so far – pointed at a Plexiglas holding tank overlooking the visitation room. Behind rectangular spectacles, his beady eyes were full of suspicion. He was struggling to keep an eye on everything going on around him. Prisoners arriving. Prisoners in the holding tank. Electronically activated doors opening and closing to allow guards in and out.

The visitation room was the size of a small warehouse. It consisted of a guard station – two officers sat at a raised desk – overlooking rows of small wooden tables and blue plastic chairs bolted to the floor. In the corners of the room were old security cameras that creaked as they rotated. There were no vending machines or toilets. The visitors had to wait outside, sometimes for hours, while all of the prisoners summoned for visits were packed into the holding tank.

Almost an hour into my wait, the visitation-room security door opened with a tremendous grinding sound. Seeing the first batch of our visitors, we scrambled to our feet. Fights almost broke out when the biggest inmates shoulder-barged their way to the front of the holding tank. We must have looked like a display of wild animals. The attention from our visitors soon changed the mood back to friendly. There was much waving of hands and blowing of kisses. In the next batch of visitors, I saw Claudia's long golden hair, pale narrow face and big eyes. My heart fluttered. She spotted me and waved. Smiling, I longed to hug her. I hoped Officer Green would let us out of the tank soon. Everything in my life had been taken away, and I was grateful to have something so precious back, even if only for a short while. On the tips of my toes, I continued to smile and wave as she sat down. She looked nervous until she flashed her long-toothed smile.

Officer Green manned the guard station as if stood on a stage, a no-nonsense look on his face. 'In a moment, I'm going to allow the inmates in.' He spoke slowly and precisely. 'I do expect you to obey the rules at all times. Posted on the wall are the rules.' Everyone's heads swivelled, and he paused for a few seconds. 'If you do not follow the rules, your visit will be ended. You will not get a second chance! There will be no passing items. Anyone that gets caught passing items will have their future visits cancelled and may possibly be charged with promoting prison contraband. There will be no hanky-panky.' He puckered his face at the few visitors snickering. 'Anyone caught kissing will lose their visit. You may hold hands. If your hands slip below the table at any time, you will lose your visit. Do you understand me, ladies and gentlemen?'

The crowd murmured acknowledgement.

'Enjoy your visits then. Officer Gonzales, please let the inmates in.'

Officer Gonzales was a slim fellow in his early 20s. A new recruit. He opened the door that allowed us into the visitation room. 'Form a straight line. Roll down your pants' cuffs. Have your IDs ready as you enter the room.'

We showed him our IDs and then formed a line at the guard station. Officer Green ticked our names off his list and instructed us to specific tables. 'Attwood, table 9.'

Rushing to Claudia, I yelled, 'I'm so glad you're here!' I noticed she was crying. 'I know. It's crazy, isn't it? I think I'm still in shock, too.' I sat down, picked up her thin hands and leaned into the musky floral scent of her perfume, filling myself with as much of her smell as I could in one loud inhalation.

'I love you,' she said, her hands trembling within mine.

'I love you, too. I wish I could show you my pink boxer shorts.'

She managed a chuckle. 'Pink's my favourite colour.'

'I know,' I said, smiling. 'So you all right or what?'

'I'm OK if you're OK,' she said, brightening up.

'I'm doing fine. It was a bit rough at first, but so far I'm not having problems. It's just the conditions suck, though.'

'Like what?'

'The A/C barely works. There's mosquitoes everywhere. The heat's the worst, though. I can barely sleep. I'm basically lying in a pool of sweat all day.'

'The food must be terrible,' she said, shaking her head.

'Red death! That's what these guys call it. Slop on rotten potatoes that have white hairs in them. It's the only cooked meal we get once a day. Breakfast's raw green baloney and mouldy bread. I've barely eaten anything since I got here.'

'Well, I've put some money on your books.'

'Thanks! Thanks so much!' I said, gently squeezing her hands. 'Now

I can buy some peanuts or something to stop my hunger pains. Some of the inmates spend the day rummaging for food. I see them going through the trash. I got lucky: my celly, Troll, gets store, so he's hooked me up with Snickers. Most people are begging him for store. Thanks for the money. It'll go a long way in here.'

'What's the people you live with like?'

'My cellmates are nice, but they've got three of us squeezed into a tiny cell. I was in Tower 2 at first. I didn't like it there. I didn't know anyone, and the skinheads were running wild. I was so nervous. But now I'm in Tower 6, it's better.'

'That's good.'

'I sat at the wrong dining table, though.'

'What do you mean?'

I explained the racial segregation to Claudia, about the heads of each race and their torpedoes.

'It sounds creepy to me.'

'Yeah, the heads decide who gets smashed and who gets to smoke and get high.'

'Cigarettes and drugs in here! How?'

'They keyster them in. That means they stick them in their behinds. The visitors bring them in in balloons and condoms. When the guards aren't looking, they pass them, and the inmates stick them in their behinds.'

'That's disgusting!'

'They put all kinds of things in there. Lighters. Needles. Knives. Nearly everyone's getting high.'

We'd just finished avowing our eternal love when Officer Green announced, 'Visits are over! Visitors, please say your goodbyes. Inmates remain seated.' Our 30 minutes were up.

It was hard to let go of her hands and watch her slip away. The feeling of being miserably alone again overwhelmed me. Most of the visitors, including Claudia, grouped by the security door. A few remained, crying, staring tenderly at the prisoners they were visiting. Claudia kept waving and blowing kisses. I struggled to put on a brave face.

'Visits are over! Did you not hear me? You all need to leave the room or else I will suspend your visitation privileges. Do you hear me, table 21? Leave now!'

When all of the visitors were clustered in front of the security door, it groaned open. They walked out, waving sadly, some, including Claudia now, were crying. They left behind an atmosphere redolent of over-perfumed women and soiled nappies.

'Inmates, stand up and enter that room over there.' Officer Green pointed at the door of the strip-search room. It was tiny and windowless. We crammed in. He locked the door and abandoned us.

There was barely any air flowing into the room. By the end of the first hour, my clothes were soaked. I felt increasingly dizzy and feared I'd suffocate. Most of us had showered before our visits, but now we were all beginning to stink again. Every time we heard the jingle of keys, we stopped panting and focused on the doors. When the jingling faded, we cursed Officer Green and returned to wallowing in our claustrophobia. He left us in there for about two hours. By the time he opened the door, I was dazed from a heat headache. I suspected it was a unique form of torture he'd devised for those of us lucky enough to have visits. It was effective: as much as I looked forward to seeing Claudia again, I was dreading spending hours in that room.

'Strip down to your boxers, gentlemen. I'm going to let you out one at a time.' His slow steady voice contained a trace of delight in what he'd done to us. 'As you exit the room, hand me your clothes. While I search your clothes, I want you to drop your boxers, lift up your ball sack, spin around, bend over and spread your cheeks.'

The stench was bad enough before the liberation of our crotch odour. In a hurry to escape the room, the men who'd disrobed the fastest were ploughing their way towards Officer Green. I didn't fancy my chances against the mass of big tattooed men, so I hung near the back. I noticed how everyone's boxers were patterned with sweat like mine.

'Drop and spin,' Officer Green said to each inmate.

Eventually, I stepped forward and handed him my stripes.

He felt my stripes for contraband. 'Drop and spin.'

I dropped my boxers to my ankles, grabbed my scrotum and raised it.

'Good. Spin around.'

I turned, bent over and spread my buttocks.

'OK. Get dressed.' He returned my clothes, and I joined the men getting dressed in the corridor. When everyone was done and grouped in the corridor, he said, 'Go back to your houses.'

I was permitted three regular visits per week. Claudia visited twice on the weekdays, and my aunt Ann joined her on the weekends. As much as I hated waiting in the strip-search room, it was a small price to pay for the visits. Claudia did everything she possibly could for me under the circumstances. Her devotion was my lifeline. She sent letters daily, and I replied with equal frequency. Outside of visits, mail call was the most exciting time of the day. The guard would place the letters on a table in the day room, and we'd mob around him. He'd yell the name on every letter, and the prisoners would be happy or sad depending on whether they received any.

May–June 2002

Hey now, Claudia!

Just got your first letter. Well, at least the first one to get through, and thank you very much. Glad to read you're occupying your time and in good spirits.

You asked about this making our love stronger, and I think that anything that does not break us up will make our love stronger. I just regret that my mess is taking your life away from you when you should be out having the time of your life. I am so sorry that you are being put through this punishment as well.

Today, I'm just doing the usual, playing chess, reading a Spanish dictionary and living off mouldy bread and oranges.

One of my cellmates, Troll, just got back from a legal visit. They're offering him eight years so he's bumming. He's such a nice guy. It sucks how their lives are taken away so easily.

My new celly, OG, is teaching me about shanks. He said a shank will save you when some 'big muvvas come for ya', but he added that shanks always get him in trouble. I think I'll stay away from shanks. I'll tell you how he carries a shank around in a later letter.

Keep writing to me as much as you can. Your letter really brightened my day up. I can't wait to see you on Saturday.

Love,

Shaun

P.S. It sucks writing with these golf pencils. They constantly go blunt and I have to sharpen them on the walls.

Hello my love,

Thanks so much for all of your love and support. Without your help I would be mental right now. I love you loads, and my whole family think you are great for supporting me. I have found 'a good girlfriend finally', that's what my mum said.

Thanks also for putting money on my books. I won't go hungry this week. Whoopee! Isn't it pretty sad when the highlight of my week is eating a Snickers bar? Thinking about Snickers is making my stomach start to rumble. Chow should be coming around soon. I've requested a veggie diet, as the meat here is atrocious. If you ever get arrested, remember to tell them you're a veggie straight away otherwise weeks of red death will kill you!

It's so boring in here. It's like an insane asylum, but, ah well, there's little I can do but grin and bear it. I read the dictionary for 2–3 hours a day, work out, play chess, eat the usual crap. I'm doing 500 push-ups a day with Sniper, a La Victoria gang member downstairs.

There is an ol' prison tale circulating that they put stuff in the orange drink to reduce our aggressiveness and a side effect is it is harder to get erections. In the shower, there is a button on the wall that you either have to press every ten seconds or keep it pressed the whole time to keep the water running. I think they designed this to make it hard to concentrate on jacking off. There is no privacy in the shower just skilful towel work. Sandals are essential, as you can imagine with 40 guys a day jacking off. I've heard stories of gangrene, swollen feet and toes getting cut off.

It's official. I'm the in-house chess champion. Twenty-three games undefeated. One of the guys I play is in cell 8. Right next to his bunk, there is an ant breakout. He wakes up with them in his sheets, crawling all over him, proper Third World style. I feel sorry for him.

[After chow]

The evening meal sucked. I traded the whole thing for tomorrow morning's fruit. I'm going to load up on Kit Kats and Snickers bars. Crap never tasted so good.

There was a fight. A guy got bloodied and his arm broke.

Signing out for now,

Love,

Shaun XXX

Hey my love,

It's 2 a.m. I can't sleep and just jumped out of bed because I have to write and tell you how special you are to me. It is your strength and love that have really helped me to cope with this situation. I am experiencing all kinds of emotions. I feel like I have let my family down and I am worthless. When I first got to Tower 2, I was hearing voices of people wanting to kill me, and I think I had a nervous breakdown that night. But after speaking to you I turned a corner. Talking to you gave me hope and meaning. You have proven to be my guardian angel.

It's starting to really suck in here because of the heat. It's too hot to work out or do anything other than lie down. I hate being treated like an animal. I constantly see other inmates cracking up mentally and being taken away. Troll tells me that now my first month is up time goes really fast.

The food has been absolutely shit for over a week now. The mashed potatoes today tasted like bleach and looked like come. I am wasting away.

A friend of Wild Man's landed in the cell next to me. He almost got in a fight as soon as he got here because he thinks there's a snitch in the pod. I went downstairs and brought him upstairs to cool off. The officers saw it, though, and locked him in his cell.

Playing chess with my celly Troll I put your pic next to the board for good luck and I won! Now we're all plugged into 104.7, and when a good song comes on OG and Troll insist we all dance. I'm getting good at dancing to rap.

I love you!

Goodnight.

Shaun XXX

My incarceration brought us so close, I proposed to Claudia. She said yes and mailed me pictures of wedding dresses she liked. I stuck pictures of Claudia under the bunk above me. Pictures I stared at throughout the day and drew strength from whenever the sadness of our separation overwhelmed me.

6

....

Phoenix is the hottest big city in America. It's against federal law for a jail to use heat as a punishment or a health threat, so, to get around this, Towers used a swamp cooler that barely worked. It was supposed to blow water-cooled air through a vent system into our cells, but the little air we received was as warm as our breath. Then in June, it completely stopped blowing. Outdoor temperatures exceeded 110°F, making us dizzy, ill and delirious. So many heatstroke victims were taken to hospital on stretchers, lockdowns were constant. At night, my skin itched, keeping me awake, and in the day I'd pass out while reading.

'Due to temperatures rising to over 110°, you're now authorised to wear only your boxers in the day room!' Officer Alston announced.

Cheering at this minuscule concession, we stripped on the spot. In our cells. On the balcony. In the day room. We paraded around in our pink boxers and orange shower sandals, comparing the rashes patterning our bodies like the mould on our daily bread. Some of the men mocked Troll for having faeces stains on the back of his boxers. Whether it was to promote his crazy act or not, he said he didn't care.

There was always an element poised to take advantage of any new liberties, and this case was no exception. Four men stripped naked, filled the mop bucket and took turns throwing water on each other. I was feeling effeminate enough in my pink boxers, and what they were up to looked like gay porn – not that I've ever seen any.

Sheriff Joe Arpaio introduced pink boxers in 1995. He claimed prisoners were stealing the old white boxers with MCSO (Maricopa County Sheriff's Office) stencilled on the rear and selling them for up to $10 in Phoenix. When laundry staff reported $48,000 worth of the white boxers missing, Arpaio had the boxers dyed pink. Arpaio said the pink boxers were too noticeable to smuggle out of the jail, causing theft to plummet. His opponents claimed the pink boxers were introduced as a moneymaking scheme and pointed out that Arpaio quickly offered them for sale worldwide, raising $400,000 within months. 'I guess I should thank the inmates for stealing the shorts,' Arpaio said. 'Their crime was the birth of a great idea.'

Prisoners were constantly on the move in the jail system. We were all subject to being rehoused within the jail itself. Sentenced prisoners were sent to the prison system to serve the balance of their sentences. (In America, jails mostly hold prisoners on remand.) Federal marshals collected illegal aliens awaiting deportation. Some prisoners bonded out. Schwartz was among the latter, and I was sorry to lose such an agreeable cellmate. In accordance with the inmates' rules, I got the middle bunk. The top one went to OG, an intimidating Mexican American in jail for trying to shank (stab with a homemade knife) someone in the prison system. OG had a Freddie Mercury moustache and no front teeth due to his penchant for fighting prisoners. He snapped at random and credited decades of heroin addiction for his paranoid delusions. His behaviour towards Troll and me ranged from threatening to shank us in our sleep because we were conspiring against him to singing and dancing with us on Saturday nights when we tuned our radios into a station that played live DJ sets from Club Freedom. Not that he didn't threaten to kill anyone on Saturday nights – he did, gleefully. He threatened everyone who complained our revelry was keeping them awake. But as most of the inmates were out of their minds on drugs, only a minority spoke up.

Even after partying for years, I'd never seen such devotion to getting high as in my new neighbours. I had no idea society rounded up its drug-addict criminals and dumped them in a place awash with the hardest drugs. The Mexicans were keystering in many ounces of crystal meth at Visitation. Troll traded commissary for some eight balls, and the dealers gave OG some for protection. As he didn't do meth, OG traded it for commissary to buy heroin with. Troll and OG transformed D10 into a drug den. No forewarning. No board meeting. We received constant visitors, about two-thirds of the pod, wanting to snort, smoke and inject crystal meth in our cell.

Choosing to do drugs had put me in jail, so taking drugs now was inconceivable. How would I survive or fight my case if drugs were scrambling my mind? While the traffic flowed in and out of our cell, I lay on my bunk doing exercises from a Spanish textbook. But the commotion made it hard to concentrate, and the visitors frowned on my sobriety. Cell visiting was prohibited, so I feared the guards would search our cell and send us to lockdown. Or even worse: charge me for any drugs found, which could harm my case and extend my stay.

Early one morning, the addicts piled into D10 as soon as the doors popped open. They'd been up all night on crystal meth, and their voices woke me up. OG was snoring on the top bunk, but Troll hadn't slept, and he began the morning ritual of dispensing them more meth.

'I'm trying to sleep!' I yelled. 'Can't you guys keep it down?'

'Who the fuck are you, telling us to shut up?' Outlaw replied.

Regretting offending the head of the whites, I tried to make amends. 'Just trying to sleep, fellas,' I said in a diplomatic tone that didn't prevent them from issuing enough threats to unnerve me from dozing off.

Joining the queue for breakfast, I had the feeling of being watched. I took my Ladmo bag to my cell and ate quietly with Troll, swilling water in my mouth to get the stale bread down. No moves were made against me that day, but my sixth sense told me not to let my guard down.

I'd been working out with Sniper for a week. He was the son of a shot-caller in the New Mexican Mafia, a member of the La Victoria gang out of Tempe, and the head of the Chicanos. Short, muscular and clean-cut, he exercised fanatically. A friendship was blossoming between us, so on the day after I'd yelled at the men in my cell, I was concerned when I saw him pacing the balcony, spying on the table of his fellow Mexican-Americans.

Keeping his eyes on the day room, he sidestepped into D10. 'Something's up with my people, dawg.'

'What do you mean, Sniper?' Troll asked from his bunk.

'I heard one of them call me a snitch, and now they're planning on rolling me up.'

'No way, Sniper! Who said you was a snitch, dawg?' Troll asked.

Sniper went back to the balcony, nodded at the Chicano table and looked at Troll.

'Your own people!' Troll said. 'Are you sure it's not just the meth making you trip out, dawg?'

'Yup.'

'Then you'd better go handle your business and put your people in check.'

Sniper dashed out, frowning as if someone had hit him in the forehead with an axe. He descended the stairs and paced around the day room like an animal circling prey. Hoping working out with him would distract him from his paranoia, I went down and we started sets of push-ups.

Glistening with sweat and circling the day room was Outlaw. He'd complete a lap, drop down, do a set of push-ups off his knuckles and do another lap. Every time he passed us, he gave me a funny look. I had no idea what the look meant and put it down to animosity from the morning I'd yelled at the men.

When Sniper went to fill his water bottle, Outlaw came up to me, quickly joined by Carter.

'Wattup, dawg!' I said, expecting them to offer me their fists to bump, but they didn't.

'I know you're new here and shit, but do you see any of the other whites working out with the other races?' Outlaw asked.

Carter folded his meaty freckled arms and shook his head.

Looking around, I realised the men were all working out in small groups of their own races. I felt a wave of anxiety. This was my second strike with Outlaw after he'd told me off the other morning. I was afraid to speak in case I made matters worse.

Sniper re-emerged and saw them talking to me.

'What should I do?' I said low enough for Sniper not to hear.

'Finish your workout, dawg,' Outlaw said, and they both walked away.

'Everything all right, dawg?' Sniper asked.

'It's all good,' I said.

'Your people turning on you, too?'

'No one's turning on no one, dawg.'

Sniper fed off my agitation. His paranoia returned. He quit the workout to pace the balcony. Afraid of him doing something he might regret, I explained the situation to OG, his fellow Chicano. We spent until lockdown urging Sniper not to fight anyone, insisting he was just high and needed to sleep it off. But the next morning, he was our first visitor.

OG climbed down from the top bunk. 'You're cut off, Sniper.'

Taking the stool, Sniper grinned like a repentant child. 'It was my first time ever doing it! What do you expect? I got a few hours' sleep. I'm fine now.'

'You slept!' Troll said, perched on the bottom bunk. 'I just listened to my radio all night.'

Picking sleep from his eyes, OG said, 'Sniper, you were about ready to smash someone last night.'

'Don't do it, Sniper,' Troll said.

'I can handle my shit!' Sniper said, folding his arms across his chest.

'Don't do it, Sniper,' I said, fearing for Sniper. I hoped the cell would clear so I could get off my bunk and use the toilet without all of them standing around arguing.

Sniper tilted his head back. 'Hell, I've done all kinds of other drugs.'

'Come on, Sniper, don't do it,' OG said, hands on his hips.

'I'm gonna prove to you guys I can handle my shit.'

We urged him not to do it.

Sniper unfolded his arms, and held out his palms. 'Fuck it! Just gimme a fucking line!'

'OK! If you think you can handle it,' Troll said, shaking his head. 'Sniper, let me sit there, and you keep point.'

On the toilet, Sniper watched for guards.

Troll tipped some white powder onto the table and snorted a line through rolled paper. 'OK, your turn.' Troll handed Sniper the tooter.

Less than an hour later, Sniper returned, paranoid. 'Homey thinks I'm a fucking snitch! I'm gonna handle my business this time!' He ran downstairs and circled the day room again.

Outlaw rushed in next, glazed in perspiration as usual. 'You wanna line, dawg?' he asked me.

'No thanks,' I said, hoping Carter didn't follow him in.

He squinted as if I'd failed some kind of test, making me uneasy. 'You wanna smoke some then?'

'I'm good thanks, dawg.'

Outlaw squatted down, whipped out a lighter, sprinkled some white crystals onto tinfoil and heated it from underneath. He inhaled the acrid fumes with a cardboard funnel, bounced up and left without saying goodbye.

'He's pissed at you,' Troll said.

'At me! Why?' I said, expecting Troll to say something about me working out with the other races.

'It's disrespectful to refuse drugs from the head of the whites. Sometimes people wanna see you do drugs so they know they can trust you. Like you're not a cop.'

'How was I supposed to know that?' I asked, convinced this was my third strike. I imagined Outlaw and Carter hashing out how best to smash me.

'You do now.'

'Sure do, dawg.' I toyed with the idea of telling Troll about my problems with Outlaw. I wanted his advice. But fearing he might yap to others and make matters worse, I resisted taking the chance.

Most of the men hadn't slept for three days, and I remembered Billy's advice: *Be careful 'cause when they've been up like this they start sketching out on each other and shit gets crazy.* The day room grew more boisterous. Men I'd never seen talking to each other before or who rarely came out of their cells were chatting about all sorts.

The first to lose it completely was a Mexican. He dashed around the day room ranting in Spanish about his arresting officer, who he swore was undercover in the pod and about to re-arrest him. A formation of Mexicans tried to prevent him from sparking a race riot by surrounding him, shadowing his movements. But every now and then he broke free from their formation, hurled himself at a random person and yelled himself to tears. He was on his knees sobbing when I noticed Sniper pacing the balcony again.

From the cell table, I called to Sniper, 'What's going on out there?'

Sniper came in, tight-lipped. 'My cellies are gonna do something to me.'

'What?' I asked, convinced he'd gone mad.

'I can't tell you, but they're gonna do it after lockdown,' he said, his eyes sad and dilated.

'Maybe you should–'

He slipped out of the cell, back to patrolling the balcony.

Carter came in next, and I figured my luck had finally gone. 'Outlaw wants to see you in his cell.'

It's come to this. I'm through. 'All right, dawg.' I got off my bunk, hoping he didn't detect how nervous I was. 'Everything all right?'

'You can talk to him.'

I followed Carter downstairs, into Outlaw's.

Outlaw was looking out of the tiny window at the rows of military tents housing female prisoners. Hearing us, he wheeled around. 'Wattup, dawg!'

Carter brushed past me and guarded the door. I didn't like having a man to my front and rear, but I appreciated Outlaw bumping my fist. *Maybe things aren't so bad? Or are they just settling me so I drop my guard?* 'What's going on?'

'We see you've not been working out with the other races, and we appreciate that.' Outlaw was standing about two feet in front of me, heaving his topless chest. His muscles and long blond hair brought to mind Thor.

Do they know Sniper has lost his mind and is in no condition to be working out? I decided to say nothing and take the credit. 'No problem.'

'Look, dawg, we know what you were doing on the streets. You've got a lotta connects. We've got no white boys bringing dope in. The Mexicans have got us by the balls. If a wood was hooking us up from the streets, we wouldn't have to deal with the other races.'

I didn't like the direction this was heading in. But what could I say? I just nodded and listened.

'Why don't you use your connects so we can step on the Mexicans? We'll pay you.'

I found the notion of dealing drugs while in jail on drug charges absurd. But safety was my priority. I couldn't just outright refuse and risk insulting the two most powerful whites in our pod. Flustered by the pressure they were applying, I struggled to find an appropriate response. I tried to say no in a way I hoped wouldn't invite violence: 'I have no way to do it.' Realising I'd opened a door from their perspective, I immediately regretted my answer. I braced for what they'd say next.

'Yes, you do,' Carter said from behind, causing me to swivel. 'Your chick's visiting you all the time. She can bring it in.'

What a nerve! Asking me to commit crimes was one thing – I probably deserved that – but enlisting Claudia! How long had they been planning this behind my back? Curbing my anger, I thought to bluff them. 'I'll have to ask her.' I figured I could pretend to ask her and tell them she said no, so it would look like I'd tried.

'We'd appreciate that, wood.'

I was a wood now, not merely a dawg. All they cared about was dope, and they'd put Claudia at risk to get it. 'I can't talk to her about it on the recorded lines, so I'll ask her at Visitation.' I'd just bought a few days.

'All right, good lookin' out, wood.' There was a con artist's tone in Outlaw's voice. But I preferred him trying to bend me to his will by manipulation rather than violence. I stood a chance with the former, not the latter.

* * *

One of the dealers became so paranoid he gave his last ounce to OG in case it were found and used as evidence against him. The users topped up in our cell. But their euphoria was short-lived. They'd been wired for so long they turned suspicious of each other. They started trading conspiracy theories and organising witch hunts. Some were even going from group to group and cell to cell insisting the groups and cells they'd just come from were plotting against them. The day room was far more dangerous than usual. Leaving my cell to use the phone, I feared getting lynched for saying no to drugs.

Troll believed the guards knew he was high and it was only a matter of time before they demanded a urine sample. He decided his best strategy was to avoid them. He hid on his bunk and sent packing anyone who popped in to see if he wanted to play cards. 'The guards know I'm always out playing spades,' Troll said, his voice shaky. 'They know why I'm hiding out.' He'd been surveying the guards in the control tower for hours. Knocking on the bottom of my bunk, he said, 'I see the dogs! I see the dogs! I see the dogs!'

His knocking was reverberating right through me. Annoyingly. 'What're you talking about?'

'The sniffer dogs are in the fishbowl!'

Concerned the goon squad had arrived, I leaned off the middle bunk. 'There's no dogs, dawg,' I said, looking down at him.

'They're bringing the dogs! Oh fuck, dawg! I'm a bust!' he said, slapping his temples.

'There's no dogs, Troll. You're sketching.'

'I see them,' he said, poking his cheeks with his fingertips.

'Troll, there's no dogs!' I said, shaking my head. 'And if they do come, it's 'cause of the way you're behaving right now.'

'Look at my pupils. Am I a bust? Am I a bust?' he said, pointing at his eyes.

His pupils had dilated into little black ponds. The whites of his eyes were strewn with red squiggles as if his capillaries were about to burst. But I didn't want to panic him. 'Take it easy, Troll.'

He gazed at the control tower again. 'Are you sure there's no dogs, dawg?'

'I thought you don't sketch, Troll. How come you're sketching?'

'I don't sketch! I was just kidding about the dogs,' he said in a fake-relaxed voice. He rolled over on his bunk, out of sight, where he could no longer see the control tower.

∙∙∙

I returned to my Spanish book.

Five minutes later: 'Dawg! Dawg! Do you see the dogs?' This went on all day.

OG had two friends in D11: Arturo and Silver Fox. Normally mild-mannered individuals, crystal meth had rendered them too afraid to leave their cell, even for chow. They stayed on their bunks, rigid and alert, like hens incubating eggs, their eyes fixating on potential threats coming through the door. After lights out, there was banging on the wall we shared with D11.

'Arturo, Silver Fox, what is it?' OG asked, climbing down from the top bunk.

'We found a note in our cell telling us we'd better roll our shit up,' Silver Fox said.

'What note?' OG asked.

'Just a note. There's gonna be trouble if we don't roll our shit up.'

'What note? What're you talking about, Silver Fox? Nobody has written a note.' OG cleared his throat, spat in the toilet, and yelled into the day room, 'Listen up! Has anyone in here written a note to Arturo or Silver Fox?'

Silence.

'See, Silver Fox. There's no note. Try and get some sleep, dawg. I'll see you in the morning.'

'All right.'

Ten minutes later, Silver Fox knocked again. 'I really should go, OG. You ain't seen the note.'

'There's no note, Silver Fox. Please listen to me, bro. You just need to get some sleep, homey. I'll see you in the morning. I've got your back, dawg!'

'All right.'

Silver Fox's knocks kept waking me up. The reassurances were the same, but OG snored through Silver Fox's final plea for help.

By doors open, D11 was empty. Arturo and Silver Fox had grown so frightened of the imaginary note during the night they'd demanded the guards move them to lockdown.

Before breakfast, guards converged on Sniper's cell. They handcuffed and escorted him to lockdown.

Troll revealed what had happened to Sniper. 'A guard caught Sniper on his bunk with his fingers in his ass.'

'What?' I asked, shocked.

'They asked him what he was doing, and he said, "I got raped by my cellies, and I'm checking the damage."'

'What'll happen to him?' I asked.

'They'll send him for a psych evaluation,' Troll said. 'There's no way the guards'll believe his two skinny-ass cellies raped that buff dude.' Troll still hadn't slept. He was convinced the guards were about to do something nasty to him. He was right.

Officer Mordhorst appeared at our door, pointing at Troll. 'You're my chow server this morning,' he said, and marched away.

'Ain't that-about-a-bitch,' Troll said, rocking on his bunk. 'He's never asked me to serve chow before. Oh fuck! He's onto me. I'm a bust. How big are my eyes, dawg?'

They were still helter-skelter, and I had to be honest in case Mordhorst noticed them. 'Still big.'

'Fuck!'

Mordhorst summoned Troll ten minutes later.

'I'm fucked! Mordhorst's gonna see my eyes and bust me,' Troll said, 'and I can't refuse 'cause then he'll know something's up, and bust me anyway, so I've gotta do it and risk getting busted.'

'Look, you don't know for sure he's onto you; just go down there and try and act normal.' I feared Mordhorst was onto him. I expected Troll to end the day in the hole. That I'd lose a good cellmate and receive a bad one.

'I haven't slept in five days! How can I act fucking normal?' Troll said, clenching and unclenching his hands.

'Just try.'

Joining the queue for breakfast, I studied Troll stood next to Officer Mordhorst. He had a hair net on. His face was trembling as he doled out Ladmo bags and milks to the inmates hounding him for extra food he dare not give. His lips were pursed, his eyes darting as if seeking a way out of the situation.

When he was done serving chow, Troll returned to D10. Stunned and shaking. 'Why me? Why'd he pick me? I've never served chow. He saw my pupils. I know he did. I'm a bust. They're gonna call me for a piss test any second. I'm a bust. The dogs were at Tower 5 yesterday. They'll be here soon. Oh fuck! Shaun! Shaun! Check out the fishbowl for me. Do you see the dogs?'

'Still no dogs,' I said.

'They'll be here soon with the goon squad.'

I feared the goon squad was coming to extract a price for all of the people going berserk on drugs.

After chow, the Mexican who suspected his arresting officer was undercover in the pod ran around the day room yelling in Spanish. He gave the Mexicans who were shadowing his movements the slip and charged at people of all races. He was stirring up a race riot, so the Mexicans subdued him and tried dragging him into a cell. This inflamed him more. He ran from them screaming, dashed into his cell, banged around and re-emerged with his mattress rolled up. He rushed to the sliding door and pounded on the Plexiglas to get the attention of the control guard. He kept looking over his shoulders as if expecting the undercover cop – the star of his delusions – to re-arrest him. When the sliding door opened, he ran down the corridor. Guards chased him out of sight.

The pod was extremely dangerous now. Someone was acting up on drugs everywhere. I stayed on my bunk, flinching every time I heard a head banged against steel or a body slammed onto the concrete. A bleeding and disorientated inmate evacuating the pod always followed these noises.

During my party years, I believed drugs were glamorous. But the constant exposure in the jail to round-the-clock drug users crushed that viewpoint out of me. I swore never to do drugs again and still haven't to this day.

Our water was off the following morning. Anticipating a raid, the majority keystered their contraband. We were all tense. I'd heard so many descriptions of the goon squad I now dwelt on my own terrible image of them. I was dreading a bunch of armed commando types storming our living quarters, stripping us naked and tearing through our belongings. The tension continued to rise. Would they come or not? Was the water simply turned off for maintenance? Why won't the guards tell us anything? Surely that means they're coming. There was a collection of us on the balcony discussing these things like village elders.

'Check this out, dawg!' Troll yelled from inside the cell.

I went back in. 'What?'

Troll pointed at his bunk. I laughed at the giant smiley face he'd made by placing brownies next to each other.

'Any food the state gives us, the goon squad are gonna trash.' Troll picked up a legal folder. 'I hid two brownies in here,' he said.

'Here they come!' everyone started yelling.

We rushed to the front of the cell. A group of big men in black shank-proof armour and protective goggles charged down the corridor. It was the Strategic Response Team (goon squad). They were even bigger than the men who'd raided my apartment. Fiercer-looking too. As they approached the middle of the tower, the prisoners downstairs started to flee to their cells. First to charge into the day room was a white man with massive tattooed biceps. He raised a shotgun and fired a thundershot distraction round that delivered a flash of light and a deafening bang.

'Put your hands on your heads! No one fucking move!'

OG shot into the cell. 'What a bunch of fucking assholes!'

Yelling at the few prisoners who hadn't made it back to their cells, the goon squad spread out in the day room. They shared the same cold expression, as if they'd come to kill us all without a scintilla of remorse. Half of them had tattoos on their bodybuilder arms and looked like they belonged in the jail themselves.

'You do not move unless we tell you to move! You do not talk to us unless we tell you to talk to us!' Some were storming up the stairs now.

'Aw, fuck. They're about to hit our cell,' Troll said.

'Fuck 'em!' OG said.

OG and Troll pressed their palms up high on the cement-block wall. I did likewise, my adrenalin surging as I relived the morning of my arrest. It was happening all over again. The bad start to a day that only got much worse.

A Hispanic goon-squad guard slammed our door open. 'Strip now!'

We got naked.

'You, turn around, bend over and spread 'em,' he said to OG. When OG had complied, he said, 'Put your boxers back on and go downstairs.' Troll and I had to do likewise.

I was descending the stairs with my hands on my head when the K9 unit arrived. The dogs barked wildly, no doubt picking up the scent of drugs everywhere.

'Keep your hands on your fucking heads as you line up against the day-room wall!'

I joined the line. Kingston emerged from his cell, his arms at his sides.

A guard shoved him from behind. 'Put your hands on your fucking head now!'

Kingston spun around, raising his arms as if to defend himself. 'Don't touch me like that, man.'

The urge to attack the guards flared up on the faces of the inmates. It gripped me too. Kingston was a good guy, and if he could be victimised, any of us could. Sensing a riot about to ignite, the guards formed a row, facing us, intimidating us into thinking twice.

Behind the wall of guards, things were deteriorating fast for Kingston. His arms were half up, as if he feared being hit again and didn't want to leave his midsection exposed. He was watching the guard who'd shoved him and didn't see the one behind him draw a Taser. As the guard he was facing said 'Do as you're told! Put your hands on your fucking head!', the Taser crackled before he had a chance to comply. The electroshock jackknifed Kingston. The guards threw him on the concrete, twisted his arms behind his back, and handcuffed him. We jeered as they dragged him from the pod. I had expected violence, but this added a terrifying new dimension.

The guards ordered us to leave the pod and throw our filthy boxers into a cart. We were herded naked down a dead-end corridor. I felt humiliated. Through the Plexiglas, we watched them search our cells. They rifled through our belongings. They dropped our bedding on the floor and trampled on it as they examined our mattresses. They flung stationery and books on the floor. They tore open our brown paper commissary bags. They confiscated our state food: fruit, bread, peanut butter, brownies (including the two Troll had hidden) . . . They checked every hiding spot with search mirrors and probe sticks. But no drugs were found, as they'd all been keystered. They did find hooch. The brewer and his cellmates were identified, cuffed and escorted to lockdown. I was worried they'd find a syringe or a shank belonging to OG, but they didn't. He'd keystered all of his metal. They marched away with plastic bags full mostly of our extra towels, bedding and clothes – our sole means of remaining somewhat clean. When they were almost out of earshot, OG yelled something about a prisoner fornicating with the girlfriend of the Hispanic goon-squad guard. They heard him, stopped and turned around. As their eyes roamed over us, we held onto our silence. They looked eager to put someone out of his misery. When they couldn't figure out who'd said it, they looked at each other, and moved on.

7

....

'Got an attorney yet, dawg?' Troll asked, breakfasting in our cell one morning in June.

'No,' I said, sat cross-legged on my bunk eating crackers.

OG was making a green-baloney sandwich on the table. 'It's gonna cost you, homey. You'd better have a lotta money stashed.'

'They seized all my money.'

'Ain't that-about-a-bitch!' Troll said.

'You're fucked then, homey!' OG said.

'You're fucked, dawg,' Troll said. 'With your charges, you've gotta get a private lawyer. They've ganked your money so you can't get a good attorney or bond out. Now they can really bend you over and stick it to you, dawg.'

'What should I do?' I asked, starting to worry. Every time I pondered a prison sentence, I felt ill. It was my second biggest concern after staying alive. I was good at thinking up ways out of situations, but the more I thought about this, the more trapped I felt. At night, I'd terrify myself over it for hours. I feared years of incarceration would bring about a heart attack or send me doolally. During the day, I tried to block it out so I could concentrate on survival. But deep down I knew I needed to deal with my legal situation in order to get the best possible plea bargain. Trials were rare, defendants winning even rarer, and those who lost at trial were punished with headline-making sentences designed to deter others from exercising their right to a trial.

'My private attorney cost 30 gees,' Troll said. 'So far he hasn't done shit for me either. I'd like to fire his ass. You've gotta be real careful.'

'One of my security guys, G Dog, told me if I ever got in trouble, the best attorney to call is Alan Simpson,' I said. 'He's supposed to know all the loopholes.'

'He represents a lotta Mexican Mafia,' OG said.

'I've heard of him, too,' Troll said. 'He's good. You should call him up, dawg. Maybe he'll take over my case, too.'

'But I've got no money.'

'You'd better find some,' OG said.

'My grandpa's paying for my attorney,' Troll said. 'Can your folks raise any cash? If this guy can slip you through the cracks in the system, it'll save you years.'

I collect-called Alan Simpson's office and gave his secretary my booking number and some brief information about my case. She assured me he would look at my charges and pay me a legal visit. When I asked about the cost of representation, she said every case was different and Alan would tell me in person. I dreaded having to turn to my parents for a large sum of money, burdening them on top of the shock they were going through.

Entering the visitation room, Alan Simpson was treated like royalty. The staff and attorneys stopped what they were doing to nod and smile at him. Some of the attorneys even rose from their tables to shake his hand and congratulate him on recently saving an innocent man, Ray Krone, from death row.

'Alan Simpson's your attorney?' Officer Green gasped, and then politely showed us to a private room.

Alan was a plumpish 50-something with a charismatic face. He smiled a lot, displaying braces. He was articulate, a quick-thinker, a born salesman. His charm put me at ease. He slapped some paperwork down on the table. 'Here's your grand jury indictment.'

'What's that mean?'

'It's a list of criminal offences the prosecutor presented to a grand jury to get you indicted before you were arrested.'

Bracing to learn the extent of my trouble, I imagined it contained every crime I'd ever committed and then some. 'I see. How bad's it looking?'

'To be honest, I've read it, and it seems they barely have a case against you.'

Am I hearing right? Barely a case against me? Am I getting out of here? 'I'm not sure what you mean.'

'They've had wiretaps set up since the beginning of the year–'

'And I've been in Scottsdale Community College, concentrating on stock trading, pretty much laying low over that time,' I said, starting to twig on.

'Detective Reid even admits that you never talk on the phone, in emails, or have people at your home. That you're beyond surveillance. They're using the gist of the conversations of the co-defendants as the main evidence against you. The prosecutor's trying to say the lack of evidence against you proves you're a criminal mastermind, too clever to be detected. So the lack of evidence against you is actually evidence against you. Which is ridiculous!' He laughed his irresistible laugh, and I joined in.

'What crimes did you actually do?' he said, switching back to serious mode.

'OK. Starting in the '90s, I threw raves and invested in club drugs, especially Ecstasy. It started out small at first, but by the time everything peaked we were bringing tens of thousands of hits in. I had a lot of money in the stock market around the time of the dot.com bubble, but when that collapsed, so did the size of my criminal activity.' I braced for him to say something like, 'If you were bringing that many hits in, you're looking at doing serious prison time.'

'Were you bringing drugs in this year?' he asked.

'No.'

'Then they've missed the boat. Are you telling me the truth? I must know what we're up against.'

'I've seriously spent this year getting back to stock trading.'

'And apparently your stock-trading data overloaded the police computers that were spying on your computer. They had to fly software engineers in from Washington.' Alan broke into laughter. 'This is a very flimsy case.'

'So what am I looking at?' I asked, my hopes rising again.

'Anywhere from probation to five years is the norm for a first-time offender with these types of drug charges.'

I gave myself probation.

'You'll be better able to help me with the case if I get you out of this hellhole.'

I liked the sound of that. 'How?'

'Well, your bond is a steep $750,000, and I think I can get it down to $100,000. Can you manage that?'

'They seized all my money.'

'You'd only need to put 10 per cent down with a bond company.'

'I think I can manage that.'

'If you're going to retain me, one of the first things I'll do is file for a bond reduction.'

'How much will it cost to retain you?' I feared his response.

'My retainer's $50,000.'

I gulped.

'It could cost more, but I imagine they'll offer you a decent plea bargain within six months. I can't see them wanting to drag this out and waste even more money on a flimsy case like this.'

I loved it when he said *flimsy case*. 'I'll have to discuss it with my parents. If it's a flimsy case, why does everyone in here I show my bond and charges to get all worked up?'

'I wouldn't pay too much attention to anyone in here. The prosecutor's overcharged you on purpose. The more mud she throws, the more she hopes will stick. This gives her plea-bargaining power. I respond by attacking the case with my motions. Because the case looks so weak, you should be offered a decent plea bargain. A plea bargain everyone is happy with.'

'How soon do you think I can get my bond reduced?'

'I can get a hearing within the next couple of months.'

Goodbye Towers! I beamed at him.

'Your next court appearance is a preliminary hearing.'

'What's that?'

'The prosecutor has to show probable cause to be holding you.'

'She already slammed me at the first court I went to.'

'She's about to slam you again, and I won't be saying anything till we see if there's any more evidence we're up against.'

'If you can get me out in a couple of months that would be wonderful.' I saw myself back at the apartment with Claudia. Eating Indian food together. Going to the gym. Making love . . .

'Can you cope with this place for a few more months?'

'I'll try.' Coping would be a lot easier now I was getting out.

After the visit, I called Claudia with the good news, and she relayed it to my parents. We were all thrilled.

June 2002

Dear D & B & Our Kags [my mum, dad and sister Karen]

Hope you are all doing good in the free world. I guess I'm over the initial shock of the situation and am settling down to the daily routine of being an unsentenced inmate. I play chess most of the day, watch TV and read. The people in my cell and pod are real nice, and I have had no problems. It's a novelty to them that I'm English.

Regarding my situation, I figured being involved with the rave scene would eventually get me in trouble. So here I am rounded up in a dawn-raid style sweep with a bunch of other people from the rave scene including Wild Man and Wild Woman. Although no stash of drugs was found, they are charging me with conspiracy, which means I was involved with a group of individuals (co-conspirators) in kind of a crime family way, and they've pegged me as the leader. Unfortunately we all get charged with each other's crimes. It is like we are all one unit, and it's a serious charge.

The police must have thought I was big time because of the money spent, the serious nature of the charges and the $¾ million bond. However, all they have rounded up is a ramshackle group of people with no money and very little drugs. They were livid; they let some of the people they rounded up go, including Claudia. The house we were at had absolutely nothing in it. They froze my retirement account, which has $20K in it, and my bank accounts and took my SUV.

They've been wiretapping us for almost six months, and during that time I have been in school and have been staying home with Claudia. They don't have much of a case, but still I'm scared because they slapped so many high felony charges on me.

Alan Simpson visited me yesterday. He's a good guy but expensive. He said it could cost $50K to fight this stuff, but in a few months they might offer me a plea bargain to avoid spending any more money. He also thinks he can get me bonded out. I could be out of here soon!

From probation to five years seems a predicted time for these types of crimes, as a first offender. Kingpins get 25 years, but it's not like there were private jets and yachts seized. Two of the guys arrested had less than a dollar on them. Anyway, Alan is applying for some kind of legal aid to assist financially, but I have to get him as much money as possible. The prison system (where you go after jail when you are sentenced) is full of people who had shitty attorneys doing ten years, and so I really am fighting for my life (and sanity) right now.

Love you all loads. Sorry for any disappointment or hurt this may have caused. Keep in touch but follow the mailing rules.

Shaun

In the letters to my parents, I hid the dangers of the jail so as not to terrify them. I also had to be careful about mentioning my crimes in letters and phone calls because the jail had access to both and any admission of guilt could be used as evidence against me.

After sending that letter in June, I prayed my parents would find the money to retain Alan Simpson. When I learned my father had to cash in his retirement account to pay the $50,000, I was relieved but also plagued with guilt. Over the years, I'd spent a multiple of that amount on drugs and partying – one New Year's Eve rave party alone had cost more than $50,000. It hurt that my parents were paying for my wrongdoing. Many of my neighbours had been disowned by their families, so I felt blessed to have such support.

The letter contained an accurate description of my involvement in drugs at the time of my arrest. The only person I could safely tell about the extent of my previous involvement in drugs was my attorney. I deserved punishment for my crimes, but for the first few months after my arrest I resented being held when no drugs were found. I desperately wanted to get out of such a dangerous environment. And if that meant beating the system due to the lack of evidence against me, then so be it. The visit from Alan Simpson reinforced my belief that I would not have to pay for my old lifestyle. Taking responsibility for my crimes was far from my mind. I still had a lot of growing up to do. I had no idea confinement was slowly mending my emotional immaturity and altering my destiny for the better.

8

....

'C'mon, Shaun, white-boy meeting in my cell right now,' Billy said just after the morning headcount.

'About what?' I asked, dropping off my bunk.

'The guards rolled Outlaw up to a pod for sentenced prisoners, so we've got no head of the whites. The woods are voting on a new head.'

'OK,' I said, hoping Outlaw's departure would stop the whites from trying to intimidate me into asking Claudia to smuggle drugs in.

We arrived at a cell packed with topless men adorned with tattoos. Swastikas. War eagles. Norse runes. Skulls. Swords. SS lightning bolts. Castles. Celtic crosses. Confederate flags. Tear drops. On one skinhead's chest: Hitler admiring Jews dying in a gas chamber.

'Look, woods,' said George, a mountain of a hillbilly who shocked us all by never wearing sandals in the shower. 'Carter's been down the longest. He's affiliated with the Aryan Brotherhood. He's the most qualified to represent our race. I say Carter should be the head of the whites.'

Oh no, I thought. Anyone but Carter. I didn't want to vote for him, but the mood was such that anyone who didn't would have been drowned in the toilet. We elected Carter unanimously. As he'd suggested Claudia smuggle drugs in, I expected things to get worse for me.

'Thanks, woods,' Carter said. 'I've got an announcement to make.'

The mood turned more serious. I expected him to command us to charge down the stairs and attack the blacks.

'I'm about to get married, and you're all invited to my wedding party,' Carter said, breaking the tension. Our laughter echoed in the day room.

Scared of sounding naive, but curious, I asked, 'How can you get married in jail?'

'Over the phone,' Carter said.

While Carter recited marriage vows on a three-way call to his wife and minister, I fetched cookies from my cell to contribute to the wedding buffet. From the balcony, we watched Carter give the thumbs-up, signalling he now had a wife. Cheering erupted in the day room. Carter raised the phone so his wife could hear. The prisoner on the phone next to Carter pulled his hand out of the crotch of his pants and patted Carter on the back.

The whites were already helping themselves to the food by the time Carter returned to D14. He led the men in drinking hooch and snorting lines of crystal meth and crushed-up psychotropic medication. The food didn't last long, and fights almost broke out over the crumbs.

Billy jumped on the tiny steel table in the middle of the cell. He undid his ponytail and let his hair down. He started dancing like a stripper, undressing himself while we sang. When he was down to his pink boxers, he gyrated his hips and lashed us with his hair. 'Congratulations, dawg!' he shrieked. He arched his back, stuck his tongue in Carter's ear and pinched Carter's nipples. 'Take a Pac-Man,' he said, putting seizure medication in Carter's mouth.

The maximum occupancy of a Towers pod was 45 men. Turnover was high, and the racial balance kept changing. What never changed was that the race with the most members picked on the race with the least. In our pod, the whites were presently the majority, the blacks the minority. Something was brewing between the two.

The day after Carter's wedding, the guards moved Gravedigger – a six-foot-four cage fighter – into our pod. Gravedigger wasn't massive, but he had muscular thickness and definition in all of the right places. He had a narrow, ill-tempered face and beady brown eyes that shone with a hunger for violence. His body was adorned with skulls, demons and racist slogans. But the tattoo that stood out the most was on his chest: the devil as a puppet-master. He was in jail for kidnapping and torturing a man who had raped one of his female friends. His presence increased Carter's smugness and the threatening behaviour of the whites towards the blacks.

Gravedigger strode into D10. 'Who's the English guy in here?'

He sounded so angry, I expected trouble. 'I am,' I said, rising on my bunk fast.

'Here you go, dawg.' He threw a small piece of carefully folded paper at me. 'It's a kite from the crazy English dude in Tower 2. I woulda sent it over from the hole, but I gave him my word I'd hand it to you personally.'

'Thanks, bro,' I said, opening it hastily.

La,

Sign up for Catholic Mass. I'll meet you there.

Love you loads,

Wild Man

Gravedigger projected his gaze at Troll. 'Hey, Troll, front me some cookies till store day, dawg.' His tone left Troll no option.

'Sure, dawg.' Troll slid one of his many brown paper commissary bags from under the bunk. 'Heard you just got out of the hole.' He extracted a rack of cookies.

Gravedigger snatched the cookies. 'Yeah, dawg. I had to smash some toads in Tower 2.'

'How come, dawg?' Troll asked.

'These two toads owed a white boy, my Russian buddy, Max. Max went in their cell to collect on store day, and they smashed him. You know the blacks ain't getting away with disrespecting our race like that, dawg, not when I'm head of the fucking whites. So I just bombed in there myself. I don't need torpedoes to fight my battles. I knocked the first one out with one punch. Motherfucker had a glass jaw. The other one shit bricks, ran into the day room like a little bitch.'

'No shit,' Troll said.

'So I'm chasing him round and round the fucking stairs with everyone watching. I caught him, put him on the floor with a kung-fu takedown and pinned him in a wrestling lock. I'm slamming his face with my elbows like this.' Gravedigger set his elbows in motion like two giant chisels. 'Blood was coming out everywhere. The guy's all fucked up, dawg. The blood around us was getting bigger and bigger. And Noble's just watching it from the fishbowl, enjoying it, waiting for backup. It took a long time for the guards to respond, so I just kept pounding him. Blood splashing all over me. Everyone watching.'

'You're no joke, dawg,' Troll said. 'You ain't nuthin' nice.'

Gravedigger glowered at Troll and left. Yet another maniac for us to contend with.

Before breakfast the next morning, Billy took me to his cell. 'I'm just giving you a heads-up, dawg. You're in danger. Shit's about to pop off in your cell.'

'What do you mean?' I asked, growing alarmed.

'Some fucked-up shit's going down with Troll. I don't agree with it, but there's nothing I can do about it. I suggest you stay out of it, too.'

'What's going on?'

'Look, Shaun, Carter and Digger's gonna smash Troll.'

I was shocked. 'Why?'

'For playing cards with the blacks and dealing too much with the other races.'

'That's crazy.'

'That's just their front so they can jack Troll. Carter and Digger owe Troll for store. So when Troll rolls up after they smash him, the debt will be squashed and they'll just take whatever store Troll has left.'

'Maybe I should try talking to Carter and Digger?'

'It's no use. They've made their minds up. If you try to get in the mix, they'll just smash you too. Look, I'm gonna tell you more, but don't tell anyone this.'

'What?' I asked, starting to panic.

'Carter's told Digger you and Troll are the two white boys least representing the white race.'

'No shit. Do you think they'll smash me too?'

'No. At least not yet. Carter thinks you might be able to bring drugs in.'

The drug thing had been nagging away at me. 'Look, there's no way I'm bringing drugs in. What should I do?'

'I really don't know. Carter's instigating all this shit. Digger just loves to fight.'

'When's this supposed to happen to Troll?'

'After breakfast.'

I returned to my cell, preoccupied. The threat to Troll was imminent, and I couldn't just look the other way and let Troll get smashed. During our time together, we'd bonded. I believed if I were in danger, Troll would at least forewarn me. I didn't know that cellmates who got along usually agreed to 'have each other's backs'. I felt that way instinctively. But what could I do? I couldn't go up against Carter, Gravedigger and their torpedoes. I would be annihilated. Our cellmate, OG, loved to fight, but prison rules prohibited him from interfering in a dispute among the white race. Wild Man was in Tower 2, at the opposite end of the jail, where he couldn't help me on such short notice. I decided to tell Troll over breakfast, to advise him to roll up to Tower 2 where I hoped he'd be better off in the company of Wild Man. Having secured Troll's safety in my mind, I was stressing about my own when Officer Mordhorst announced: 'Chow's in the house! Line up at the door with your IDs!'

In the day room, the friction between the blacks and whites was palpable. When Mordhorst left to serve the next pod, Carter yelled at SmackDown, a trained fighter and the head of the blacks, 'You need to stop sweating the woods, dawg!' SmackDown had been bullying members of every race out of commissary. Carter was telling SmackDown to stop bullying the whites or else. The day room hushed.

From the blacks' table, SmackDown yelled, 'Who've I been sweating?' He spoke like an East Coast rapper.

'I can't name names, dawg,' Carter said, 'but as the head, people have been complaining about you bulldogging them.'

'I ain't bulldogged nobody!'

'That's not what people are saying.'

'Well, if fools have got a problem with me, they need to come and tell me to my face.'

'That's what I'm talking about, dawg. The people you've been sweating are afraid of you.'

'Fuck 'em then!'

'You need to keep yourself in check! People are sick of your bulldogging!'

'I ain't putting myself in check, dawg. You can go fuck yourself, too!'

'You calling me out, dawg?'

'Hell, yeah, I'm calling you out! Ain't no punk-ass white boy telling me how I'm s'posed to behave round here.'

One of the worst things you can call someone in jail is a punk. A punk is a sex slave who can be traded or rented out. Being called a punk left a head of a race no choice but to fight. If a head didn't fight, he'd get smashed and moved out by his own race. I didn't envy Carter's position – SmackDown had never lost a fight in the jail. Troll told me that the guards had previously expelled SmackDown from our pod for fighting, but he'd smashed so many people in so many other pods he was right back where he'd started out.

Everyone stopped what they were doing and joined their races. Whites. Blacks. Mexicans. Mexican Americans. Four armies posted around their heads, poised for war.

'You'll see who's a punk!' Carter yelled, tilting his head back. 'Let's take this to cell 3!' Cell 3 was under the stairs, making it less visible to the guards and the most popular spot for fights.

The residents of cell 3 rushed inside and shifted all of their property under the bottom bunk so it wouldn't get damaged or bloodied.

'What're we waiting for?' SmackDown swaggered into cell 3 and assumed a boxer's stance. He had the word SMACKDOWN tattooed on his right forearm.

Carter charged in and spun SmackDown around. SmackDown almost lost his balance but steadied himself and delivered a hook to Carter's head, sloughing the cockiness from Carter's face. A flurry of desperate kicks from Carter got nowhere. SmackDown simply shifted slightly, frowning, remaining focused, biding his time. A jab struck Carter's head and set him bouncing all over the place. Dodging punches, he looked as if he were doing some wild dance. Then he lost his footing and stumbled forward. Carter took another blow to the head. He crouched and lashed out with a kick aimed at SmackDown's groin. As if anticipating the kick, SmackDown shifted out of the way. He moved into the perfect position to land an uppercut on Carter's chin. *Bam!* The audience gasped. Carter's knees buckled, but he didn't fall. SmackDown moved in closer and threw more blows. Carter leapt away, dashed out of the cell and tottered back to the whites' table. His face plastered in disbelief as he sat down.

Standing in the cell doorway, SmackDown yelled, 'What the fuck was that? Get back in here! We ain't through!' He was panting and flaring his nostrils like a stallion in heat.

Voices rose from all of the tables: 'Handle your business, Carter!'

'Finish the fight, dawg!'

'You can't just run away from a fight like that!'

'Yeah, Carter, get back in the cell!'

Carter's face blushed. 'I went in already.' He could barely speak. It was all coming out in spurts. 'We fought. He won. I handled my business.'

Yelling rose from all of the tables: 'What the fuck?'

'You're supposed to be the head of the whites!'

'You have to fight, dawg!'

Even his own torpedoes turned against him:

'You're our head!'

'You're making us look bad to the other races, dawg!'

'You have to go back in!'

'Go back in, Carter!'

'I already fought,' Carter said, his face crimson. 'He fucking beat me!'

'Fucking punk-ass bitch!' SmackDown yelled. 'Get back in here, motherfucker. I'm calling your punk-ass out, you fucking bitch!'

Gravedigger rose from his seat and put his hands on his hips. Glowering down at Carter from his great height, he shook his head. The jeering stopped. As much as I disliked violence, I was rooting for Gravedigger to smash Carter right then. I figured it would end the threat against Troll and me. Gravedigger shook his head, and said in a low voice, 'Man up, wood.' He intensified his gaze.

As if the possibility of being smashed by his own race had just dawned, Carter stood up. 'Fuck it! I'll fight him again.' He returned to cell 3.

SmackDown had his breath back. He retreated into the cell and raised his fists. Carter raised his. SmackDown feigned a few jabs. Lacking energy, Carter skipped around like a man whose heart wasn't in the fight. He seemed resigned to his fate, which soon arrived in the form of a cross to his left eye. He swayed, dropping his guard. He was kicked in the leg and blows pulverised him. But he wasn't knocked out. He couldn't stand it and again dashed from the cell in such a hurry that he collided with the stairs. The prisoners jeered. Panting and disorientated, he leaned forward and rested his hands just above his knees.

Gravedigger marched up to Carter. 'Roll yer shit up! I'm the new head of the whites! Does any of you woods have a problem with that?' He panned his eyes from white to white prisoner. No one objected.

Much to my relief, the threat to Troll and me did indeed leave with its instigator. Carter limped out of the pod with a battered face, a rolled-up mattress and all of his property. Billy told me Carter's property included photos of his new wife that he hadn't shown to the whites. If he had shown the photos to the whites, they never would have crowned him their head. She was Mexican American.

9

The prisoners respected Lev Egorov because of his tough aura and association with the Russian Mafia. He was short, had a solid physique and cropped brown hair with flecks of grey. Right down to the wrinkles on his forehead, he had the look of a KGB agent. Introduced to chess as a child, he was an enthusiast I played almost every day. As immigrants, we bonded quickly. The topics of our lively discussions ranged from geopolitics to the corruption in the legal system. When a battered East European arrived at our pod – a Muslim from the Balkan Peninsula who didn't fit into any of the four major racial categories and had been smashed everywhere he'd been housed – Lev rounded up some of the saner whites, including me, and we agreed to protect him. Unfortunately, the guards moved the Muslim a few weeks later, and he was beaten and hospitalised, and we never saw him again.

Lev was the only person I ever saw in the jail criticise the addicts to their faces. In his deep angry voice and strong Russian accent, he'd yell, 'You fucking Yankees have sucked your brains out by doing dope! If the Yankee didn't do the dope, maybe the Yankee would have more intelligence. The dope is destroying this country. It is the greatest weapon against the Yankee.'

It's generally not a good idea to ask prisoners what their charges are until you get to know them. Questions along those lines from newcomers can make the more established feel disrespected – and the common answer to disrespect was usually a punch to the face. Burning with curiosity as to what Lev was in for, I waited until I'd known him for a few weeks before I popped the question: 'How did you end up in jail?'

'Ha! First, let me tell you the story of how I came to America.'

'OK,' I said, sitting on my bunk.

'I deserted the Russian army and ended up in a jail in Germany. I contacted the American embassy and offered to trade them knowledge of the Russian military for US citizenship. They agreed, and I signed a two-year contract to work for the CIA. I did this to save my sister's life.'

'Save your sister's life?' I asked, confused.

'She was stuck in Russia dying from the effects of the Chernobyl accident. I came here, introduced her to a Yankee, who married her so she could come here legally and get the correct medical treatment. The Yankee doctors cured her, and now she is living here and has remarried and has her own family.'

'Good for you, man!' I was so tired of hearing farfetched crime tales, Lev's story nourished my soul. 'So how did you end up here?'

'Almost ten years ago, I was involved in cocaine in Arizona. Someone murdered my business partner. I went looking for the murderer. I entered the house of the murderer's brother with a gun. The murderer was not there. The brother was, and he called the cops, and they charged me with assault with a deadly weapon and attempted kidnapping.'

'Assault and kidnapping?'

'Yes, because he said I pointed the gun at him, which I didn't. But I did shoot the floor when I was yelling at him. I was arrested and released. They didn't do anything for years, so I thought it was dropped. Then they recently extradited me from Washington, where my family lives and where I was working as a mechanic.'

I wondered why some people were arrested, released and then rearrested on the same charges years later. I imagined bureaucrats in police departments reopening certain cases to fill their quotas. 'That sucks, that they'd have Washington ship you back years later.' His case was so old I sympathised. His actions, such as risking his personal safety to stand up for the Muslim, led me to believe he'd matured from that life of crime into a well-meaning person.

Lev was my next workout partner after Sniper. Using a towel, we tied the broomstick in the day room to the handle of a mop bucket full of water. Holding the stick horizontal, we did a variety of weight-lifting exercises. We wrapped our pink socks around sections of the metal-grid stairs to make handgrips for pull-ups. In his youth, Lev had won prizes for gymnastics, and his ability still showed. He breezed through sets of pull-ups, starting with 50 reps, working his way down to 30 – with many onlookers awestruck – and he always dismounted gracefully. I'd grow tired around five pull-ups, and he'd support my back so I could do more. At first, my lats remained sore for days, but that soon wore off, and I was surprised by the increased strength I felt in that region.

* * *

The heads of all of the races arranged a chess tournament. Each contender contributed one commissary item of food to the jackpot. Outside of the jackpot, the inmates bet heavily on the two favourites: Lev and me.

To put my mind in overdrive prior to the tournament, I ate several brownies. I punched a bag made from toilet rolls in a sock that I'd hung from the top bunk, stopping only when my knuckles bled. Psyched up, I bounced down the day-room stairs, shadow-boxing, singing 'Eye of the Tiger' by Survivor, my eyes mad-dogging Lev the whole time. I took a stool at one of the steel tables and commenced my first game, radiating chess expertise.

Surrounded by onlookers – half of them yelling advice that would have caused anyone who took it to lose the game, the rest telling them to shut up or else – I beat all eight contestants, including Lev. I expected to receive the jackpot, but Gravedigger, who had bet on his cellmate, Lev, said that the top four players now had to play three games each against each other. In the zone and feeling invincible, I agreed.

Lev and I crushed the competition and commenced playing each other. Concentrating on the available moves, the opportunities each move presented, Lev's possible responses to each move and my responses to his responses, I could almost feel my neurons firing. About ten minutes in, I had to stand up to stop trembling. The atmosphere intensified as we each won a game. Due to the large amount of side bets, the audience remained riveted as the third game began. Mid-game, my energy level subsided, and the audience's cockfight wisecracks started to get to me. I knew I was in trouble. But Lev was also taking longer to move and making silly mistakes, so I banked on his brain being more frazzled than mine. My morale sank as I made a series of moves I regretted and lost some key pieces. Sensing my downfall, Lev's supporters, egged on by Gravedigger, heckled me all the more. When I saw Lev could checkmate me in three moves, I positioned my king for a stalemate, while staring blankly at the board so as not to betray my sneakiness. But Lev knew me well enough to see through that strategy. Biding his time, he checkmated me. As the crowd mocked me for losing, I almost collapsed from mental exhaustion. Lev congratulated me on being a worthy opponent, and secured the jackpot (mostly melted Snickers and Kit Kats). 'You played well and deserved to win,' I told him. Vowing never to let that happen again, I ordered my first chess book.

* * *

A Space Hopper of a youngster moved into an upper-tier cell. Eighteen-year-old Alejandro, a 400-pound half-Mexican half-Native American, had shot an AK-47 at a car full of rival gang members, all teenagers, who'd ventured into his westside neighbourhood. Some of his victims were in critical condition, and if any of them died he would be facing a sentence of death by lethal injection.

Every night, just in time for the beginning of the news, Alejandro emerged from his cell with a look of dread and positioned himself at the back of the two dozen or so noisy prisoners clustered in front of the TV on the day-room wall. When the news started, he'd move forward as if yanked by its familiar jingle. Sweating more visibly than the rest, he'd urge everyone to hush. Out of deference for the gravity of his situation, the heads of all of the races would order their youngsters to shut up. By the time the condition of his victims was reported, the unusual quiet – which in the jail meant something bad was happening to somebody somewhere – had drawn the attention of the card and domino players and even brought the hermits from their cells, doubling the size of the audience. I was sure that all of the men watching from the balcony and every corner and table of the day room were thinking the same as me: *Will a victim die? What's it like to be facing the death penalty?*

Alejandro would stand there, arms folded, his bulk swaying slightly, with a fear in his eyes as if he were not looking at a TV that barely tuned in but at a gun pointed at him. The prisoners usually remained quiet, except for the night a reporter revealed that one of Alejandro's bullets had exited through a girl's nipple. That caused many groans and expressions of displeasure. The reports invariably ended with his victims in critical but stable condition. None dead. After digesting this, Alejandro would set off relieved. He'd trudge up the metal-grid stairs, the hermits disappearing into the cells in front of him and the noise in the day room picking up behind him.

The heat made him sweat and stink so much his race held a meeting about whether to get rid of him. Bad hygiene could get you smashed by your own race. In Alejandro's case, a compromise was reached. Under threats of violence, Alejandro had to take a shower every few hours and afterwards members of his race coated him in baby powder.

Sensing a frightened child inside the gunman, I was one of the first to befriend him. 'How much is your bond for shooting those people?' I asked.

'Only ten gees, homey,' Alejandro said.

'Ten grand!' I said, envious. 'I've got drug charges. Mine's three-quarters of a mill.'

'That's way too much for drugs, homey. They got me on attempted murder. Hey, I'm gonna get bonded outta here real soon.' In a lowered voice, he asked, 'Think I should go on the run, homey?'

'I can't be recommending that. It could open me up to new charges. But I think even if none of your victims dies, they're going to put you away for a long time. I'm not recommending you do anything illegal, but if it were me, and my bond was only ten gees, I'd disappear into Mexico and *never ever* come back to Arizona.'

'I've been told I'm dead as soon as I touch down on a prison yard.'

'How come?'

'That hood's got a hit out on me now for blasting their homies. And my victims have family members in the prison system.'

I didn't know what to say to comfort him. Hearing he was facing multiple life sentences and possibly the death penalty had given me a sense of relief that I wasn't in that much trouble. I steered the conversation around to parties, and he reminisced about his rave experiences.

To see a doctor you had to beg a guard for a form called a medical tank order. If the guard was in a good mood he might give you one on his next security walk. You then had to return the form to the guard, who had to sign it, and hope it survived its journey through various departments to the medical staff. The medical staff decided who got seen and who didn't. Depending upon how serious they deemed the nature of your complaint, they'd call you to Medical in a few days' time at the earliest, call you weeks or months later, or not call you at all. The medical staff operated under the assumption that most of the sick inmates were fakers. They often turned away genuine cases, resulting in deaths and life-threatening situations.

Someone decided Lev was the closest thing we had to a doctor. Inmates from all of the races inundated him with demands for medical treatment due to a menace from the insect world: spiders that crawled on us during the night and bit while we slept. The culprit was rarely seen. Some thought it the brown recluse, others the Arizona brown. Whatever the spider, the result was always the same: during the first few days, the bite would slowly expand from a small white blister to a pus-oozing sore; over the next few, tissue would slough away from the abscess leaving a sunken ulcerated crater, exposing underlying tissue. These holes were sometimes as broad as the palm of a hand. Other side effects included fever, chills, vomiting and shock.

Alejandro was so big, his flab crept up and down the wall as he breathed during his sleep. With scant room for spiders to manoeuvre around him, he was inevitably bitten. His written requests for treatment were ignored. When the pus began and Officer Mordhorst rebuffed his pleas for help, inmates from all of the races began to sympathise.

'Give him treatment!' Gravedigger yelled at Mordhorst in the day room.

'He must go to Medical. Look at his damn back! He must see a Yankee doctor,' Lev said.

'It's getting worse and worse,' Alejandro said, his face pinched.

'It's growing. Look! There's pus coming out,' OG said.

'I already told you guys: the Medical Unit does not treat insect bites. That's the jail's policy,' Officer Mordhorst snarled.

'That's fucked up, dawg,' Troll said, playing spades.

'You're shit outta luck,' Billy said to Alejandro.

'You're burnt,' Gravedigger said.

Later that day, Lev entered my cell. 'These damn Yankees think I am a doctor.' He seemed strained yet proud. 'Now they want me to take care of Alejandro's spider bite. Will you help me?'

'How?' I asked, honoured to be included.

'Gravedigger and the others are going to hold Alejandro, so the big bastard doesn't move, while I squeeze the pus out, and I need from you some salt and perhaps you will help me put salt on the wound?'

Revolted by the pus aspect, I didn't think twice about helping my friend: 'Count me in.'

Plagued by outbreaks of mouth ulcers due to stress and malnourishment, I'd been collecting the tiny salt packets served with the chow because gargling salt water temporarily relieved the burning sensation the ulcers caused. I retrieved the salt packets from under my mattress and followed Lev into the day room.

The bullet-wound scars on Alejandro's back paled in comparison to what looked like a baseball of yellow plasma trying to exit his body. I was flabbergasted that a spider had caused that. When Lev fingered the wound, thick yellow pus ran down Alejandro's back, triggering my gag reflex.

'That's fucking gross!' Billy said.

Gravedigger smiled.

'It hurts like fuck! Are you sure you know what you're doing?' Alejandro asked.

'Trust me. I was in the Russian military. This wound is easy for me.'

'He ain't no doctor!' yelled the big hillbilly George, sitting with the TV-watching crowd. 'The commie bastard'll make you worse!'

'The irritation will be less when I am finished. Someone bring me toilet paper!' Lev caught a toilet roll launched from the balcony, unspooled some and swabbed up the pus. 'Men, I need you to hold him steady,' he said in the tone a commander reserves for troops entering battle.

Gravedigger yanked Alejandro's right arm and locked it between his forearms and biceps. Two men secured Alejandro's left side.

Lev pressed his thumbs against the wound.

Alejandro moaned. The wound gushed. 'It hurts,' he whined.

'It hurts! Ah, good! It will hurt less when I am finished.' Lev pressed harder, freeing more pus. I wondered if he knew what he was doing.

'It fucking hurts!' Alejandro said, his face scrunched.

'More toilet paper!' Lev's eyes followed the pus streaking down Alejandro's back like egg yolk.

Sweat was streaming from Alejandro's short black hair, converging on his neck, branching into tributaries on his body and coagulating with the baby powder coating his skin.

Passing Lev toilet paper, I hoped that was the last of the pus.

'We done yet?' Alejandro asked, swaying, destabilising the men holding him.

'Keep him steady! We are not done! The poison is still coming out! More toilet paper, please!' Lev boomed.

I quickly unspooled more toilet paper. 'Here you go.'

Lev cleaned up the fresh pus, and applied pressure to the rim of the lesion.

Groaning like a dying elephant, Alejandro shifted, dragging along the men holding him.

'We need more guys to hold him,' Gravedigger said.

Everyone in the day room stopped their activities to watch more volunteers steady the big man.

'I think that is it. One moment! Let me see. No! No! We are not done.' Gazing like a fanatic, Lev discovered a new region of pus to finger.

Alejandro groaned and shifted again. He looked as if he was about to faint.

'More toilet paper!' Lev yelled.

'That must be it,' Alejandro said, sweat dripping from his ears and chin.

The prisoners eased their hold on Alejandro.

'Wait, men! Let me see.' Lev thrust his fingers into the sore. The ejaculation of pus, the largest so far, surprised Lev, delighted Gravedigger and shocked the rest of us.

Alejandro stumbled forward, tugging everyone holding him. They steadied him again. It seemed a pint of pus had come out by now.

'More toilet paper!' Lev massaged the area, exhausting the supply of pus. 'Now I will apply the salt.'

I tore open the tiny packets, tipped salt into Lev's palm and cringed at the prospect of what he would do next. Lev sprinkled salt onto the wound and rubbed it in. Alejandro wailed so loud the hermits rushed from their cells.

'There. Thanks to my Russian military training and the solidarity of my Yankee and Limey assistants, you are all fixed up now.' Lev smiled.

With their bee stripes stained by a combination of pus, sweat and baby powder, the men released Alejandro to much applause. Alejandro swayed but didn't collapse.

Alejandro's back improved. He made bond and was released, but I had a feeling I'd see him again.

10

....

In July, Officer Alston stopped by my cell with a smug smile and a copy of the *Phoenix New Times*. 'Have you seen this?'

'No,' I said, bracing for him to drone on about something boring.

'You're the cover story! English Shaun's Evil Empire. Don't tell anyone I gave you this. Read it. I've got some questions for you later on.' He handed me the newspaper and continued his security walk.

Ba-dum-ba-dum-ba-dum went my heart when I saw the cover: a portrait of me resembling Nosferatu with four of my co-defendants, including the Wild Ones and Cody (my head of security), in the foreground, my arms encircling them like an evil puppeteer; in the background, a horde of tiny ravers in a strobe-lit inferno dancing with their arms in the air. I couldn't believe it. Frantically turning the first page, I tore the newspaper. I scanned the contents page. There was a nine-page article titled 'The Evil Empire'. Stunned, I climbed onto my bunk and began combing through the article as fast as I could. Curious. Bewildered. Afraid. I needed to know if there was anything that might damage my case.

It was mostly the accounts of ravers, some who knew me, some who didn't and were making stuff up. When I read that the prosecutor had classified me as a serious drug offender likely to receive a life sentence, I went into shock. I had thought I was getting out – my attorney had filed for a bond hearing – and now I was facing 25 years due to a serious-drug-offender classification. I added a 25-year life sentence to my 33 years of age: 58! I'd be near retirement age when I got out! I considered my life over. I wanted to throw up. When I'd finished the article, I thought I'd read about some arch-villain in the Marvel Comics I'd collected as a child.

Crushed by the threat of a life sentence, I dreaded the impact of the article on my parents. The criminal behaviour I'd hidden from them over the years had burst out into the open. Even worse, the article portrayed me as a cross between Tony Soprano and a vampire, not some hedonistic stockbroker gone wild on drugs. Wanting to prevent my parents from reading it, I dashed down the stairs to call my aunt

Ann. She was aware of it and the Internet version. *Holy shit,* I thought. *An Internet version!* She said there was no way to prevent my parents from seeing it if it was on the Internet. She wanted to forewarn them before they found out from a less friendly source. She tried to calm me down by pointing out that no one would believe such an over-the-top article. She rang my father and emailed him the online version.

The article caused my mother to have a nervous breakdown. Her mental deterioration began after giving a lecture. In the staff room was a group of foreign students waiting to see their tutor. She imagined they'd read and were talking about the article. 'They all know!' she screamed, darting at the students. Busy at their computers, her fellow teachers stopped what they were doing to watch my mother shouting abuse and pointing at the students until someone calmed her down. My father rushed to the college to take her home, and she ended up on medical leave from work.

Her initial anger at what she saw as my lack of concern for my family turned inward into a deep depression. She could not understand how I could have done this to my family. Her anger turned to shame and guilt. She was ashamed of what the son she'd been so proud of had done and didn't want anyone to find out I was in prison. She kept the secret for months, not even telling her only sister. At home, she lived in fear of her house being vandalised by people who'd read the article. She imagined the words 'DRUG DEALERS' daubed across the front of their house. Every time she went near a newsagent, she was afraid to look at noticeboards or stacks of papers, thinking I'd made the headlines in the UK. She thought her friends would turn against her and she'd lose her job.

Her sympathetic GP gave her anti-anxiety medication, which helped her sleep and blocked out to some degree the constant unease she felt about my safety. Overriding the guilt and shame was her concern for me. From the moment they found out, my parents gave me unconditional support. There were no recriminations. No blame. They were just there for me. They never complained about any of it. I still live with the guilt of this unforeseen consequence of my lawbreaking.

With numerous counselling sessions and cognitive-behavioural therapy, my mother learned to deal with the situation. When she did finally break down in tears at work, she let the whole sorry story come out to her manager, Jill, who could not believe how she'd kept it all to herself for so long. From that moment she received nothing but support from her co-workers, friends and family, as she gradually told them all.

My father, who always appeared strong, suffered panic attacks, and my sister ended up having counselling. During one of the sessions, her counsellor suggested she write me a letter expressing the deep anger she felt about what I'd done to my family. The letter was ten pages long, and Karen waited a week to pluck up the courage to mail it.

In the letter, Karen told me she was furious about my uncaring and selfish behaviour towards our parents before my arrest. She reminded me how I hardly ever called them, how I constantly lied to them and how they never knew what I was doing. She accused me of behaving as though I didn't care about them at all.

She asked why I'd married Amy without telling our parents and why I thought it was acceptable to be so secretive even though I always expected them to bail me out whenever something went wrong.

She lambasted me for not paying off Mum and Dad's mortgage when I was rich, for not trying to make their lives easier and for blowing an absolute fortune on my raver friends. She reminded me that this was a time when our parents should have been slowing down, taking it easy, enjoying a holiday home with grandchildren, and instead they were spending a large part of their lives frantic with worry about me, their entire life savings sucked up by lawyer's fees.

She wrote that I'd been a constant disappointment to her, that she felt rejected during our childhood and years later, whenever she came to the States for a visit, and that she was hurt by my lack of interest in her life. She admitted she'd only come to visit me and Amy in Tucson because she'd thought it would be good for Mum and Dad for the whole family to be reunited. Yet I had still managed to almost ruin that trip with my 'fucked-up life'.

She wrote that the person I was before my arrest didn't deserve the deep love and devotion of someone like Claudia. I had wrecked Claudia's life with my selfish behaviour, so how could I talk about loving her?

She also questioned my present behaviour, my pronouncements about living a good life, and asked whether I had really learnt what a massive impact my behaviour had had on everyone. She reminded me that Mum and Dad had been ill with stress, all their plans for the future had been shelved, and that she too had become ill from the stress of seeing how badly Mum and Dad were doing.

She told me they were all furious for being dragged into my mess and angry that after everything Mum had said about Wild Man, I had ignored her, flown him to the States and supported his behaviour.

Finally, she wrote that she'd never bothered telling me how much I'd upset her in the past, as she didn't think it was worth it or I was capable of understanding. She told me she hoped I'd changed and not just somehow intellectualised a change by reading about how a good person should behave. She would only be able to tell when I got out.

Reading her letter threw my mind into turmoil. I knew I deserved it, and many of the things she said were true.

The guards circulated the *New Times* article in the jail. They cut out pictures and posted them to the Medical Unit's noticeboard for all to see. When Claudia came to visit, some guards harassed her about the article. Officer Alston pulled me out of the pod, asked what I'd really done and said he didn't believe I fitted the newspaper's portrayal of me as the Antichrist. He said I should have committed my crimes in his hometown of Chicago, where they only arrested black people. I appreciated his sympathy but not his racism. My infamy spread throughout the jail. Inmates asked for my autograph and put me on the phone to say hello to their wives and girlfriends. At breakfast time, I received extra milk and cheese from trusties eager to serve 'English Shaun' – a persona I was regretting ever having created. Even Gravedigger stopped by – drunk on hooch and in an expansive mood after knocking out a Mexican who'd been defecating in the shower – and offered to have smashed any of my co-defendants I thought might cooperate with the prosecutor.

Alan Simpson said the article had damaged my right to a fair trial in Phoenix, and he filed some motions. The judge issued a gag order on all the agents of the state involved in my prosecution, including the prosecutor and Detective Reid. But the damage was done, and I felt dissatisfied with the outcome of the motions.

Making matters worse, a second group was arrested – 39 more co-defendants – increasing the size and complexity of my case. The prosecutor told my attorney that there was too much legal discovery on the case to be printed out. The tens of thousands of pages of police reports on the 'Attwood Organisation' would have to be downloaded onto computer discs. The motion Simpson had filed to reduce my bond, which had raised my hopes of getting out of the jail, was denied. The growing complexity of the case, he said, meant that I would probably be in jail for at least a year.

As the legal situation deteriorated, my attorney's initial optimism faded and so did mine. Even though the prosecutor didn't have much of a case in the beginning, Simpson said, so many people were being arrested some would inevitably agree to testify against me. With a life sentence over my head, I now expected to serve prison time for my sins. And deservedly so. But I at least wanted a speedy resolution so I could be transferred to the prison system, where conditions were better than in Arpaio's jail (according to the prisoners who'd been there). Coming to terms with having to do up to a year in Arpaio's jail wasn't easy. I feared for my health, safety and sanity.

July 2002

Dear Love,

Just finished chow. The rice was skanky. Luckily I saved half of a breakfast brownie, but I feel bad after eating that crap. We have no air conditioning and showers still. I am writing literally stuck to my clothing, and all of my chocolate bars have melted.

Besides that, everything else is going good today. I'm 2–2 with the Russian chess champ, and I just got back from church where I saw Wild Man and had a good sing-a-long.

The whole pod was buzzing when I walked upstairs with boxes of my case paperwork. Thanks to that and the *New Times* article, I'm getting more status than ever now. At classes and church, I'm getting more hellos and fist shakes than ever. People were bowing down in church whispering 'Evil Empire'. People love talking about raves and the scene.

If I could sue the *New Times* and get some funds then I wouldn't feel as financially helpless as I do now. I feel sick to my stomach that my parents are paying my legal bill, and I would do anything to take that burden away from them.

In one of your letters, you say the weeks are going faster. Well that's certainly the case. The August court date will be here in no time, and we'll have a better idea of what's going on. One of the guys in the pod used Alan Simpson for his previous case. He shot at people in a Circle K and was looking at 15 years. Simpson got it down to three years.

In one of my classes, we talked about freeing ourselves from our bad apples. That we are trees. Bad apples include drugs, violence, etc., even fear of flying. She says we must get rid of all our turkeys as well. Those are people encouraging us into negative environments and people making us feel guilty or bad so that we will help them. Well, I guess I have been growing bad apples and been surrounded by turkeys for quite some time. This experience should free me of all that so I can be with you 100 per cent.

Love,

Shaun XXX

Dearest Fiancée,

Today is a very strange day in jail. No sooner had I called you than they declared headcount, and no sooner had I got back on the phone than they declared lockdown. Whilst sitting bewildered in my cell, a guard came by. He said hello and explained that something had happened. I asked him if someone had been murdered, and he said he wasn't allowed to answer that question.

So here I sit. Troll is passed out on the bottom bunk. OG is on the top bunk contemplating whether he'll be struck down by God if he uses pages from the Bible to roll cigarettes with. Both lie in their pink undies. The pod is unusually quiet. People are miffed. First they took our food, and now we are trapped in our cells. The noise of the constantly leaking water from the shower pierces the silence. Every now and then an inmate listening to the radio joins in with a partial song. There's no mail today. No visits are allowed on lockdown. The spirit of the pod is in dismay.

Troll just rolled out of the foetal position and blurted, 'Where am I? What day is it?' He giggled and coiled himself back up.

Chow should be here soon: the first and only opening of the cell door for the evening, aside from the continuous headcounts. Yesterday's chow was cowboy beans, two meat tostadas, and watermelon, carrots and onions mixed together in a greasy sauce. I used the bread provided with my breakfast to make bean sandwiches of which I ate five. I traded my two tostadas for two juices with other white inmates. The juices are half ice and are gone in a few swigs but in the unairconditioned environment provide excellent thirst-quenching. Even after the juice is quickly drunk, I utilise the ice in the cups by dropping it into used plastic bottles, which are filled with lukewarm tap water to hide its tepid taste. Nothing is wasted except when the food is so bad the returned trays pile up with the uneaten garbage.

I love you dearly and deeply,
Shaun

11

....

Church on the Street started as usual at Towers jail. We were sat in rows of plastic chairs in a large bare room without any windows, singing along with the chaplain, Pastor Will, who insisted, in the face of numerous obstacles put up by the jail, on coming in to hold a weekly Christian outreach service. Pastor Will was an ex-Vietnam vet, Satanist and alcoholic whom God had restored to His flock in 1976. In drainpipe jeans and a lumberjack shirt, tiny Hillbilly Ed was strumming his vintage guitar and tapping pointy snakeskin cowboy boots against the concrete. There were no guards present, affording more privacy for the devout to commune with God and the less devout to misbehave.

THERE IS POWER, POWER, WONDER WORKING POWER
IN THE BLOOD OF THE LAMB;
THERE IS POWER, POWER, WONDER WORKING POWER
IN THE PRECIOUS BLOOD OF THE LAMB.

WOULD YOU BE FREE FROM YOUR PASSION AND PRIDE?
THERE'S POWER IN THE BLOOD, POWER IN THE BLOOD;
COME FOR A CLEANSING TO CALVARY'S TIDE;
THERE'S WONDERFUL POWER IN THE BLOOD.

Clutching the Bible, Pastor Will took a few steps forward. His keen eyes, bulging and bloodshot, appraised the audience. 'Tonight this is God's room. This is our church. This is the time and place to worship Him, and I expect you all to behave yourselves – especially the scoffers and mockers in the back row.' Pastor Will's eyes scanned the back row and halted on a known disrupter of religious ceremonies: Wild Man. Wild Man stopped whispering loudly to me and smiled dementedly at Pastor Will. The expression on Pastor Will's sun-baked face soured, his gaze intensified. When Pastor Will got through shaking his head at Wild Man, his eyes settled on the Christians in the front row. Most of them had brought rosary beads and soft-bound Bibles. Some were adorned with tattoos of crucifixes, Jesus and the Virgin Mary. The communing of eyes between him and the devout restored a calmer look to Pastor Will's face. 'You see, scoffing and mocking was predicted in the Bible. The scoffers and mockers were expected during the End Times. How many of you are familiar with Revelations?'

All hands shot up in the front rows, not so many in the middle, at the back, none.

'If you've read Revelations—'

Two men burst through the door right behind Pastor Will, startling him. One, a Keith Richards type in tight-fitting black clothes and a headband, unsheathed a guitar with a gay-pride rainbow sticker on it and didn't speak or seem to alter his facial expression. The other was bald and beaming a smile not of this earth. Through Lennon specs, his eyes radiated happiness. His cheap white T-shirt proclaimed: I LOVE JESUS. He wore sandals worthy of an apostle and well-faded jeans.

Regaining his composure, Pastor Will said, 'Some of you may already be familiar with Jumping Bill.'

The bald man raised his hand and intensified his smile. The inmates who recognised Jumping Bill clapped as if we were in for a treat.

Pastor Will gazed for a few seconds at the two new arrivals tuning their strings. 'I'm just gonna step outta the way and let Jumping Bill take over.'

Jumping Bill centred himself in front of the congregation. His partner remained several metres behind him near the wall. 'How many of you love Jesus?' Jumping Bill whispered.

Only the front rows responded.

'How many of you love Jesus?' he said a little louder, nodding at us. More rows responded.

'How many of you love Jesus?' he said even louder. He strummed his guitar and lunged forward.

Most of us responded.

He smiled over his shoulder at his partner. His expressionless partner responded with a barely perceptible nod. Rotating his head from side to side like a mannequin, Jumping Bill engaged us with eyes that said, *I am about to open the gates of Heaven for you*. Still in the lunge position, he began rocking back and forth as he sang in a soothing whisper:

> WORTHY IS THE LAMB
> WORTHY IS THE LAMB

YOU ARE HOLY, HOLY
ARE YOU LORD GOD ALMIGHTY
WORTHY IS THE LAMB
WORTHY IS THE LAMB

Jumping Bill leapt into the air, surprising us. His guitar flew out to one side. He dashed down the aisle, casting the net of his smile over the rapt audience. Strumming faster, he homed in on the back row. He stopped in front of various men, nodding and smiling, not saying a word, melting the meanest looks from faces. When my turn came, he looked so happy, I thought, *My God, I took drugs to feel like that.* The force of his smile was so strong I couldn't stop smiling back at him. His aura made the hair on my arms stand up. Then he ran to the front of the room. Back to rocking in the lunge position.

'Repeat after me, everyone!' he shouted, and then sang, 'Worthy is the lamb.'

'Worthy is the lamb,' we chimed in.

'You are Holy, Holy,' he sang.

'You are Holy, Holy,' we repeated.

We cheered when the song was over.

'Excellent! Excellent!' he said. He played more songs. He whispered to God. He sang loudly. He wept. He sang in Spanish. He danced and dashed around the room. 'OK, everybody, at the end of this song I want you all to jump up and down with me as high in the air as you can.'

When he shouted 'Jump, everybody!', he jumped, and some men began to pogo. Others looked around the room as if wondering what to do. I decided to jump. It seemed the right thing to do. I jumped alone in my area, embarrassed at first but then joined by a few others whose jumping eased my self-consciousness. Smiling at Bill and the other men jumping, I was momentarily free from the stress of my case and the environment. I was free to push down hard on my feet and spring as high in the air as possible. Free to land in a way that jolted my body and sent my anxiety out in shockwaves through my feet. There was an irrational joy sparkling in the eyes of the other men jumping, and I knew my eyes looked exactly the same. I was finally at one with the insanity of the place.

'You are going to be free-free-free-free . . . ' Jumping Bill yelled. 'C'mon, everybody, jump with me!'

Around the men that were already jumping, many more joined in.

The mass of jumping men expanded across the room. Late jumpers were enthusiastically matching the intensity of the early jumpers. Even Wild Man was jumping and yelling, 'The devil is in me!' The men jumping nearest to Wild Man gave him a wide berth lest he injure them. IDs shot from the top pockets of some of the jumpers. Men pushed and shoved each other and play fights broke out. When shower sandals and chairs were launched across the room, Pastor Will called order. Much to my disappointment, Jumping Bill and everyone stopped jumping. I was back in the jail.

When Pastor Will stepped back, Jumping Bill yelled, 'One more time! You are going to be free-free-free-free . . . '

The cheering men jumped again, converting the room into a punk-rock concert. To a boisterous ovation, Pastor Will announced the end of the service. Most of us had stopped jumping by the time the guards rushed in to investigate the commotion. They commanded us to return to our pods, but we were so many and they were so few we ignored them. Basking in our defiance of the guards and the afterglow of jumping, we lingered to hug Jumping Bill.

12

··········

Returning from court, OG breezed into our cell singing 'Another One
Bites the Dust', grinning in a self-satisfied way that didn't look right on a
man lacking both front teeth. His case had been dropped. To celebrate,
he tied a towel around his arm, clenched his hand several times and
shot up a massive hit of heroin. He sang until 2 a.m. that night, and
tickled my feet every time I fell asleep.

Troll and I prayed we wouldn't get another maniac like OG for a
cellmate. Our prayers were answered in the form of Doug, a mellow 50
year old who'd spent half of his life locked up. He was short, thin, with
gentle blue eyes and a large nose reshaped by ancient prison fights.
Caught with a tiny amount of black-tar heroin, he was facing five years
for violating the terms of his parole. As Doug had done more time than
all of us, the other inmates respected him. Even Gravedigger stopped
by to congratulate us for having 'an all-white cell with a well-respected
wood'.

Around the time Doug arrived, our pod received the biggest man at
Towers jail: Houston, an ex-pro footballer. Six foot eight, he towered
over everyone and was crowned the head of his race by virtue of size.
His presence put an end to the day-room affronts on the blacks – even
Gravedigger modified his behaviour. When there was a black-on-black
dispute in a neighbouring pod, the guards took Houston over there to
settle it. I was wary of chatting with him because of what the whites
might do, but he insisted on telling me about travelling the world with
his football team and the partying he'd done at Stringfellows nightclub
in London. Along with his sports success had come a cocaine addiction.
Drugs had destroyed his career. He'd been arrested selling cocaine to
finance his addiction. I told him I'd thrown my stockbroking career
away to party. After chatting with Houston, I returned to my filthy cell
with the two addicts, dwelling on what I'd lost.

Houston wasn't with us for long. Trouble brewed as soon as he was
moved to another tower to promote 'racial harmony'. Lev told me about
Gravedigger's plan to have SmackDown – who was now the head of
the blacks again – smashed. After smashing Carter, SmackDown had

behaved himself for a few weeks but was now bullying commissary from members of every race again. There were few men in the pod that SmackDown hadn't tried it on with. Knowing that smashing the head of a race was a declaration of war on every member of that race, I expected mass violence.

SmackDown cornered me in D10 when I was on the stool writing a letter to Claudia. "Ey, England, I saw you get store. Gimme some Snickers till store day, dawg, and I'll pay you back two-for-one.' In shower sandals and bee-striped pants, he stepped towards me, reducing the distance between us as if to pressure me into saying yes. He inhaled volubly, expanding a broad and powerful chest that rose from his narrow waist like a triangle.

Troll had previously warned me that if the prisoners knew I'd give them store, there'd be a line at the door to take my commissary. 'I've only got enough to last till store day, dawg,' I said, hoping he'd leave it at that.

SmackDown stepped closer, breathing the full weight of his presence down upon me. 'You don't trust me 'cause I'm black. You don't think I'll pay you back,' he said, anger rising in his voice.

Tensing up, I paused to think what to say. 'That's not it at all, dawg. I'll starve in here if I give my store away,' I said, which was true. It was also true that I didn't trust him, and he knew it. He was trying to milk that truth. But the reason I didn't trust him wasn't racial, it was because I could count on the fingers of one hand the amount of people I could trust in the jail.

'Y'all motherfuckin' racists up in this cell.'

Fearing he'd try to exploit any emotional reaction, I strained to remain pleasant. 'Look, dawg, I can't eat the red death and green baloney. I'll starve if I give my store away,' I said, determined to hold my ground.

'Fuck, man, all I'm asking for is one lousy Snickers.'

'If I give my food away, I'll run out before store day and end up hungry.'

Troll walked in. 'Wattup, dawgs!'

'I'm motherfuckin' hungry,' SmackDown said. 'Got any honey buns?'

'Best I can do is a few soups, bro,' Troll said, reaching under his bunk for a commissary bag.

The soups sent SmackDown on his way, but I knew he'd be back. A part of me appreciated what Gravedigger was about to do. It was the same part that rejoiced when SmackDown smashed Carter and Gravedigger sent Carter packing. SmackDown had threatened my food – something I no longer took for granted. I felt hassled and understood why so many were against him.

Gravedigger used the numerous incidences of SmackDown bulldogging inmates to organise a meeting for the heads of all of the races except the blacks. He told them that if a torpedo gave SmackDown the standard ultimatum, 'The fellas have decided you need to roll your shit up or else we'll roll it up for you. What's it gonna be, dawg?' SmackDown would probably smash the torpedo and claim he'd earned the right to stay in our pod. To get the job done properly required three torpedoes to corner SmackDown and more to wait outside his cell just in case. Eager to get rid of SmackDown, each head volunteered a torpedo to smash him.

While on the phone in the day room, I noticed men gathering suspiciously on the balcony. Most of the blacks were engrossed in a card game downstairs as three torpedoes – a white, a Mexican and a Mexican American – entered SmackDown's upstairs cell. More torpedoes guarded the stairs.

'Each of the races have decided you've gotta go, SmackDown,' yelled the white torpedo, a tough 40-year-old ranch hand from Nebraska. 'Now roll your fucking shit up!'

'For doing fucking what? Who wants me to fucking roll up?' SmackDown yelled, shifting away from them.

'Come on, SmackDown, let's do this the easy way, dawg.'

'I ain't fucking rolling up!'

The white torpedo dashed behind SmackDown while the other two approached from the front. He put SmackDown in an upright headlock while they punched SmackDown's head and stomach. SmackDown lurched backwards, sandwiching the white torpedo between himself and the wall. He flicked his head forwards and then backwards, instantly breaking the white torpedo's nose. Noisy crosses, jabs and uppercuts fermented into a bloody mess. The yelling and pounding of knuckles against flesh caught the attention of the blacks, who charged halfway up the stairs before the torpedoes began pushing them back down. One of the blacks weighed about 400 pounds, and he fell down the stairs, knocking men out of the way like a bowling ball striking pins, dragging more men into the fight. Two of the blacks fought their way past the torpedoes and onto the balcony. Inmates of all races emerged from the upper-tier cells and fought those two blacks. The battle for the stairs was raging below them, and the fight at the bottom of the stairs was spreading throughout the day room. Several blacks were still trying to gain ground on the stairs until a hefty Mexican American attacked them from behind with a mop stick. Everywhere I looked, a black man was bravely fending off multiple assailants. As if he were the personification of the Satanic puppet-master on his chest, Gravedigger was enjoying the spectacle from his cell downstairs. I later learned he'd opted not to fight so the disciplinary officer couldn't find him guilty of inciting a riot and send him back to lockdown.

Mordhorst turned the phone lines off. 'Lockdown! Lockdown, now!' he yelled over the speaker system. 'This is a direct order: lockdown right now!' Everyone ignored him, so he put on a gas mask.

Knowing Mordhorst was on his way to the day room to spray us all, I tried to get up the stairs behind Troll and Doug, who were struggling to elbow through the fighting men. Struck by flailing arms, I raised my forearms to shield my face. Progress was impossible: we'd advance a few steps and get pushed back down. The torpedoes at the top of the stairs were pushing the blacks down onto the rest of us. I'd never been in the thick of a room full of people fighting. Caught up in the atmosphere, I was soon elbowing and pushing men of all races away with increased force. I felt the rush of the battle as I did what was necessary to try to get up the stairs. Also motivating me was fear of Mordhorst, who was descending the control-tower stairs wielding a giant canister, seconds away from entering the day-room door directly behind me.

Sane guards waited for backup before entering a riot situation, but not Mordhorst. Watching over him in the control tower, Officer Alston activated the sliding door to our pod. As Officer Alston yelled 'Lockdown!' over and over, Mordhorst turned sideways to get through the half-open door and charged into the day room. The Mexican pulling ninja moves with the mop stick was the first to be sprayed. An awful smell assaulted us, as if a thousand bird's-eye chillies were being deseeded all at once. The spray scattered the men from the stairs. Falling over each other, eyes smarting, my cellmates and I rushed into D10 and slammed the door. From the safety of the cell, I watched Mordhorst, resembling an invader from the Second World War, dashing around fumigating the combatants as if exterminating vermin. Coughing and wheezing prisoners rushed into cells. Many locked down in the nearest cells they could find just to escape from Mordhorst. The Mexican and

Mexican American torpedoes slipped out of SmackDown's cell just before Mordhorst got there. Mordhorst locked the door and sprayed the cell for a good few minutes.

'I'm fucking blind!' SmackDown kept yelling.

By the time backup charged into Tower 6, Mordhorst had put out half of the riot. The backup guards dragged out anyone still fighting.

'My eyes are killing me,' I said, panting by the cell door.

'Wet your towel and wrap it around your head,' Doug said. 'It'll stop the spray. Blink as much as you can, so your tears wash the crap out.'

I put a wet towel around my head but left a gap to monitor the day room. Guards were ascending the stairs, hurrying towards the fighting noises still coming from SmackDown's cell. The guards opened SmackDown's door and rushed in, yelling orders to stop fighting. They emerged with SmackDown.

'You'll all be fucking sorry for pulling that three-on-one bullshit when I get back outta the hole!' he yelled. Hardly able to open his eyes, he otherwise looked unscathed as they escorted him to lockdown.

Then they brought out the white torpedo whose bleeding nose was pointing in a new direction.

'Your nose is crooked,' mocked a guard.

'Can I fix it before you handcuff me?' the white torpedo asked with a polite cowboy twang.

The guard looked perplexed. The white torpedo placed the palm of one hand against the side of his nose, and struck his nose with his other hand. It made a crunching noise. Holding his hands out in readiness for the cuffs, he smiled with satisfaction.

13

....

My parents have always liked hiking. Prior to my arrest, they'd booked a walking holiday in Switzerland together with some friends. Due to my incarceration, they cancelled the holiday, losing their deposit. They didn't want to waste money that might be needed by my attorney. They said they'd rather jump on a plane to Phoenix, but I told them not to come. I didn't want them forking out thousands in airfares, and I didn't want them to see me in the jail. I was ashamed. But Mum was determined to make the trip, so to save the cost of two fares, she booked to come on her own. Putting aside my dread of her seeing me in there, I looked forward to her visit and wrote to her about my excitement. I appreciated her determination to travel 5,000 miles.

When her first visit was called, I was excited but also had great fear. I worried that when she saw me – malnourished and in bee stripes – she might have a second nervous breakdown. My situation was a far cry from her last visit when I was living in a mountainside home, jumping in my swimming pool first thing in the morning and eating at fancy restaurants every night.

I first glimpsed my mother from the visitation holding tank. She looked smaller and more fragile than when I'd last seen her. Struck by guilt, I was determined to reassure her, so I put on my widest grin. She was sat at a table in the visitation room, pale and tired, looking around expectantly until she spotted me waving. Momentarily, her eyes lit up and the sadness left her face.

Officer Green gave his speech to the visitors, and I was allowed into the visitation room. I hastened to Mum's table. 'Thanks so much for coming,' I said.

Tears started to fall, but she quickly fought them back. I could tell she was shocked by my appearance. Unlike me, she couldn't hide the sadness on her face. 'You look as though you've lost weight,' she said, appraising my sunken cheeks and skinny frame. 'Are you getting enough to eat?'

'Thanks to Claudia, I'm getting Snickers, peanuts and peanut butter from the commissary,' I said, maintaining my smile even though I was devastated by what I'd done to her health. 'How was your journey?'

'Long and tiring, but it was worth it to see you.'

'I really appreciate it.'

'I had to come. I had to see you in the flesh. I needed to know you're all right.'

'I'm all right. I was in shock at first, but I've adjusted. The longer I've been here, the more allies I've made, and that's what keeps you out of trouble. The *New Times* article – as exaggerated as it was – gave me a lot of credibility with my neighbours.'

'So in jail, everything's turned on its head. What's bad is good and vice versa?'

'Kind of. Well, actually, only in some cases. Sex offences and crimes against kids can get you killed in here. But if you're a murderer – and you've not murdered a woman or a kid – then you're at the top of the pecking order.'

'And Alan Simpson, what's he saying?'

I didn't want to burden her with the stress of my legal situation. 'He said my case is going to take longer to resolve than we originally thought, and that's because it's a complex case.'

Mum started to look worried.

'Alan's one of the top attorneys in Phoenix. I'm sure he'll get me the best possible plea bargain at some point. It's just a matter of waiting it out. I really appreciate you and Dad paying his fee. If you can't afford a private lawyer here, you're pretty much dead and buried.' She looked even more concerned, so I changed the subject. 'So how's your stay gone so far?'

'Everyone's been so helpful. It's fortunate that I can stay at Ann and Donny's house. They've been so kind, and Claudia's been an angel.'

'I know. I don't know how I'd cope without her visits. She comes here all the time and writes every day.'

'She picked me up and drove me here and is waiting to take me back. She said she'd do that every visit and drive me anywhere I want to go afterwards. We'll go to eat after I get out.'

'Good. She'll enjoy spending time with you. She told me she'd look after you.'

'How she copes with getting in here I don't know. It's horrendous. It's so distressing seeing the people in the waiting room, mothers with toddlers and small babies, crying and restless, all crowded together in a hot stuffy waiting room. It's dirty and littered, and the toilets are a disgrace. We were sat there for hours waiting for my number to be called.'

'Claudia's told me about some of that stuff. She's going through it every few days. I'm so lucky to have found someone so caring.'

'And when I was finally called after going through security, feeling the heavy door close behind me, shutting out the world, I felt an inkling of what it must be like to be a prisoner.'

'At least you can go back out through that door,' I said, glad to see her smile. 'There's people been in here for over a year.'

'Held on remand for over a year?'

'Yes, over a year. Can you believe it?'

'The system here stinks! The guards treat the visitors like dirt. They're abrupt. They look down on everyone. It's so unfair. A lot of the women waiting are Mexican and obviously poor. They've committed no crime, but they're treated like criminals. Outside, we drove past a woman pushing a pram down the dusty road. Too poor to afford a taxi, I suppose. The officers in charge of Visitation are rude and ignorant. Which, having a boss like Arpaio, doesn't surprise me. The nastiness comes down from the top. I don't want any special treatment, but they just don't seem to care.'

'There are plenty of snidey ones.' I glanced over my shoulder. 'Like Officer Green over there. When the visit's over, he locks us in the strip-search room for hours. It's a bloody nightmare. But some of the guards are OK. Some hate working for Arpaio and aren't afraid to tell us.'

'I suppose it takes all sorts, and they're probably not paid very much. The dress code gets me. They complained this shirt reveals my collarbone and were about to refuse me entry. I had to plead ignorance about the dress code. They allowed me in – only because it was my first visit – but warned me to cover my collarbone next time. I can understand them banning miniskirts and cleavage but not collarbones. Who's going to get excited by my collarbone? I hate to think of it!' she said, her face brightening up. 'We drove past Tent City, too. I couldn't believe what I was seeing.'

'Arpaio's real proud of Tent City. If you think we've got it bad, imagine those poor buggers out in the desert in old army tents left over from the Korean War. The news reported temperatures in the tents of over 130°. And because it's outdoors, the gangs get weapons and drugs thrown over the fence.'

'If this were a developing country, I'd understand it. But not in America. No one would believe it.'

'Arpaio does what he wants. The old fogeys in Sun City keep voting him back in 'cause he's out doing tough-on-crime PR stunts every week. But in reality, he's all spin. He's created an environment that just breeds more crime. There's no hope for youngsters coming here. They get recruited by the gangs, and are soon shooting up drugs like everyone else and contracting diseases like hepatitis C.'

'You've been writing a lot about the food. Are you sure you're getting enough to eat?'

'Yes, I told you, Claudia's putting money on my books. The guys with no money on their books are constantly begging everyone else for food.'

'Starving people in the land of plenty. It's shameful.' My mum talked about how my dad and Karen were coping. 'They're both still shell-shocked and just taking it a day at a time. Karen's working hard. She'll be a top journalist some day. But she gets upset and anxious for your safety. You hear so many tales about violence in prison. I try not to think about it.'

'Being in here is like being in a video game: you just have to work your way through it and you've constantly got all this danger around you. But so far – it's like I have a guardian angel or something – I've managed to get through unscathed.'

'It's a relief to know you're safe. That someone's looking out for you.'

'I'll be OK. Try not to worry. The longer I've been here, the more friends in low places I've made.'

We both laughed.

'Your dad is just getting on with it. What else can he do? He's strong, and although he's worried sick about you, he keeps positive, which helps me survive each day. We are a strong family, and we won't let this pull us apart. You know we love you very much, and we'll do anything to get you out of this mess.'

'Thanks,' I said, overwhelmed by her kindness.

Officer Green announced visits were over.

'I'll phone you at Ann's tonight,' I said.

'I'll look forward to it. I love you. Take care.'

'Love you too.'

During her two-week stay, my mother visited at every opportunity, sometimes with Claudia, sometimes with my aunt Ann. She got used to the ordeal of getting in and out of the jail. She even befriended some of the people she met in the waiting room. Although I was traumatised by my legal situation, her visits began to restore my hope. I found her constant expressions of support reassuring. I was sad when she returned to England.

August 2002

Dear Claudia,

We are on 24-hour lockdown because a fight broke out this morning. I'm not sure what happened, but a bloodied little Mexican emerged from the shower area after some thumping noises were heard. For once the guards were on it right away and locked the whole pod down.

Despite lockdown, we've been in good cheer. Rather than give us our chow room-service style, each cell was called down the stairs. This led to a kind of frenzied atmosphere. As each three cellmates went on their walk down the stairs to get their chow, the rest of the pod hollered and screamed obscenities. Troll walked down the stairs with his bum hanging out to massive applause. When Kenny, who's always asking me to spoon with him on his bunk, went down we all screamed, 'Slut, slut, slut!' Ah, the small joys of mocking the system. After chow, another guard came in and threatened a 72-hour lockdown if we didn't shut up.

The chow was gross, love. I ate two cabbage sandwiches and had to eat an extra Snickers bar to fill up. I eat a Snickers for lunch because we get no lunch. I order seven a week so I'll run out early now, but I still have plenty of nuts left, so I won't starve.

Gravedigger didn't get a bond reduction, so he's been depressed. My Russian friend Lev is having to take his case to trial, so he's also pretty depressed. Troll got granted mental-health status, so he was in good spirits today.

August is here now, and my court date. I wonder if I'll ever get to listen to the wiretap evidence. It would be nice to hear the full extent of the calls so that I can find out what was really said as opposed to the police's hang-the-bastard interpretations. I'm not expecting much from court. The let's-scare-the-new-inmates-to-death procedures are likely to continue. If the prosecutor could, she would up the 25 years I'm facing to the death penalty. I expect some offer of many, many years designed to scare me and make me feel like I'm getting a deal later on when they reduce it.

I L U forever,

Shaun XXX

Dearest Loveliness,

So court was just a continuance yet again. Surprise, surprise. I've slept about 2 hours in the last 24 hours with the up-all-night court routine. At least Alan said I've been doing good work in these legal visits listening to the wiretaps. I feel more confident after listening to the calls because I'm not really on many of them or saying much. It puts things in perspective.

The guards played a prank on Wild Man this morning. Out of 50 inmates they chose him and Gerard Gravano, Sammy the Bull's son, to be chained together. Gerard seemed nice, though, and we got to ask him more questions about his Ecstasy ring case, which is similar to ours. Apparently, most of his co-defendants have agreed to work with the prosecutor. I hope that doesn't happen in my case. Alan said we'll find out when the prosecutor starts offering them sweetened deals to testify against me.

It's so hot in here tonight, it's insane. Sweat is just dripping down my face as I write this. It keeps dripping on the paper and fucking my writing up. I pray that they will fix the fans soon. I drink tonnes of water all day long. I'm so sick of the swamp environment and the new mosquito invasion. I'm going downstairs in a minute to do a few hundred push-ups with the boys. I'm trying to do more exercise each week despite the hot conditions. It just requires three showers a day. The exercise helps me stay sane.

After two nights of cabbage sandwiches I couldn't eat, tonight's meal was emu burger, soggy rice and corn on the cob. I took one bite of the emu burger and gave it away. I am out of Snickers, so I ate two rice sandwiches so I would not starve.

The guys two cells down from us got searched today. They had to strip to their pinks and were then handcuffed and taken downstairs. As the guard searched, we heckled him. An hour later we were handcuffed and taken downstairs, and our cell was searched. They took our spare towels and sheets and stuff. That sucked. We had to sit at the dining table in our pinks while the inmates tormented us for ten minutes, yelling stuff like, 'Look at his ass. Nice ass. Search his ass. It's in his ass!' I guess we have to suffer everything in here at least once. Oh, love, you're so lucky to be in the free world. The depths of depravity in here get worse.

We are so bored at nights we name a letter then have to think of movies beginning with that letter. Each letter can last up to an hour, so we only do one or two letters a night.

Ta-ta!

Shaun

XXXXXXXXX

14

....

'Don't get too attached to anyone in here 'cause they're always moving us around, and it hurts when you're split from dudes you just made friends with,' Billy, the hippy who'd vouched for me, had told me. To promote racial harmony following the riot, the guards moved half of our pod to other towers, including Troll, Doug and Lev to Tower 2. Losing my cellmates and my chess partner on the same day brought home Billy's advice. I'd defined myself through friendships with relative strangers – primarily those three – and without their companionship buoying my spirit I felt lonely.

Into D10 the guards moved Busta Beatz, a young Mexican American who thought he was a rap star and arrived with a pet cricket in a box. He had an Eskimo look about him. A round face. Slanted chestnut eyes. Short spiky black hair. His skin was an Etch A Sketch of mismatched tattoos, including smiley faces on his fingertips, BUSTA in rickety writing on one forearm and BEATZ on the other. After taking his psychotropic medication, Busta Beatz would circle the day room with a vacant stare and rap. His attorney had filed a Rule 11, so he was undergoing tests for severe mental impairment. Something the psychiatrist should have taken into consideration for Busta Beatz's Rule 11 was his love of red death. He couldn't get enough of it! It was common courtesy for anyone who couldn't eat his red death to give it to Busta Beatz. He received up to ten trays daily. By tray pickup, he was usually still eating, so he would bag the red death, put all the mustard he could scrounge into the bags, bite the corners off the bags and squeeze the red death into his mouth. This food lasted until the next day and made our cell stink of decaying meat.

Curious about this bizarre character who delighted in catching me off guard and pulling my pants down, I asked him about his life.

'I'm State-raised. Foster homes, dawg,' Busta Beatz said. 'When I was 11, I was kidnapped off the streets by a guy and a chick. They took me to a house and made me take crystal meth. They kept me there while the guy raped me and his friends raped me. They'd suck me off and give me crystal and tell me everything was gonna be all right.'

I was shocked. 'Hey, look, you don't have to tell me this stuff if you don't want. I was just–'

'It's all right, dawg. I can deal with it. They raped me for three days straight, then just dropped me off where they found me, so I went back to my foster parents. After that, I started to run away a lot. Did drugs. Sniffed a lotta paint. To buy paint and drugs, I shoplifted and robbed houses. I ran away to Phoenix where I didn't know anyone, ended up living on the streets, mostly West Van Buren. The paisas there recruited me for their gang, Doble. They gave me a gun, so I'd go to 35th and Van Buren and stick-up shoppers. Doble took half. I kept half for paint, drugs and fast food.'

'So you were busted for sticking someone up?'

'No, for breaking into an empty house I was gonna sleep in.'

I encouraged Busta Beatz to get some books to improve his reading. He read erotica to a mosquito he kept on a small island of soggy toilet paper under an empty peanut-butter container. Worried the mosquito might escape, he ripped one of its wings off. Feeling sorry for it, he attempted to feed it a morsel of Snickers, but the mosquito backed away.

'Bad mosquito! Don't walk that way! I'll have to punish you again.'

He rolled six inches of toilet paper to the diameter of pencil lead and hovered it over the mosquito's rear. 'You are not being a good slave! I'm going to have to spank your bottom again! Here I come!' He tapped the mosquito's rear as if the toilet paper were a cane. 'Good slave! No! Bad-bad-bad-bad slave! I'm gonna have to spank you again.' He did this for two days until the mosquito died – and then he ate it.

During the night, lying stomach-down on the cell floor, he wrote rap songs in the company of his cricket, which couldn't jump away as he'd removed its legs. Practising his raps in a loud whisper, he often woke me up.

His most popular rap with the inmates was 'Dead Body Hoes' – about him defiling the corpses of famous women including Christina Aguilera and Britney Spears. The inmates demanded he rap that song every day.

When Claudia's next visit wasn't announced at the prearranged time, I waited a few hours and telephoned her.

'What're you doing home?' I asked, worried.

'They wouldn't let me in,' she said.

'What?' I asked, furious.

'It's really hard to visit. The staff are always giving me a hard time, and today one in particular had a problem with the way I dressed.'

I could tell she was about to cry and assumed she'd been insulted or possibly sexually harassed by a male guard. 'Who was it? Which guard?'

'Some fat lady at the front with attitude from hell.'

'What did she say?' I asked, angry at the female but relieved it wasn't a man.

'She said don't try to come here no more unless I follow the rules for outfits and dress properly, so I started crying and asking her how I broke the rules, and she told me something along the lines of my shirt being too tight, you can't show your boobs, or something. Yeah, like, basically, I'm not allowed to be showing the shape of my boobs. I wanted to show her the shape of my middle finger.' We both laughed. 'I was dressed like a schoolteacher trying to come there, and she's telling me my clothes are too form-fitting.'

'Take no notice. She's probably just jealous of your looks.'

'Do you know if that counted as a visit?'

'I don't know. I'll put a grievance in if it did.'

'I wanna come down as soon as I can, next visit. I hope you don't mind me in a baggy shirt. What makes me mad is half the other people come in wearing shorter or less clothes, and tighter than I do, with no problem.'

'I'm sure they'll let you in next time, love. I really appreciate what you have to go through to come see me.'

Claudia was allowed to visit, but no matter what she wore, that particular guard continued to harass her.

15

....

Young Marco was a new arrival to our pod. Within days of him moving into cell D15, he had the guards fetch two of his friends, Paulie and Hugo, from other parts of the jail to join him. No one was quite sure how he'd arranged this – I was flabbergasted – but rumours soon spread that he was the son of a Mafioso and bribery was involved. Someone said he'd won trophies for kickboxing, but he didn't look the fighting type. He was short, with an innocent look about him, and usually smiling. He had large affectionate eyes and eyelashes long enough for women to envy. His thick brown tresses and olive complexion made him look unlike anyone else in the jail. From a distance, he seemed unimpressive, but close up the self-confidence he radiated swept you away. He was in for punching someone. We shared the same attorney, Alan Simpson.

Lanky and with stately slicked-back salt-and-pepper hair, Argentinian Hugo idolised Marco and acted in the capacity of his butler. The son of Italian immigrants, he spoke Italian, Spanish and English fluently. Although in his 40s, he was prone to emotional outbursts, which he put down to his South American upbringing. He wrote love letters to his wife signed in his own blood. He often wept during church services and while listening to inmates tell sad stories. He was facing deportation to Argentina, where he claimed he was blacklisted as a political dissident and the government would execute him on arrival. I paid him cookies to teach me Spanish, a language I was determined to master.

The stocky Italian New Yorker Paulie looked like a typical Hollywood Mafia goon. He had beady brown eyes, a boxer's flat nose and hairy sausage fingers that dealt out a nutcracker of a handshake. Every few days, he vented his anger on Hugo, much to our amusement. But like Hugo, he was prone to crying, especially when talking about how much he missed his wife and kids.

Much to the astonishment of the guards and inmates, a drawing of the Italian flag and a sign went up on the door of D15: LITTLE ITALY. I couldn't believe my eyes and laughed out loud the first few times I saw it.

As Gravedigger had been moved to Tower 2 following the race riot, we had no head of the whites. A white-boy meeting was held, which I wasn't invited to. I knew the whites were voting on two candidates: Marco and Bolts, the skinhead with a tattoo of Hitler admiring Jews dying in a gas chamber on his chest. As most of the Aryans had been moved out of our pod following the race riot, Marco won the vote by a narrow margin, a result that amazed and gladdened the other races and me. Bolts was peeved, and I feared jail movements were such that it was only a matter of time before there were sufficient Aryans to launch a coup d'état on Little Italy.

"Ey, England," Paulie said, entering D10 with a scowl that made me squirm on my bunk. 'I've come to you 'cause I know you're the only one in here that'll give me a straight-up fucking answer.'

'What is it, Paulie? You know I'll help you if I can,' I said, sitting up fast.

'You promise me you'll tell me the truth no matter what I fucking ask?'

'Of course I will.'

'Well, then. Tell me this then: do I have a fucking anger problem?' He stared at me as if he were a lie detector equipped to punish a wrong answer.

I pushed thoughts of *Why me?* out of my head and searched for something safe to say. 'Here's what I think, Paulie. You're a really nice fella, but you do get a little excited every now and then. You're an emotional person and everyone likes you.' I hoped he'd leave it at that.

'So you're saying I do have a fucking anger problem then?' he snarled.

I paused to find a better answer. 'I try to stay as calm as possible during stressful situations, but I can see how you handle things a little differently and like to speak what's on your mind.'

He looked up as if in deep thought. 'So are you saying I *do* or *do not* have a fucking anger problem?'

Cornered, I risked being more specific: 'I'd say you don't have an anger problem, but you do get angrier than most of us.' I studied his face.

He scratched his chin. 'So you're saying I do have *a little bit* of an anger problem?'

The jokey high-pitched way he'd said *a little bit* encouraged me to mimic him. 'Maybe *a little bit* of an anger problem, but nothing to lose any sleep over.'

He leaned towards me, and I flinched. His hand appeared to be coming for my face, but it found my shoulder. Rocking my shoulder, he said, 'Thanks, England. I really appreciate your honesty.'

Much to my relief, he marched out of the cell. He stomped down the day-room stairs towards Hugo, who was standing watching TV. He stopped when his face was inches away from Hugo's and yelled, 'England said I don't have no fucking anger problem!' He thrust his palms at Hugo's chest, knocking Hugo over a table. I felt partially responsible. 'You don't know what you're fucking talking about!' Jabbing his finger into Hugo's face, he yelled, 'Don't ever talk shit to me again about no fucking anger problem!'

Into D14, Marco moved another friend, Nick, a Golden Gloves boxer, who'd won many fights in Tower 5. Slightly bigger than Paulie, his handsome, friendly face made him seem less fierce. He puzzled the inmates by obsessively shaving all of the hair from his arms and the back of his hands with a stolen razor he kept hidden in his trash bag. When he wasn't knocking people out, he was mild-mannered and an erudite conversationalist. I discovered he traded the stock market, and we began sharing finance books. Our fiancées befriended each other at Visitation.

When Nick invited me to his cell to drink the juice of stolen oranges freshly squeezed by Hugo, I figured we were close enough for me to ask about his charges. 'You seem out of place here, Nick. How'd you get busted?'

'I was set up by my fiancée's ex,' Nick said, perched on the bottom bunk.

'How?'

'He's a rich guy, a martial-arts expert. He was hassling Susan, so I pulled out a knife, and he tried to kick it out of my hand and it got stuck in his foot. Not only did he call the cops and say I assaulted him, he filed a police report saying I stole 500 thou from him. Then he filed an insurance claim to get the money.'

'How come the cops aren't busting him for that?'

'The cops are in on it with him. He's paid them off. So I've got armed robbery and kidnapping and all these charges for defending Susan.'

Before my arrest, I thought dirty cops were a figment of movie-makers' imaginations, but I heard many stories in the jail that rang true.

'Did I ever tell you about my first day at Towers?' Nick asked.

'No. What happened?'

'You're gonna love this. After suffering two sleepless nights at The Horseshoe, they finally ship me to a cell at Towers. It's a nightmare. I'm exhausted, but it's still before lockdown. Anyway, I'm trying to sleep, and I hear two black inmates next door arguing over a pair of slippers. One says, "Whose are these shoes?" The other says, "Them's my motherfuckin' shoes." Then the other one shouts, "Well, they're my motherfuckin' shoes now!" I hear "Oh no, they isn't," and "Oh yes, they is." I'm thinking, *What is this madness?* and then it gets worse. One says, "You touch my motherfuckin' shoes and I'm gonna stab your ass." The other says, "You ain't gonna fucking stab nobody – no, sirree!" "Don't make me do it," shouts the other. I hear "Don't lay one finger on my shoes!" and then I hear a scream, *"Aaggghhhhhh!"*, and one of them comes rushing out of the cell with a golf pencil stuck in his chest. I'm thinking, *What am I doing here?*

'Anyway, it quietens down. I'm lying there, tired, but still too nervous to sleep, and then they call "Lockdown!" This homeless-looking guy enters my cell and gets on the bunk below me. I'm finally trying to get some shut-eye, and I hear this weird noise. I do my best to ignore it, but on it goes. I still can't sleep. I'm really curious, so I peep down over the end of my bunk and see this guy jerking off.'

'Wow! I haven't had a celly like that yet,' I said. 'It's probably just a matter of time.'

'Fortunately, Marco knew where I was, and he got me moved to Tower 5 the next day. There was a lot of crazy violence in Tower 5, but nothing's as bad as the shock of your first few days of being in jail.'

Due to Nick's association with Marco, the guards allowed his visits with Susan to exceed the maximum time allowed. If Claudia were to arrive at Visitation with Susan, Nick said, he could have the guards extend my visits, too. Visitation time was golden, and I was honoured to be included with Marco's perks. I desperately wanted to break the news to Claudia but couldn't on the recorded phone lines or in a letter the mail officer might intercept, so I waited until her next visit. She was delighted. Showing up at the jail with Susan even put an end to the harassment from the female guard.

During the extended visits, Nick and I monitored the guards. Whenever they were distracted, we leaned forward and kissed our fiancées above the newly installed table divides. Stealing those kisses became the highlight of our week.

'I got five kisses in,' Nick boasted, as we walked back to Tower 6 after the strip searches.

'Only three,' I said.

'Marco gets legal visits,' Nick said.

'What do you mean?'

'Look, you can't tell anyone what I'm about to tell you.'

'You can trust me, Nick.'

'He had Officer Hoover put his girlfriend into the computer as a legal visitor.'

'You're kidding!'

'She came dressed in a business suit and they both got put in a private room.'

'Lucky bastard! I can only imagine what he got up to in there.'

'Officer Hoover told him not to go all out and get caught having sex, but they fiddled with each other, and she gave him head.'

I was flabbergasted. Every week I'd heard an incredible story about Marco, but this one topped them all. 'I've never seen an inmate run the guards like him.'

'They won't do it for me. Marco has more pull. Don't mention this to anybody. We don't want to get Officer Hoover fired.'

November 2002

Dear Mum and Dad,

I hope all is well over the pond. I'm sat on the arse-aching steel stool with my tiny golf pencil.

There's no reprieve from the noise in here. 'Lockdown! Go to your cells. Find your favourite partner! It's 10.30! Lockdown!' blurts out over the ancient intercoms, and everyone trudges back to their cells. Inmates slam their doors with excessive force and retire to their bunks.

Someone in cell 15 is singing 'Rudolph, the Red-Nosed Reindeer' to the whole pod. The sense of humour in the American prison system is far more acute than in the average American sit-com. There are some hilarious inmates, a lot of cynics and much black humour. Something that breaks the ice on an otherwise bleak pond. There is hope for America after all. Some of them are bloody funny.

The unfortunate newspaper article and the consensus that anyone throwing raves just wants to have a good time has certainly helped my ability to communicate with other inmates. Many of them have attended raves at one time or another, and they're eager to tell me about it. The novelty of being housed with an Englishman is also a good talking point.

The stress of not knowing what is going to happen to me is psychological torture. It's the worst part of being an unsentenced inmate. I dream every night of personal disasters. I dream of being chased, confined, killed. I dream of nothing else.

I really appreciate your kind acts, your love and support, and I am deeply sorry for the emotional trauma this has put you through. I am lucky, though, to have been brought to focus on what really matters most to me, which is by no means my party-animal friends. You have saved my life, or a good portion of it, and have flown halfway round the world to support me. You have given me inspiration when there was only despair. This situation has completely changed my outlook on life. Gone is my complacency. I now realise how precious every moment is in the outside world. To suffer this pain, to bring me closer to my family and make me enjoy my future time with them, is but a small price to pay. Maybe all of this was necessary for this purpose.

Hopefully things will be resolved soon and I will be getting on with my new life, with Claudia as my wife, happily trading stocks. That is all I ask for.

Thank you so much for everything,

Love Shaun

16

....

I wouldn't wish jail on any of my friends, but when you're in there it's always a pleasure to run into one. I was happy to see Joey Crack, who I knew from Tempe, in Tower 6's punishment pod. As a favour to me, Marco used his influence with the guards to move Joey Crack into my cell. Emaciated by drug abuse, Joey Crack arrived with a face as gaunt as an Afghan hound's. He was taller than me, high-spirited and prone to unusual behaviour. He shocked the inmates and guards by inserting the circular bottoms of black chess pieces into his ear lobes, as if he were following the fashion of voodoo tribesmen.

Joey Crack liked to alter the jail-issued postcards that showed Sheriff Joe Arpaio in a variety of publicity poses. On the bottom bunk, I looked over at Joey Crack on the concrete, surrounded by tiny body parts he'd cut from magazines with a stolen razor, sticking a pair of breasts to Sheriff Joe's jowls. His glue was soap shavings mixed with the high-fructose corn-syrup jelly that came in the Ladmo bags. His cards were in high demand. Most of them made it out of the jail – the guards usually laughed at them – but some were intercepted, deemed illegal due to the alterations, and Joey Crack received numerous verbal reprimands for promoting contraband.

'So what adventures have you had in Towers?' I asked him.

'I landed in Tower 5. I'd only been in the pod maybe a couple of weeks at the most when a bunch of tobacco and meth was keystered in and for some reason half the damn pod decided my cell was the spot to converge and do their deals. I had no direct involvement or prior knowledge of these dodgy deals; however, once it was there, I found myself right smack-dab in the middle of the whole mess. Mainly, I was concerned with the tobacco end of things, but I was willing to partake in some of the ol' naughty,' he said, referring to crystal meth.

'Oh dear.'

'So here we all are – Mexicans, whites, everyone, all together in my cell. One guy has about a gram of crystal meth dumped out on my desk and is in the process of chopping it all down into lines for a select group of us to do – and, yes, I was one of the selected. Then we hear a door opening and see a DO coming straight for the cell.'

'Oh no.'

'As to be expected, all the idiots in the cell begin to filter away in a very obvious manner, leaving just a couple of us there. The Chicano at the desk who was chopping lines thinks quick and simply sweeps the entire pile right onto the floor before Officer Flores makes it inside to see what's going on. The cop comes into the cell and right off the bat asks where the cigarettes are. I've got a whole bunch tucked into my pretty pink socks, but I'm trying to hold onto them. What it comes down to, though, is if somebody doesn't give up something then Flores is gonna shake everyone down and find a lot more than just some tobacco.'

'What did you do?' I asked, leaning closer to him.

'I'm elected to give my stash up for the good of everyone else, with the promise of being compensated for my troubles.'

'What a hero.'

'Sounds good to me, so I go for it. I give up my bounty, but it's too late. The officer decides to strip search those of us still in the cell. The remaining inmates were myself, a Mexican named Chevvy, and Kyle.'

Excited to hear the name Kyle, I asked, 'Kyle, the youngster who all the stories are going around Towers about him knocking people out and making them crap themselves?'

'Yeah, he's a kickboxer. I have loads of stories about him to tell you. Anyway, Kyle's skinny butt cheeks were packed with tobacco, a lighter, weed, speed and a spot of black-tar heroin. To say the least, we were shitting bricks. We were taken into the hallway and down to the closet where they keep all the mops and things. Then we're made to get naked.'

'Together?'

'No, one by one. Kyle was last. Somehow, by the time he is up to flaunt his stuff, the cop runs out of steam and doesn't really look too hard at his asshole.'

'He's lucky.'

'That sure was close, but we're not out of the woods just yet. The cop decides that Kyle is the guilty party and I was his fall guy – which was dead on. The cop cuffs us both, lets Chevvy go and takes us to the hole pending investigation. Had he only known the fun we would have in there! As soon as the door slams behind us we are unloading Kyles's ass and making plans to party.'

'I don't know how you can party in here. It's too depressing. Being around all these needle junkies has put me off drugs.' I'd never seen my party friends from a sober perspective, as I was usually higher than most of them. Being forced to live with so many out-of-control addicts was a constant reminder of what drugs can reduce people to – cementing my earlier decision to stay sober.

'Not me. We got all spun out on speed in the hole and played cards for the entire day while smoking cigarettes like they're legal. No worries. No regrets. It's just Kyle and me doing what we do best. Well, it's only a matter of time before something bad comes our way. It's maybe seven or eight at night, and the cop on duty makes his rounds. He can't help but notice the stench of smoke wafting from our cell. He opens the door and makes us vacate the cell so that he can conduct a search.'

'Oh no.'

'He finds nothing, and we all but laugh in his face. About an hour or two goes by, and we're not taking any precautions – just blazing till our lungs ached. The cop is not letting us get away with our blatant disregard for the rules. He pops our door and searches the cell again. This time he finds a big knot of tobacco on my bed, barely hidden under my sheet. He then writes us yet another ticket with a suggestion on it for a further 30 days in the hole. Does this little incident deter either of us one little bit?'

'Probably not.'

'No, no and no! We refuse to obey, and nobody can stop us. Before Kyle unpacked his ass, we covered every place on the door where smoke might escape. We did it with toilet paper and toothpaste.'

'Very crafty.' Every time I heard a story like this, I wondered why Sheriff Joe Arpaio didn't offer ways for the inmates to channel such inventive qualities into constructive activity. Then maybe some of them would have stood a better chance in society.

'It worked, but only for a day or two. On day two, we are practically out of our minds, and we decide a little heroin and Klonopin cocktail is in order to level us out. For me, it does the trick, but for Kyle, it merely sends him over the edge. Every time the cop walks by, I'm awakened by Kyle beating his head against the door and screaming that he's going to hurt himself. They take him to go see the psych, but he returns shortly after and seems to be somewhat better. The next day, they let both of us out, but before departing the both of us agree that I'll take this write-up as well, seeing as how the tobacco was found on my bed. From there I got moved to T2, where I knew people like Wild Man, so I was happy.'

'Wow! What a grand entrance you made to Towers,' I said, hoping that he wouldn't get too crazy on drugs in my cell.

'Yeah, and here's what happened next. A few days later, a hearing officer comes to see me about the write-up. I tell her that the contraband was all mine, but she twists my words and tries making it seem as if I put the blame on Kyle. Then there's all kinds of rumours that he wants me smashed for blaming the smokes on him. *Whatever!*' Joey Crack paused. 'Nothing happens, but a couple of weeks later the cop that found the tobacco in the hole gets a hard-on to fuck with me and search my cell. When he does, he finds an extension on my pencil made from postcards and tape. Here comes another write-up and another trip to the hole.'

'How lame.'

'Yeah, but this jerk puts the pencil in an evidence bag and tells me it's a shank. Pure BS, but it still got me 15 days in the hole. That's how I made it to Tower 6 and ended up here with you.'

After the evening chow, Joey Crack was pacing, warming up to describe one of Kyle's fights, when Little Italy filed into the cell. The Italians looked almost dapper in the brand-new bee stripes they'd bribed from the laundry officer.

'Wassup, fellas!' Marco said.

'Wassup, dawgs!' I said, offering my fist from the bottom bunk.

'Wassup, Joey Crack and England!' Paulie said, grinning and winking at me.

'Wassup, dawgs!' Joey Crack said.

There was much bumping of fists, and then we urged Joey Crack to tell the story.

'Yeah, Crack, how many guys has Kyle made shit themselves?' Paulie asked.

'I wasn't present when Kyle knocked the shit out of those guys. I missed those gems,' Joey Crack said. 'I was, however, front and centre for many good smashings he inflicted. My personal favourite is the one I call "The Naked Cage Match", which I must admit, I somewhat helped to instigate.'

'How d'ya manage that?' Paulie asked.

Marco took the stool. The rest leaned against the wall, settling in to hear the tale.

'It was gonna happen regardless, but I had to put my own two cents in to make things more entertaining. I don't remember what the original beef was about, but then again what does it really matter – Kyle just loves to scrap!'

'Hold on a minute,' I said. 'What's this Kyle look like?'

'That's the thing,' Joey Crack said. 'He's just a skinny youngster. He doesn't look like much of anything, so these big dudes pick on him, and he always smashes the shit out them. So anyway, there's this guy who's having some kind of problem with Kyle. Kyle takes this guy into a cell and touches him up. Seconds later they both emerge and this guy has some bumps and bruises, so we make him get into the shower to clean himself up. When he gets out, wrapped in only a little pink towel, he proceeds to tell us that he's OK and that Kyle hits like a girl!'

'Oh no!' I said.

'We know exactly where this is going,' Marco said, grinning.

'Saying that was hilarious enough considering he's standing before us with his face swelling black and blue. But he also tells us that if he had been ready for it, Kyle wouldn't have stood a chance. We laughed our asses off, and then we informed Kyle that he had been incompetent in not properly smashing his opponent. The guy's walking around protected only by his little pink towel, talking all kinds of shit about Kyle. We warn the guy that he might want to get dressed ready for the next round, but of course he fails to listen. Kyle comes rolling in full of piss and vinegar ready to do battle and make up for not doing things right the first time around. Then suddenly – *bang!* Kyle knocks the fool for a loop and we all spill out of the cell in order to make room for this little rumble. As expected, the towel falls to the floor, and now we've got ourselves a naked cage match!' Joey Crack's voice intensified. 'Kyle throws the buck-naked guy into a headlock and proceeds to beat his face into disfigurement. You've never seen anything so funny as this little naked man grunting like a baboon in distress trying to escape from Kyle's fists of fury. Lucky for the little bastard, Kyle didn't go too far. He simply needed to show him that not only could he beat him down once but he could do it twice, and with the challenger being buck-naked, he put icing on the cake by keeping a straight face the entire time.'

'That's a hell of a story,' Paulie said.

'There were plenty more fights, but one was pretty much the same as any other after a while. One thing that never changed, though: Kyle was always the one who came out on top.'

Marco's crew listened to Joey Crack tell stories about the Wild Ones. Intrigued by these stories, Paulie added that he'd heard about Wild Man and asked us to arrange a meeting with him. I sent a kite (a note smuggled through the jail by inmates) to Wild Man, requesting his presence at the next Catholic Mass to meet Little Italy.

17

....

The high demand for Catholic Mass was not from prisoners seeking absolution from their sins but from those eager to exchange gossip and drugs with their friends from other towers. Problem was, only ten men were allowed to attend from each forty-five-man pod. And when the guards announced 'Catholic Mass! First ten at the sliding door only!', dozens charged for the door, leading to much squabbling, pushing and occasional bloodshed. Fortunately, when it came to the battle for the ten spaces, my friendship with Marco gave me an advantage. Marco had so much inside information he often knew the actions of the guards in advance. So ten minutes before the guards were due to announce Catholic Mass, Marco told Joey Crack and me to line up at the sliding door with all of Little Italy. With the Italians eager to meet Wild Man, we set off.

In a black cassock and white alb, tall bespectacled Father O'Donnell greeted us at the door of the windowless religious-services room. He wasn't his usual chirpy self. We rushed past him, secured the back row of plastic chairs and waited for the other towers to join us. When Tower 2 arrived, Wild Man gave me a bear hug and sat in-between Joey Crack and me. The seats filled quickly, and the latecomers had to stand.

'This is Wild Man,' I said to the Italians.

'Ah! So this is Wild Man! We've heard so much about you,' Paulie said in his gruffest voice. He leaned across me to shake Wild Man's hand, crushing my stomach and tilting my seat back.

'In the name of the Father, the Son, and the Holy Spirit . . .' Most of the inmates trading gossip hushed as Father O'Donnell started the introductory rites. As the Mass progressed, he seemed more serious than usual, and before the distribution of Communion he explained why. His mother was on her deathbed in hospital, and he asked us all to pray for the restoration of her health. Her illness had arisen unexpectedly, and Father O'Donnell wept as he described her condition. Tears streamed from Hugo. His sobbing attracted so much attention that he buried his face in his hands and bowed his head. At either side of Hugo, Marco and Nick turned teary-eyed. Marco made the sign of the cross and closed his eyes. Paulie wept openly, rubbed his eyes, dried them off, calmed down, looked at Hugo and wept again. Marco patted Hugo on the back. The more Father O'Donnell sobbed, the more the audience reacted. Some wept. Some offered sympathy. I felt moved but not enough to cry. The crying peaked when Father O'Donnell started sputtering. He paused to regain his composure then travelled the rows feeding the men Communion, which they devoured in the hurried manner of starving people. When Father O'Donnell reached the back row, Hugo swore we would all pray for his mother and that she would recover. Revisiting the subject of Father O'Donnell's mother provoked another round of tears from Little Italy. We received Communion, and Father O'Donnell headed back to the front.

'What's everyone crying for?' Wild Man said. 'Look how old he is. His mum's got to have one foot in the grave by now. She's probably 100 years old.' The congregation tsk-tsking only encouraged Wild Man. He spat an intact Communion wafer into his hand, put it over his left eye as if it were a pirate's patch and yelled, 'Look at me! Ha-ha-ha-ha-ha!'

Prisoners stopped praying and craned their necks to watch Wild Man.

'You're all fucking sinners! You don't fool me! You're all going straight to hell!' Wild Man's maniacal laughter drew more attention.

Inmates elbowed each other until the majority had turned around to look at Wild Man. Reactions from Little Italy ranged from an appalled Hugo to an amused Paulie.

Wild Man removed the Communion wafer from his eye and launched it at Father O'Donnell, who was approaching the front of the room with his back facing us. The onlookers steered their heads, following the trajectory of the Body of Christ. It ascended steadily. When it skimmed the ceiling, a few men whoa'd. The skim should have knocked it off course, but it continued on, descending at a steady rate, arcing relentlessly towards the priest as if under the guidance of an invisible evil hand. Just as Father O'Donnell placed down the ciborium, a few arms from the front row shot up but failed to stop the wafer from hitting the priest square in the back like a perfectly aimed Frisbee. The congregation gasped. Wild Man said, 'Bull's eye!' The worshippers shook their heads or snickered, but no one spoke up against Wild Man. Nick and Marco were speechless. In a show of disapproval, Hugo took his seat to the front row.

'He's a fucking lunatic,' Paulie said, grinning. Then he whispered in my ear, 'He's worse in real life than he is in Joey Crack's stories.'

Fortunately, Father O'Donnell didn't notice the Communion wafer roll across the floor and settle under the table he'd set up with holy water and Christian pamphlets. When Mass ended, Hugo discreetly pocketed it.

Wild Man continued his antics in the corridor. 'Fucking church, eh? That priest can kiss my arse!' He dropped his pink boxers and mooned the prisoners, failing to notice the arrival of a female guard.

'You're on report! Give me your ID!' she yelled, her face pinched. She called backup, who handcuffed Wild Man and led him away.

The following week, Wild Man was still in the hole, unable to join the rowdy cheering in Catholic Mass when a joyous Father O'Donnell announced his mother was out of hospital and on the mend.

18

....

By the end of 2002, Marco and his Praetorian guards seemed to have more control over Tower 6 than the jail administration. Every day, the guards chose Little Italy to serve chow and turned a blind eye when they stole the leftover Ladmo bags and trays and divvied the food out to the heads of all of the races. They were applying Troll's law – *he who controls the food controls the prisoners* – on a mass scale. Business was booming for the 'two-for-one store' Marco ran out of D15, which enabled inmates to buy commissary provided they repaid double on 'store day' – the day of the week our commissary orders were delivered. Whenever the goon squad was due to raid our pod, Marco knew in advance. During such searches, the guards confiscated our extra clothing, towels and sheets, but Marco simply had the next shift walk Little Italy to the property room. They would return with mountains of fresh laundry, grinning triumphantly.

Marco dealt with disgruntled inmates sympathetically. He presided over the kangaroo court of white-inmate conflicts, and when he banished inmates from our pod or decreed they must settle things by fighting, everyone later commented on how fairly he'd adjudicated. His power was such he could have the guards move any inmate in or out of our pod, and he was inundated with requests from inmates wanting to move. They mostly wanted to move into our pod, which was humming with the vibrancy of Little Italy.

Settling into a disciplined study and exercise regimen was helping the time go by for me. Lying on my bunk at angles that minimised the discomfort of my bedsores, I read for hours. At first, the abundance of time to read rekindled my teenage obsession with stock-market books. But then a prisoner urged me to read two novels: George Orwell's *1984* and Aldous Huxley's *Brave New World*. Prior to my arrest, I had considered reading fiction a frivolous pastime. The last novel I'd read was *To Kill a Mockingbird*, required reading in high school. But in the dystopian jail environment, I related to Orwell's Big Brother and Room 101. Reading Huxley, I saw parallels in my life with the characters taking grams of the hallucinogenic drug soma and orgying. These books dramatised two things I hadn't stopped dwelling on since my arrest: the excesses of my lifestyle and the justice system.

I'd been doing yoga exercises almost daily since I read *Yoga Made Easy* sent by my sister, Karen. At first I saw the book as an attempt at effemination and hid it under my mattress to avoid being mocked. But Karen insisted I give the basic postures a try, and I felt so relaxed after stretching my cables I kept coming back for more. I was soon proficient in postures such as the cobra, forward bend, cat, dog, side bend and seated spinal twist, and I yearned to master the harder ones.

As well as working out with Marco, I established a second workout partner, Burklev, a Canadian of Yugoslavian descent who'd been arrested on his bicycle after policemen in a parked vehicle noticed him turn a corner without signalling. The police had insisted on conducting a search and found a water bottle with a small quantity of methamphetamine dissolved in it and a pool-cleaning chemical in his backpack. Classifying his bicycle as a two-wheeled vehicle, they'd charged him with operating a mobile meth lab. He claimed to have been a pro bodybuilder, but meth had taken its toll on his physique. He was six foot five, and with a smoothly shaved head and face he resembled a giant matchstick. For weights, Burklev and I used the mop bucket like I'd done with Lev. By attaching a towel to the mop handle, we performed rowing, curling and shoulder exercises. Other than Mordhorst, most of the guards didn't mind us working out with the mop bucket in the corner of the day room. Every now and then one yelled through the speakers 'No working out with the cleaning supplies!', which usually meant his superior officer had entered the tower.

The glut of drugs and cigarettes in Tower 6 was thanks in part to the keystering skills of the car thief Magoo, a tall, bespectacled hippy with a spattering of crystal-meth sores on his face. He prided himself on his ability to stuff long packages into his anal cavity. Magoo set himself up as a mule for hire. His fee: a percentage of what he smuggled in. At Visitation, I watched Magoo observing the guards through his thick-lensed glasses. When a querying visitor distracted Officer Green, Magoo received some cellophane-wrapped packages under the table, which disappeared into his trousers. He didn't even flinch as he deposited them deep enough in his behind so as not to peek out during the strip search. He received numerous visits each week from strangers bearing such packages and never got caught or sent to a dry cell to defecate, even though after each visit he walked in a bandy-legged, leaning-back way as if he'd been speared in the behind.

The sense of community spirit in our pod rose even further when we adopted a needy youngster named Slopester as our son. Eighteen-year-old Slopester had been living on the streets of Sunnyslope, a crack and crystal-meth hub of Phoenix, with his younger sister. With his mouth closed, he resembled Christopher Walken. But he smiled constantly, displaying a graveyard of brown teeth. Caught shoplifting clothes from Dillard's in Paradise Valley Mall, he'd pulled a butterfly knife on an employee. Arrested in the parking lot, he was charged with assault with a dangerous weapon. In Durango, a minimum-security jail, the gangs had preyed upon him. After receiving numerous tickets for fighting, he was reclassified to Towers jail.

Marco put him to work offering a hand-laundry service. The jail replaced our laundry once a week, but in the meantime our underwear and towels collected filth and sweat. For one item of candy, Slopester hand-washed two items of clothing. 'Bleach is free,' he tittered as he closed his sales. Prior to visits from Claudia, I took advantage of his laundry service. I also paid him to barter for state cheese, but he brought me so much it repeated on me for hours, and I had to tell him to stop. Needed and cared for, Slopester blossomed. We rejoiced to see him so happy. Other youngsters took notice of his growing importance, and he became the king of the waifs.

The atmosphere grew increasingly circuslike, and newcomers added to the furore. Kyle came from lockdown. His last fight had yet again resulted in his opponent defecating. Upon regaining consciousness, his opponent had been ordered by the head of the whites to clean the faeces off the floor before he rolled up. Kyle and a skinny African American did daily back-flip shows off the chow tables. The competition between them delighted us.

Christmas was the most depressing time of the year for inmates. The majority longed to be celebrating with their loved ones. But the antics of our Italian Mafia rulers made Christmas the best it could be under the circumstances. On Christmas Eve, we paraded around singing 'Felice Navidad' and our favourite Jumping Bill songs. A few days later, seeking adventure outside the pod, Marco field-tripped most of the whites to Muslim services. We outnumbered the Muslim congregation.

Anticipating a race riot, the frightened imam radioed the guards. But Marco settled the imam down, sent the guards packing and encouraged the imam to teach us the Arabic alphabet. At the end of the service, we knelt with the Muslims in prayer to Allah, and the imam invited us back.

With exuberance running so rampant, Joey Crack had to take his shenanigans to another level. He wanted a Prince Albert piercing, so he sharpened the end of a paperclip, spent a few seconds studying his penis and then stuck the paperclip into his frenulum and out of the urethra. The blood trickling into the toilet didn't deter him from shoving a tiny silver bar through the hole he'd made. I never thought I'd see the day when I'd stop what I was doing to stare at a man's penis, but it's hard to concentrate on writing when such things are going on around you. Sitting on the stool, I was amazed he had the nerve/insanity to gore such a precious organ.

Some inmates were astonished, others sickened as he walked onto the balcony waving blood-stained hands, blood dripping from his penis, with an intoxicated look in his eyes. 'Look, fellas, I've put a bar in my cock, and 'cause the bar's straight it feels like it's ripping me apart. So what we've gotta do, fellas, is, I'm gonna put my cock between the cell door and the wall, and then I want someone to put their fingers in the same spot, 'cause we need to close the door on my cock, and hopefully the door will bend the jewellery, but I don't want to completely close the door and crush my cock, so if one of you guys has your fingers in the same spot then we can judge how far we can close the door without anyone's fingers or cock getting hurt. Got it? Who'll put their fingers in the door, and who'll slowly shut it?'

Slopester volunteered to put his fingers between the door and the wall. Joey Crack inserted his penis and positioned the silver bar, so that the force from the closing door would bend it. Magoo slowly closed the door. The jewellery slipped twice and the audience in the day room gasped over the fate of Joey Crack's penis, which looked as though it were being crushed between the door and the wall. The jewellery held steady during the third attempt, and the bar bent.

'That's fucking great! My cock doesn't feel like it's being ripped apart any more, but it's gonna hurt like hell when I take a piss! Thanks, fellas!'

December 2002

Dear D and B,

Thanx for the Xmas card. Very groovy. I hope that everyone has a Merry Xmas and a Happy New Year. It was good to talk to you both last Wednesday.

So the madness in the courts continues. It amazes me how things are developing. It is obvious to me that I was arrested without a case prepared. I was arrested in the hope that they would find evidence and hence be able to form a case. They were so bloody confident. Detective Reid's words were that I was a big name from the rave scene and that he was sure the raid would vindicate the charges. He didn't have to say that to me.

Further confirmation is that the prosecutor is now trying to stop Alan from playing the wiretaps. Isn't this the evidence against me? Isn't this a good thing for the prosecution to hear the evidence against me? In normal circumstances one would think so. This action confirms that they created a case by selecting a misleading choice of wiretaps and are now worried about being exposed.

Apart from court, everything plods along as usual. I've now been in Towers the longest in my pod out of the whites.

I talked to Claudia about St Bede's for our wedding, and she sounded very excited with that idea. She said she has seen a picture of St Bede's already. I'm so glad Karen and Mum really liked Claudia when they met her. I feel like I'm doing the right thing this time.

The pod is freakier than ever in its composition of inmates right now. There's 'Big Gay', a 300+ pounds roly-poly homo. There's John the Baptist, a skinny 6 ft 4 in. hippy/Jesus-looking type who stores a diamond in his arse. Three Sopranos live in cell 15, and there's a guy here who runs the Aryan Church. Yes, it makes for an interesting Xmas.

Sometimes I think I've gone completely mad and that I'm actually in a mental hospital but don't really know it. The vibe here is mighty amusing. John the Baptist runs around screaming 'Repent!' and another inmate makes a realistic voice of a baby crying all day long. It fooled the DOs. The effect of walking into my pod is similar to walking into the pub from *Boys from the Blackstuff* when Shake Hands and the whistling guy are in full effect. Good character-building stuff.

Love you loads,

Shaun x

19

....

Under Little Italy's rule, many prisoners were acting as if jail wasn't such a bad place to be after all. I hoped the good times would last but feared the inevitable backlash. In the New Year, the mood shifted.

Shortly before lockdown, the Mexicans were tossing a grapefruit. A poor lob resulted in a missed catch, and the grapefruit flew over the head of its intended recipient and hit Magoo in the leg. In accordance with the jail code of not backing down from any act of aggression, Magoo retaliated by lobbing the grapefruit at the Mexicans. Four of them stretched but failed to catch it. It travelled over them and hit their leader, Carlo, in the head as he played spades. When the shock wore off Carlo's face, he gave Magoo a stare of death. The Mexicans advanced towards Magoo.

Seeing what had happened, Marco dashed between the Mexicans and Magoo. 'Look, he never meant to hit you with the grapefruit like that. And I apologise for it being a wood that threw it.' Turning to face Magoo, he yelled, 'You need to apologise!'

'Nobody is telling me what to fucking do!' Magoo said, and stomped up the stairs to his cell.

The Mexicans looked at Marco, and Marco said, 'Please don't get involved. This is white-boy business now.'

The next morning, Burklev and I were under the stairs doing pull-ups when I noticed Marco's crew gathering at either side of Magoo's door. Officer Mordhorst was just finishing walking our pod, and as soon as he exited the sliding door Paulie entered Magoo's cell and the familiar thumping noises commenced. A few minutes later, Paulie emerged, panting like an over-walked pit bull. Everyone in the day room looked up at Magoo's door. Magoo emerged, dishevelled, battered, minus his glasses, swaying like a drunkard. 'What the fuck was that all about?' he yelled. He turned but not in time to see a right hook hit his chin. The fist belonged to Wedo, a muscular Mexican-American covered in Aztec tattoos who had taken a dislike to Magoo prior to the grapefruit incident. Wedo then slammed Magoo's head against the iron railing running along the top tier with such a clunk that many of us gasped. Wedo kneed Magoo in the groin, and Magoo collapsed on the balcony.

'You need to roll your shit up!' Paulie yelled at Magoo.

Magoo grabbed the iron railing, pulled himself up, staggered into his cell, gathered his property and re-emerged with his face starting to swell. From the stairs, he yelled for the guards in the control tower to open the sliding door. The guards let him out but didn't lock us down, which was the normal procedure when someone had been beaten up, and I couldn't help but wonder whether the officers had known what was going on.

Magoo was still in the corridor waiting to be rehoused when Slopester strutted up to Wedo and said, 'That was white-boy business. You Chicanos shouldn't be getting in the mix. That was for us woods to handle.'

'So fucking what? Are you gonna fucking do something about it?' Wedo snarled.

Inmates usually went to the cell under the stairs to fight, but Wedo and Slopester traded blows in the day room. Marco's Praetorian guards charged over and stopped the fight. Minutes later, Wedo and Slopester were sharing a cigarette in a cell together.

A few days later, Paulie returned from Visitation boasting he had just smashed a chomo. Later the same day, he called a female guard who'd reprimanded him a 'fucking cunt'. For disrespecting staff, he was transferred to the Madison Street jail to go on the loaf programme – two meals a day of leftover food cooked into burnt bread that smelt like shoe polish.

A brunette beauty started working at Tower 6, stirring up much excitement. When she did security walks, the prisoners stopped what they were doing and stared at her as if under mass hypnosis.

'You're not gonna fucking believe this,' Joey Crack said.

'What? Marco was outside smoking with the guards again while we were all locked down and asleep?' I said.

'No, no, much better than that. Kyle's having an affair with the new female guard.'

'No way! I don't believe it.'

'It's true. It's fucking true, but don't tell anyone.'

'She's gorgeous, too. The lucky bastard. Nah, I still don't believe it.'

'Look, if you don't believe me, then how about I go get him, and he can tell you himself?'

'All right.'

Joey Crack returned with Kyle, who was beaming.

'Good job, Kyle. Is it true?'

'Yup.'

'How did you manage this? Come on, tell me everything.'

'Don't tell anyone else, OK?'

'OK.'

'I'd never seen Officer Magnuson before until she woke me up one morning at two to go to court. I was dreaming, and as I woke, I looked up and saw her beautiful face – as if she was an angel. I couldn't stop thinking about her ever since that moment. On the way to court, I wrote down a love poem. I wanted to give it to her the next night. I discussed it with my celly first, and he told me that no harm would come and that I should go for it. The next night when she was doing a walk, I passed her the love poem, and guess what? She wrote one back to me.'

'She did what?'

'She wrote back, and that's when I knew she liked me. I'll show it you if you want.'

Kyle reached in his shirt pocket and pulled out a bundle of letters.

'I took a chance and it worked,' he said, as if he could hardly believe his luck.

'So what have you guys been getting up to?'

'Not full sex, but we've been hugging and kissing, and she's now started sending me dirty letters.'

'No way!'

'Yup! Read these.' Kyle handed me some letters written in ink on paper clearly not provided by the jail.

'She's recently divorced and wants a serious relationship. Problem is, I'm about to get a 12-year sentence, so I guess there's not much hope. She even called my mom and told her that she's in love with me.'

'Bloody hell!' I said.

The first letter started out stating her family situation but with that out of the way, she got down to describing how good she was at oral sex.

'Good grief! Are you sure you didn't pay someone to write this stuff?' I asked, unable to peel my eyes from the sexual fantasy unfolding.

'Tonight she's working. Stay awake and watch the fishbowl. She'll be winking at me and blowing kisses.'

'It's all true,' Joey Crack said.

'While my cellies are sleeping,' Kyle said, 'I get naked and stand on the toilet and dance for her.'

Glad he'd found some happiness, I worried about him telling too many people. 'You're crazy! You best keep this on the DL, or else some jealous inmate will try to sabotage it. Strange things happen in here, but this is great. You're a lucky man indeed.'

During the night, I watched the fishbowl. I spied Officer Magnuson winking, smiling and blowing kisses in the direction of Kyle's cell. Imagining him standing on the toilet dancing naked, I chuckled.

Also that night, Officer Magnuson tipped Kyle off that the goon squad was coming to shake us down. Kyle alerted the pod, and everybody keystered their contraband before the goon squad arrived.

A few weeks into the affair, Officer Magnuson was reassigned to another tower, probably a result of Kyle telling too many people.

'Now Magoo's gone, I've been asked to take some visits,' Joey Crack said.

I didn't like the sound of this. 'You really want to risk getting busted bringing drugs in, getting another five years added to your sentence?'

'It's just tobacco.'

'That's what they tell you! Think this through, man. It's not worth the risk.'

'I already gave them my word.'

'Who?'

'I've been asked not to tell you about it. I've said too much already.'

'I don't know, Joey Crack. I'd pull out if I were you.'

Joey Crack went to Visitation and never returned. Rumours of his arrest circulated faster than smokes. Listening to certain men in the day room bemoan the fate of their drugs while expressing zero concern for Joey Crack, I guessed who'd hired him. Angry with those men, I paced the cell expecting the goon squad to raid my home at any moment because Joey Crack was busted. But a few hours later, Joey Crack showed up grinning, lifting my bad mood.

'Everyone's saying you got busted,' I said.

'Listen to this. I go to the visit and the guards are suspicious from the get-go 'cause I don't know who my visitor is, and she usually visits someone else. Anyway, I find her. She's some sketched-out twitchy tweaker. She tells me the package can't be delivered 'cause it's too big, and she doesn't have it with her.'

'Good.'

'I was relieved, 'cause after speaking to you, I wasn't wanting it to happen. It seemed out of sorts, and my gut feeling was not to do it. So we're at the table for all of three minutes when a guard comes over and says, "I think there's something going on that shouldn't be." They know her face 'cause she usually visits some guy who has non-contact visits. They tell her I'm gonna be searched, and if anything is found on me she'll be charged with promoting prison contraband and our personal favourite: conspiracy. I'm laughing 'cause we have nothing on us. I'm stripped naked and nothing is found.'

'Good.'

'Then a female is brought to search my visitor. I'll never forget the look on her face! She was truly scared beyond all control. Her jaw was twitching, her lips doing something I can't put into words, and her hands were everywhere.'

'Uh oh.'

'I realised then that she might have told me a fib. They search her. I'm told to get against the wall, interlace my fingers on top of my head and slowly move to my knees. Later, I found out she got busted with meth, tobacco and weed.'

'Your new friends in here were more concerned about the package getting seized than your welfare.'

'I know. The main guy's more concerned about losing his dope than his own girlfriend getting busted and going to jail. It would have been ugly if she'd passed the package. Never again. No way.'

Officer Mendoza appeared at the cell door. 'Roll ye . . . ye . . . yer shit up! You're g . . . g . . . going back to the hole.'

'For what?' Joey Crack asked.

'Conspiracy and susp . . . sp . . . icion o . . . o . . . on of attempting to smuggle drugs int . . . int . . . into the jail system.'

20

....

Every time you receive new cellmates, you have to adjust your routine to accommodate theirs. I preferred cellmates who spent a lot of time in the day room so I could concentrate on reading and writing in the cell. I received two such cellmates after Joey Crack was sent to the hole and Busta Beatz moved out.

Little Honduras had short black hair, friendly brown eyes and spoke little English. He was accused of being a coyote: paid to escort illegal aliens into Arizona from Mexico, part of a Mexican Mafia organisation that used cell phones to communicate with lookouts stationed on mountaintops in order to avoid Border Patrol agents. He was arrested for allegedly holding at gunpoint a freshly smuggled Mexican who'd refused to pay the coyotes their fee. Charged with armed robbery, kidnapping and extortion, Honduras was facing 15 years yet seemed calm about his case. '*Tengo suerte!*' – I am lucky! – he often remarked. His Mafia boss hired him an attorney, who advised him not to sign a plea bargain or to cooperate. He spent most of the day out of the cell with the Mexicans. To improve my Spanish, I often joined them in the mornings watching soap operas called telenovelas. The racists asked me questions like, 'Why're you celling with a wetback?' I ignored them. Some of them griped about me watching the TV with the Mexicans, which I found odd because the most-watched TV show by all of the races was *Caliente* – a dance-music show on every Saturday morning, so esteemed that a group of prisoners would fiddle with the wonky TV set five minutes before the show began to tune it in as best they could. Even the bigots couldn't resist the lure of señoritas in skimpy bikinis shaking their hips to house music.

My second cellmate, Stalker, was in his mid-30s. He was slightly bigger than Honduras but made of much frailer stuff. After the breakdown of his 12-year marriage, he'd gone on a crystal-meth and alcohol binge. He started following his wife around, leaving messages threatening her life. She played them to the police, who charged him with stalking. Unlike Honduras, Stalker never stopped fretting about his case. Sometimes, he broke down and sobbed. Over and over I reassured him that a prison sentence wasn't the end of his life. Even Honduras pitched in with, '*No problema. Poco tiempo.*' No problem. You won't get much time.

Stalker delighted in plaguing us with his flatulence. He claimed he intentionally withheld his farts all day so he could unleash them on us after lockdown at night. He usually signalled their arrival with fits of giggling. He'd let one round off and there'd be silence until the stink was almost gone and then he'd let loose again. Time-released farts. They were especially bad after he'd eaten red death. The best Honduras and I could do to protect ourselves was to hide our heads under our sheets. But the potency of his farts was such that defensive manoeuvres with sheets only minimised our suffering. And with his average run of farts lasting close to an hour, we had to surface at some point. It was through this torment I learned some less polite Spanish phrases:

'*Pedoro.*' (Fart man.)

'*Culo mugroso.*' (Filthy ass.)

'*Culo sucio.*' (Dirty ass.)

Stalker's rapid-cycling bipolar disorder was such that one minute he'd be spitting out farts and giggling himself purple, and the next he'd be telling us through trembling lips how it was best he slash his wrists so he didn't have to go to the big house. I read his paperwork. Sexually abused as a child, he'd used alcohol and drugs to self-medicate multiple mental disorders. I encouraged him to sign up for the few classes available and tried to coach him into thinking positively. 'I know that everything's gonna be all right. I'm lucky to have you two buddies as cellmates,' Stalker would say, raising my hopes for him, only to disintegrate into suicidal madness ten minutes later.

January 2003

My Darling,

I'm riding the rack because my bum is so sore, sorry about the writing. Today I woke up with massive swollen tonsils and screamed, 'Get me out of this bloody place!' The day started with 'Chow's in the house!' Tuesday is peanut butter. I was hungry because last night I gave my whole macaroni tray away for a pack of chocolate chip cookies. After grabbing my Ladmo bag, I put it on my bunk and jumped in the shower (which is finally fixed). I was first in the shower and then went back to the cell to eat the chow.

My cellies had already eaten theirs and were back asleep. No sooner had I finished chow and laid down to read than they shouted 'CAB class! Roster only!' Returning from Confronting Addictive Behaviour, they stripped us of our boxers and we pleaded for rec but to no avail. I then hopped on my rack and did a Spanish crossword and conjugated some Spanish verbs. I ate an orange and some peanut butter. So I was studying, and they locked us down for the plumber. He worked and we had a headcount. When they took us off lockdown, there was an immediate scramble for the phones, so I'm sorry I wasn't able to call you. Shift change came, and we commenced working out. We have to wait for shift change because the morning guards will not let us work out with our tops off. After working out came 'Chow's in the house! Diets first!' Burnt veggie burgers. I soaked them in the sink, and they were so burnt I had to swill water in my mouth as I ate them. I hope my burnt veggie burger breath has gone for your visit tomorrow.

See you soon,

Shaun XXX

P.S. Last night I discussed Stalker's revolting farts (*los pedos*) with Honduras. We cracked up and couldn't stop laughing.

21

··········

'Everyone, roll up! All medium-security inmates in Tower 6 are moving to Towers 2 and 5!' Officer Mordhorst announced.

'Moving all of us! I don't believe it!' I said, scrambling off the bottom bunk.

'They're gonna split us all up, and we're gonna have fucked-up cellies,' Stalker said. 'I really like you guys.'

'Here's as good as it gets,' I said, and joined the worried prisoners gathering on the balcony.

The guards assigned my downstairs neighbours to various pods and cells in Towers 2 and 5. Everyone seemed to be upset with the move except for Little Italy – meaning they were up to something. I feared being rehoused and having to adjust to new cellmates.

Then the announcement came: 'Everyone on the top tier, grab your shit, you're moving to the top tier in Tower 2, A pod.'

The tension on the faces of the men on the balcony melted into many incredulous smiles. Marco winked at me, and I knew he'd arranged for the top tier to be moved as one, so Little Italy would remain intact.

The upper tier in 2A was empty due to a race riot ignited by the Aryans. As we moved in, the Aryans from the lower tier announced a mandatory white-boy meeting. As we were all new arrivals, we fell under the rule of their existing head of the whites: Iron Eagle. Dreading the new rules the Aryans would enforce, I joined the white-boy meeting in a crowded cell downstairs. Marco was present, meekly sizing up the Aryans, no doubt running the calculations for his next power play.

'Any woods kicking it with the other races are gonna get smashed,' said Iron Eagle. He was a muscle-bound 30-something with a shaved head and an angry look on his square face. He had a big swastika on his chest surrounded by a pattern of white-supremacy tattoos. 'That means no playing cards with them, no going in cells smoking with them, no selling commissary to them. If you've got money on your books, you need to be breaking bread with your own race, helping the indigent white boys out. Also, we heard some fucked-up rumour about a bunch of woods in Tower 6 going to Muslim services. If you woods know who the race traitors are, we wanna know about it.'

The eyes of Iron Eagle and his torpedoes roamed over us. I felt my face turn red. No one volunteered that all of us white new arrivals to Tower 2 had gone to Muslim services with Marco that day.

The next day, Iron Eagle cornered me in my cell. 'Hey, dawg, how about kicking in some store for the indigent woods?'

'Sure, dawg,' I said, resting my golf pencil on the tiny table. 'What do you want me to order?' I had no problem helping out penniless inmates. I remembered how strangers had offered me stamps, writing supplies and hygiene products when I'd arrived at Tower 6.

'Some toothpaste, so they don't have to use that state shit.'

'I'll put it on my commissary list.'

'What about hooking me up with something to eat, wood?' He had a violently hungry look in his eyes, common in the jail.

If I fed him, he'd take it as a sign of weakness and be back for more every day. If I didn't, he might take it as a personal affront. 'I'm low on store, dawg. How about I order you a rack of cookies for store day?' I'd agreed to his demands but on my terms. He'd have to wait a week for the cookies to come from commissary, and, with the friction between the Aryans and Little Italy, a lot could happen in a week.

'Good lookin' out, dawg.'

I smiled as if happy to oblige.

As the week progressed, the hostility of the Aryans towards Little Italy increased. The Aryans had slightly greater numbers, so Marco went on a recruitment drive. He received a kite from the head of his Praetorian guard, Paulie, who'd finished the loaf programme at the Madison Street jail and wanted to be moved from Tower 5. Marco had him moved in the next day. Paulie wept in Marco's arms and then went cell to cell on the upper tier bear-hugging everyone. Crushing me with his body, he said Marco needed to speak to me. Eager to find out what Marco wanted, I followed Paulie to Marco's cell.

'How many people have been arrested in your case?' Marco asked.

'I stopped counting. They arrested them in groups. The last group was 30-something, and they're still arresting people.'

'You've got co-defendants all over Towers?'

'Yes.'

'And you're their ringleader?'

'Alleged ringleader.'

'Yes, alleged ringleader. After the Aryan Brotherhood and Mexican Mafia, you've probably got one of the biggest crews in the jail system.'

'I know, but I'm not trying to run anything as it could be used as evidence against me.'

'I've got a proposition for you.'

'What?'

'Shit's about to go off between my people and the Aryans. Look, Shaun, we work out together, and I know if something goes off, you've got my back. But I was thinking it would be safer for all of us if I moved some of your co-defendants into this pod.'

I felt a mix of excitement at the prospect of joining forces with Little Italy, along with apprehension about where it might lead. Deciding the more friends I had in my pod, the less chances of anyone picking on me, I said, 'Good idea.'

'Cool.'

But as soon as I'd committed, doubts crept in. 'But isn't going up against a prison gang way out of our league?'

'Yeah, but we're not in prison. This is jail. It's far more every man for himself here. The Aryan Brotherhood are far stronger in the prison system than in the jail. Most of their shot-callers are locked down in the state's super-maximum prison. A lotta the guys in here are just wannabes. I don't see the Aryans here attacking us if we have greater numbers. If I move your people in, I need to know will they have my back?'

'Of course, Marco.'

'Then draw up a list of who you want moved in.'

'I'll get right on it. Wild Man would be at the top. And Maddox, he's six-seven and almost 300 pounds.' Wild Man's presence would intimidate most of the prisoners, but I feared he might instigate trouble with the Aryans just for the hell of it.

I compiled a list and Marco moved Maddox, Joey Crack and Grady (one of my youngest security guards from the raves) into one cell. He tried to move Wild Man from the hole, but the computer system prohibited him from being housed in the same pod as me, so he ended up in the adjacent pod, 2D. Joey Crack also had Marco move Kyle the kickboxer over. At Durango jail, a gang of youngsters had smashed my oldest co-defendant, Little Ben. He'd been moved to Tower 1, so we moved him to Tower 2. Little Ben – yet another co-defendant I'd never met – was an old-timer Wild Woman had bought drugs from.

He arrived with a cut and bruised face. My crew was now six strong in Tower 2. Although Wild Man was in the next pod, Marco had the guards let Wild Man visit our pod for hours on end, and people took notice. The inmates nicknamed us the Evil Empire, after the title of the *New Times* article.

The five Aryans and torpedoes were not enough to move against ten of us. And none of them dared challenge Wild Man and Maddox, who stood out like a bear and a Cyclops. When he wasn't in our pod, Wild Man often came to the window in 2D to chat with me in sign language, surrounded by a band of thugs. Wild Man had shaved his eyebrows off to pay a gambling debt and looked like a monster. Another regular at the window with Wild Man was Troll, who'd recently signed a plea bargain for almost ten years and was sporting a bruised face after getting smashed over drug debts.

Unable to take us all on, the Aryans picked on the smallest of us, Little Ben. They sent Bam Bam, an overgrown hick with a husky voice and scaly facial skin, to extort tobacco from him. Bam Bam cornered Little Ben in his cell. The first I knew about it was from the familiar sound of a body getting thrown around. Used to that sound, I dismissed it as just another fight. Then Slopester ran into my cell: 'Bam Bam's smashing Little Ben!'

The rest of the Aryans were trooping up the stairs as I rushed from the cell, my adrenalin going like crazy. Little Italy, my co-defendants and Kyle were stampeding across the balcony to Little Ben's. I got there just in time to see Marco threatening Bam Bam, who was about six inches taller and broader than him. I'd never seen Marco so angry. He was roaring in a deep voice, fists balled, pumping his chest further out with every heavy inhale.

The Aryans tried to push their way through us to get into the cell, but we stopped them. Surprised by our resistance, Iron Eagle assured us we were all dead as soon as we stepped foot into the prison system. I shuddered at the prospect of running into Iron Eagle in prison, where I'd be after sentencing. My bravery dwindled as I imagined the Aryan Brotherhood shanking me to death in the shower.

Inside the cell, the argument between Marco and Bam Bam was about to get physical, and outside Kyle was feinting jabs at the Aryan torpedoes. The *thud-thud-thud* of Marco converting Bam Bam into a punching bag prompted the Aryans to plough into us, restoring my courage. It was more of a pushing match than a fight. Surrounded by large friends, I pushed into them. I was equal parts animated and terrified. Then the fists I'd heard so much about went to work. Kyle let loose a flurry of blows worthy of an X-Man. Blood splattered from an Aryan torpedo's nose. More blows knocked the torpedo back, his eyes fading in and out as if his brain were shutting down like an old computer.

The control guard's voice crackled out of the speakers, 'Lockdown right now!' The older Aryans yanked Iron Eagle back, and they retreated. The guard kept yelling lockdown. Paulie pulled Marco off Bam Bam, and they got back to their cell just as the backup guards filed into the day room. I was afraid of getting caught and punished for being a part of it, and also worried about Iron Eagle retaliating against us. I envisaged the Aryans picking us off one by one. The guards had seen the fight on the balcony, so they only cuffed and extracted Kyle and the torpedo he'd smashed. We remained locked down for the rest of the day, but we didn't lose any more men.

Wild Man heard what had happened and offered to smash Bam Bam at Catholic Mass, but Marco said no. A few days later, the guards moved Iron Eagle to Tower 5, further incensing the Aryans, who accused Marco of working with the guards. But Bam Bam continued to menace Little Ben. Wild Man came over to our pod and blatantly cheated at cards while playing Bam Bam. 'You cheatin'-ass punk!' was all Wild Man needed to hear from Bam Bam. Wild Man picked Bam Bam up, twisted and pile-drove him head-first into the chow table. Wild Man broke his own thumb. Maggoting around on the floor, Bam Bam was out of action. The Aryans didn't attack Wild Man, as it looked like a one-on-one fight over a card game, and such fights were routine. A guard escorted Wild Man and Bam Bam to the hole. I spoke to Marco, Marco to the guard, and the guard brought Wild Man back with no disciplinary action. Bam Bam never returned.

There was nothing the few Aryans left in our pod could do now. We vastly outnumbered them. They didn't object to our decision to crown Marco the head of the whites, and their behaviour towards us slowly became more respectful. We'd shown we would fight back, and the gangs respect that when it suits them. I still didn't feel safe, though. If I were moved to another tower without my co-defendants or Little Italy, the Aryans could easily get revenge.

In the back rows at the next Catholic Mass sat my friends, Little Italy and Aryans from various towers who knew what had happened. Now they outnumbered us. With them was Carter, who hadn't regained his swagger since being smashed by SmackDown. Father O'Donnell had to keep stopping the Mass to hush Wild Man, who was incapable of whispering quietly. The Aryans from our pod had associates from four pods present – including one with flames tattooed on his head – and we expected a war to break out. But instead of attacking us, the Aryans laughed at Wild Man throwing his Communion wafer around and disrupting the service. They even praised Wild Man for smashing a baby shaker – the baby had been blinded in one eye and suffered a broken arm according to the legal paperwork.

'The doctors took me off the Thorazine and told me I'm normal. I'm normal!' Wild Man boasted in a voice loud enough for all to hear. 'Everyone who says I'm a Rule 11, you don't know what you're fucking talking about! I'm not a Rule 11!' Demonic laughter. 'I'm fucking normal!' More laughter. 'If the doctors say I'm normal, then I must be fucking normal!'

'That Wild Man's fucking crazy,' said Clubs, a portly redneck, the oldest Aryan from our pod. 'But I fucking like him. He reminds me of me at his age.'

Later on, Clubs paid me a visit and described how he'd nailed a man to a wall and hit golf balls at him. He was especially proud of how well dressed he'd been that day and what fine clubs he'd used.

22
··········

Alejandro, whose pus-filled spider bite I'd helped salt with Lev, was rearrested for threatening witnesses and housed in pod 2D next door to Wild Man. Facing a sentence in excess of a century for shooting multiple teenage gang rivals with an AK-47, he said he regretted not going on the run in Mexico while he was out on bond.

The guard who selected him and Wild Man – with a combined weight of about 700 pounds – to serve red death must have been a prankster. In the corridor, besides steel feeding carts stacked with 180 trays, the ravenous twosome put on hairnets and proceeded to steal everyone's dessert – a stale but beloved chocolate-chip cookie. Watching them shove cookies into their mouths until their cheeks were stretched to capacity, and then hide plastic bags full of them inside their trousers, the inmates banged on the Plexiglas, shook their fists and mouthed threats, but the twosome just laughed them off. The angry prisoners blamed the guards for the disappearance of their cookies, and the two big men were never allowed to serve chow again.

Young Officer Hernandez – who'd recently purchased a video game heavy on British slang – started yelling on his walks, 'Oh no, it's the filth!' in a mock English accent. The prisoners made a sport of parroting him. Mesmerised by this, Slopester sought to consult the man he assumed was the resident expert on matters of English slang: me.

'When Baptist does his walks, I call him the filth and he goes bright red. I need more shit to throw at him. What do they call prison guards in England?'

'Screws.'

'What other bad words you got?'

'You could call someone a plonker, a pillock or a daft git,' I said, without giving a second thought to the consequences.

Slopester left giggling over the new additions to his vocabulary. He used them to devastating effect on Officer Baptist, an averagely built, effeminate 40-something who wore big square glasses. Slopester's barrage sent Officer Baptist scurrying out of the pod. Worried he might call the goon squad, Nick and I asked Slopester to behave himself. Which he did for a few hours, but when Baptist was supervising the inmates serving red death, Slopester opened up on him again in an English accent: 'Look who it is! It's the filthy screw! He's a pillock and a plonker, too!'

The laughter in the day room rose to the lead paint peeling off the ceiling.

'Yeah, that filth . . . I mean filthy screw. What a daft git he is!'

Officer Baptist's face turned purple – a show of weakness the inmates pounced on with more fake English accents: 'Who's the filth?'

'That pillock Baptist is!'

'He's a filthy fucking screw!'

'Who's a screw?'

'Who's filthy?'

'Baptist!'

'He's a filthy screw and a plonker.'

Startled by everyone joining in, Officer Baptist panicked. 'You, lockdown,' he said to Slopester, in a wimpy way as if close to tears. He stepped out of the sliding door, fumbled with his radio and urged Officer Hernandez to close the door from the control tower.

Slopester refused to lockdown.

'Everyone lockdown!' Officer Hernandez announced.

As a dozen men hadn't been served, the prisoners threatened to riot.

'Lockdown now!'

Backup guards ran into Tower 2 and tried to force us back to our cells by yelling and waving pepper spray at us. As more arrived, we retreated. The last men in their cells were those who hadn't been fed.

The next day, those who hadn't eaten complained to the shift commander, who rewarded them with double rations of red death. Marco reprimanded Slopester. The jail enrolled Officer Baptist in assertiveness classes. The classes apparently worked: he was promoted to Sergeant Baptist.

March 2003

Dear Claudia,

It was nice to see you in court today, albeit briefly. I am shattered. I hate the post-court jetlag effect. It makes you feel so shitty and miserable. The judge denied the evidentiary hearing/remand motion.

That made me feel a little despondent as well. So I guess we file motions attacking the wiretaps next. We also must argue against us being tried in groups, which is not a good or a fair idea. All this bad news from court is terrible. I just want to know what's going to happen to me, so I can make plans for when I'll be in your loving arms. I'm so weary; I know I sound down today. I'm sure I'll be back to normal tomorrow for when you and Aunty Ann visit.

All the guys are downstairs watching *Goodfellas*. They're all wannabe gangstas. The whole pod is out. Standing room only.

I love you,

Shaun XXX

The commander of the jail discovered that Paulie had been moved from Tower 5 to Tower 2. He moved Paulie back to Tower 5, and Slopester with him. A few days later, Marco had the guards on a different shift move Paulie and Slopester back again. They returned teary-eyed and to much fanfare. This incensed the commander, and a tug of war began whereby every few days Paulie and Slopester were moved from one tower to the other. In the end, Slopester was allowed to stay but not Paulie.

Hugo found out he was going to be released, and Marco was sentenced. The release news purged a depression from Hugo, who had expected to be met by a death squad if deported back to Argentina.

The guards moved all of the sentenced inmates in Tower 2 to Tower 5 – except for Marco. He'd arranged with the guards to stay in our pod until his penultimate day at Towers. Hugo roped a banner across the upper tier to prevent access to Marco's cell. The banner read: 'V.I.P. Visits by appointment only!' The banner flabbergasted inmates and guards, especially when they watched Hugo attach and reattach it to let people in and out. But the newly assertive Sergeant Baptist was having none of it. He arrived on the scene with the afternoon shift change, pounced on the unprotected banner and tore it up. When the Italians emerged from their cell and surrounded Baptist, he must have forgotten his assertiveness training because he went red and trembled. Watching him slink away, the Italians mocked his timidity and told him he needed to retake the assertiveness classes.

As the day of Marco's departure neared, the inmates and even some of the guards saddened. We felt that the close community and minimisation of violence he had engineered were about to end. I was

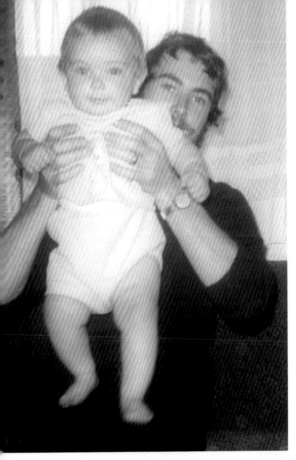

Me at eight months old
with my dad at our
house in Widnes,
Cheshire, 1969.

My mum, my sister Karen
aged eight and me aged
thirteen in Portugal, 1981.

With Hammy in Majorca, 1984.

Graduating from Liverpool
University, July, 1990.

Dressed to go raving in Manchester, 1989.

Working as a stockbroker at 3101 North Central Avenue, Phoenix, 1991.

My first home
– Piedmont Road,
Ahwatukee Foothills,
Phoenix.

My first sports car
– a Toyota Supra,
1994.

With my aunt Ann, who smuggled the blogs out of the Madison Street jail, 1995.

My second sports car – a twin turbo Mazda RX7, 1995.

With Wild Man, raving at the Celebrity Theater, Phoenix, 1995.

After-partying with DJ Mike Hotwheelz, Ecstasy supplier, 1998.

With my ex-wife, Amy, 2000.

My mountainside home in Sin Vacas, Tucson, 2000.

Le Girls Cabaret, Phoenix, 2000.

Getting a foot massage on Ecstasy, 2000.

Claudia, 2002.

With Wild Man shortly before our arrest in 2002.

Inside the maximum-security Madison Street jail.

Publicity photo shot in London,
May 2010, in Arpaio's famous
black-and-white bee stripes.

Me and Wild Man, April, 2010.

I'm sharing my story with young people as a cautionary tale
about getting involved in drugs and crime.

Orpington College, 16 March 2010.

St Columb's College, Derry,
Northern Ireland, 24 March 2010.

home and that someone had picked on my harmless little cellmate.

Later on in the day room, Busta Beatz barged into Bruce Lee – a mellow Jehovah's Witness who'd been my neighbour since my arrival in Tower 6 – who was eating his red death with the Mexicans. The Mexicans all rose fast as if to set on Busta Beatz.

'Beatz, you need to apologise to Bruce Lee,' Nick said, springing to his feet.

'I ain't apologising! Are you gonna fucking make me?' I found it hard to believe Busta Beatz had snarled at Nick like that, as Nick was trying to help him find his foster parents. Even worse, he'd 'called out' Nick by posing a question that left only one response in jail when directed at a head of a race: to fight.

Nick told Busta Beatz to see him in A7, the cell on the end of the bottom run he preferred to fight in as it was the furthest away from the control tower. As they entered A7, the day room hushed to tune into the music of violence. When the fighting lasted much longer than usual for Nick, the whites expressed concern, and the hermits emerged from their cells. The fight dragged on, and more prisoners clustered in the day-room's vantage points. Rooting for Nick, I saw him pin Busta Beatz against the wall, yelling 'Give up! Give up!' Busta Beatz surrendered, but as soon as he was released he leapt on Nick, who subdued him again. Ten minutes later, both were still fighting and exhausted. Nick put Busta Beatz in a headlock and urged him to give up again.

'I give up. You win,' Busta Beatz said. Nick turned to leave the cell, panting as if he'd just sprinted several hundred yards. But Busta Beatz sprang onto the small table as if he were Spider-Man and jumped on Nick's back. Nick threw him off fast, his face contorting with fury. He unleashed punch after punch on Busta Beatz's face. Punches that would have knocked out an average man.

Blood gushed and streamed all over Busta Beatz's face. Blood splattered on the walls. A volley of punches forced Busta Beatz backwards, cracking his head against the wall. I worried Nick might kill him. As Busta Beatz lost his balance, Nick pounded his head relentlessly until he fell unconscious.

'Fuck, I think I broke two of my knuckles,' Nick said, emerging from the cell half-covered in blood. He spat bloody saliva and pieces of teeth onto the floor.

The Mexican Americans filed into A7 and roused Busta Beatz, who was barely able to stand: 'Go back to your cell and clean yourself up.'

He staggered out of the cell, painting the concrete red with a trail of blood.

The Mexicans, including Bruce Lee, thanked Nick for standing up for their race.

Over the following days, Nick's hand swelled up to the size of a grapefruit, and Busta Beatz's face ran the hues of purple and blue. Nick declared he would never fight another Rule 11 inmate again.

A week later, the Mexicans saw Bruce Lee on the news. The report claimed that he and his wife had molested their own daughter. While Bruce Lee was at court, Carlo, the head of the Mexicans who'd shared a cell with Bruce Lee for a year, ordained the usual justice for a sex offender. Usually, such beatings were over in minutes. But the Mexicans – who'd been the least violent from what I'd seen – worked on Bruce Lee for half an hour. They timed it to start right after a guard had done a security walk through our pod. When the thudding and stomping sounds began, it sounded like a normal smashing, but then there were questions yelled harshly in Spanish, followed by Bruce Lee pleading for mercy, and eerie wails of pain as they tortured him. When they let him go, he stumbled to the sliding door soaked in blood from his hair to his feet. He was unrecognisable. When the door opened, he took a few steps and collapsed. The pod wasn't even locked down, probably because the guards approved of sex offenders getting smashed. Sometimes I heard they even tipped the prisoners off.

Gigolo Harry, a tall, handsome Englishman in his early 40s, transferred from Durango jail to Tower 2, into an adjacent pod. Signing at him through the Plexiglas, I arranged to meet him at rec. Early next morning in the cool outdoor air, we walked laps in an area enclosed by tall buildings. Above us, the rising sun we couldn't see was illuminating a square section of sky and making the razor wire atop the buildings glisten like tinsel.

'How long you been in jail?' I asked.

'Three years,' Gigolo Harry said in a posh voice.

'You're kidding?' I said, shocked anyone could be held for that long without a trial, fearing it could happen to me.

'Three years. I'm dead serious.'

'Bloody hell! How come?'

'I said something the judge didn't like.'

'You did what?'

'Get a load of this. It was my sentencing hearing about two years ago, and the judge was lecturing me about how lucky I was to be in this bloody free and wonderful land. He said that instead of realising how privileged I was to be here and behaving myself, I'd taken advantage of wealthy American ladies. He put the US on such a pedestal I was thinking his spiel was the standard crap he pitched to the Mexicans. I politely reminded His Honour that I was not from a Third World country but rather from one of the most advanced countries in the world. He got angry when I alluded to the British Empire, and he rudely told me to shut up. I became rather emotional, and I couldn't control myself any longer, so I said to him, "Excuse me, Your Honour, but if my studies of history are accurate, and correct me if I am mistaken, then if it wasn't for us – the English – then you Americans would be speaking bloody French right now." That didn't go down very well with the judge. He cancelled my sentencing hearing, and I've been here ever since. I was in Durango for three bloody years. Everybody knows me. I've become a bit of a legend!'

'You've got more balls than I have to speak to the judge like that. I couldn't do it. You give new meaning to the phrase, "Lock 'em up and throw away the key." What were you arrested for?'

'I was a bloody gigolo!'

'What?'

'A real-life gigolo.'

'How'd you get into that?'

'I met some 40-year-old American bird who owned car dealerships, and she started to solicit me to go on trips with her. I was running my own business, and I told her I'd lose thousands of dollars if I were to go away for a few days. So she offered me $10,000 to go on a dirty weekend with her, and I never looked back. She started buying me all kinds of expensive things and telling me she loved me and I was the best thing she'd ever had.'

'Bloody hell! That's a lot of money!' I said, amused and intrigued by his story.

'Well, get this then. She obviously ranted and raved about my performance to her friends, and then she started introducing me to them. They were all rich middle-aged women who were married to wealthy business-owners. Anyway, I saw to it they acquired my number, and I started getting all kinds of calls offering large amounts of money to go on secret liaisons. Things just snowballed, and women started having me over to their houses. A few times, the husbands nearly caught us at it. I was making a bloody fortune from these women, much more than from my business.'

'So how did you end up in here?'

'Well, I am charged with stealing some paintings from one of the women, including a Monet.'

'How much was the Monet worth?'

'A lot of money. I've been stuck in jail since then, and nothing ever happens.'

'You should contact the British Embassy in LA and see if they can help you.'

'The state of Arizona doesn't care. This is the state that executed those German lads and didn't even inform the German Government.'

'I read about that.' The state of Arizona had flouted international law by failing to notify Germany that two of its citizens, the LaGrand Brothers, had been jailed for armed robbery and the murder of a bank manager. The German authorities found out too late. By the time the World Court in The Hague issued a stay of execution, one brother had been executed, and the other brother was gassed to death the day after the stay was issued.

'They were trying to give me twenty-five years at first, and I got it down to five, so I'm hoping that five will come back again. If I get five, I'll be out in a matter of months with my back-time taken off.'

Attempting to reduce the misbehaviour in Tower 2, the guards rounded up suspected troublemakers and moved them to Tower 5. Wild Man, Alejandro and Joey Crack ended up as cellmates in Tower 5, where a guard with a reputation for being tougher than Mordhorst woke them up every day at 6.30 a.m. by blasting the national anthem over the speakers.

At church, I asked Joey Crack for an update on Wild Man and Alejandro.

'Wild Man's back in the hole,' Joey Crack whispered to me on the back row.

'What for this time?'

'Me, Alejandro and Wild Man were all in the cell together, and the guards decided to do a cell search. Wild Man was told a number of times to shut up, but he continued to be his insane obnoxious self. He kept running his mouth till the cop had had enough. The cop asked him to face the wall, place his arms behind his back, and he refused.'

'Oh no.'

'So the cop pressed his panic button and within seconds 20 COs came running in ready for the worst. They surrounded Wild Man with their pepper sprays out, but he just stood there laughing at them. A cop said, "Do you want to do this the easy way or the hard way?" Wild Man looked them up and down, and waited till they were just about to spray him, and said, "Let's try the easy way."'

'What a nutter!'

'He loves the attention. He just laughed in their faces.'

'How's Alejandro?' I asked.

'He got 46 years.'

'Holy shit! How's he handling it?'

'They've moved him to a suicide-watch cell at the Madison Street jail. He didn't handle it well at all, and Wild Man made it worse by tormenting him the whole time.'

'What do you mean?'

'During the trial, Wild Man woke Alejandro up at all hours of the night for absolutely no reason and pelted him with rotten grapefruits. Alejandro was too preoccupied to react much.'

'That's way out of order.'

'Alejandro had to get up after midnight and go to court all day long, so he was only getting a couple of hours' sleep. He ignored Wild Man, which sent Wild Man crazy 'cause he wasn't getting a reaction.'

'Good for Alejandro.'

'Wild Man ended up smashing grapefruits all over the cell floor, so Alejandro would slip around as he got ready for court.'

'I'm sure he works for the Devil.'

'The insanity never stopped. The citric acid stained the floor, and Wild Man started hallucinating, saying he was seeing faces of every sort on the floor.'

'I told you he's a Rule 11.'

'Another thing I noticed about Wild Man is a strange 6-6-6 system that he keeps. He had a picture of Wild Woman taped above his rack, and all day long he tapped it in sets of 6-6-6. What he was trying to achieve, I haven't the slightest, but it's what he does.'

I was in the visitation room sitting at a table alone, listening to wiretaps playing on my attorney's laptop, when Wild Man showed up to meet his attorney. He had no eyebrows, a goatee and a shaved head. His attorney was sitting at one of the little visitation tables close to me. I didn't let on to Wild Man so she wouldn't know I was there. Her face puckered when she saw him. I turned down my headset volume so I could eavesdrop.

'Hello!' Wild Man said in a deep giddy voice. He sat down opposite her and shook her hand.

'How're you doing, Peter? How's the broken thumb?' she asked, shaking her head at Wild Man's thumb that had turned blue and shed its nail.

'OK. Everything's OK,' Wild Man said.

'As you know, the prosecutor's offering eight years. Considerably less than the 25 you're facing,' she said in the tone of a used-car salesperson.

Wild Man nodded. 'I never got busted with no drugs. Don't you only get the 25 if they can show 25 grand in drug sales?'

She sighed. 'Not necessarily. Who's been telling you this?'

'Co-defendants.'

'I know Attwood's telling you this,' she said. 'He has a paid attorney. He'll tell you anything, but in the end you'll be the one that ends up doing the time. You're best taking the plea now. It's the best you're gonna get.'

Many of the co-defendants had told me that their public defenders were saying similar things, so I was unsurprised yet keen to hear what else she might say about me.

'As this is my first plea, I'd rather roll the dice and see what happens.'

'This is your life you're gambling.'

'It's not like I haven't heard that before.'

'Quite frankly, I think your co-defendant, Attwood, is going to get a lot of time, and he's going to take you down with him.'

As much as I expected her to say something like that, it was frightening to hear it.

'Save yourself while you still can! I can get a settlement conference with the judge and prosecutor. See if we can work out a deal if you like?'

'Uh, OK. But I didn't get caught with any drugs. I won't do more than five years.'

'The prosecutor's a very reasonable woman. But from eight down to five, I just don't know. Let's just go ahead and set the settlement conference, shall we?'

'Uh, OK, if you ask for the five. I like the food here, me.'

'The food?' she asked, surprised.

'In England, you just get bread and water.'

'How about next month for the settlement conference?'

'They feed you bread and water all week long. I love the food here, especially the potatoes. People complain about the food, but I love it. I can't get enough of the red death.'

'Peter, you're completely crazy. Now let's get back to the settlement conference. With good behaviour – do you think you're capable of good behaviour, Peter?' she asked as if talking to a child.

Wild Man looked over his shoulder as if she were talking to someone else.

'If you sign for eight, with your back time and the 85 per cent kickout, you'll actually do closer to five.'

'Uh, OK.'

'I'll go ahead and schedule the settlement conference then.'

'In England, they feed you porridge. This is like hotel food here. We had bean burritos last night. I love the food, me.' Wild Man leaned towards her, his eyes demented.

'Peter, you're completely crazy.' There was fear showing on her face now. 'I have to go. I'll be in touch. Bye!' She stood, up and left without shaking Wild Man's hand. She'd been paid to represent Wild Man, yet he felt that she had not properly defended him. He got the impression that she just wanted him to sign a plea bargain.

Big Wood was a shot-caller (one of the heads of the whites) from Buckeye prison. Caught with marijuana and facing new charges, he was sent to Towers and assigned to Nick's cell. He was a massive man but had a mellow disposition that made him someone you could reason with. Nick and Big Wood got along. After breaking his hand on Busta Beatz's face and losing pieces of his teeth, Nick was weary of being the head of the whites. He passed the mantle to Big Wood, who commanded respect due to his reputation in the prison system. Big Wood ordered the whites he didn't like to roll out of the pod, got the rest to behave and then set about stopping the nightly fellatio shows in 2B, a neighbouring pod where after lockdown a Native American transsexual could be seen from our cells bobbing his head between the legs of a white inmate sat on the toilet at the front of the cell. Prior to Big Wood's arrival, bored prisoners had enjoyed yelling running commentaries on these performances. But Big Wood sent a kite to the head of the whites in 2B saying the receiver of the oral sex was disgracing the white race and must be smashed if it continued. It stopped immediately.

Honduras, whose plea bargain had dropped from double-digit years down to five, notified us that he would be leaving soon as all of the witnesses in his case had disappeared. His prosecutor offered him a final plea bargain for two years, which he laughed at. He knew they had no evidence against him, so he called the prosecutor's bluff. A few nights later at about 2 a.m., our cell door opened, and a guard shone a torch on us.

'Jose! Roll up! Roll up! Immigration are here to pick you up!'

Awakened by the guard, I shook hands with Honduras.

'*Buena suerte*, Honduras,' I said. Good luck.

'*Buena suerte, mi compañero de cuarto.*' Good luck, my roommate. 'See! I told you, *tengo mucho suerte.*' I have much luck.

'*Si, que suerte tienes.*' Yes, what luck you have.

'*Que Dios te bendiga, Inglaterra.*' God bless you, England.

'*Que Dios te bendiga tambien.*' God bless you also.

'*Adios.*'

I was glad Honduras had beaten the system. Surrounded by mayhem, he'd kept his cool, remained sober, prayed to God and shown nothing but respect to everyone.

A few days later, Stalker was sentenced to three and a half years. He would serve just over two, which I hoped would be long enough for him to overcome his desire to resume stalking his wife. If you must stalk someone, I told him, do a celebrity next time and we'll get you on *Oprah*.

April 2003

Dear Claudia,

Here I lie. Riding the rack. Writing to you and listening to Spanish love songs on Amor 100.3 FM.

Last night, a big young guard came in and looked at your pics. He said, 'Ahhhh, these are the famous sexy pics,' and was nice to me. Then 20 minutes later, after lockdown, he bombed into my cell and ripped down our clotheslines. What a U-turn! I guess he was either jealous or felt guilty for being nice to me.

I had a full day today. Razors at 7 a.m., followed by rec at 7.30. It's nice jogging at 7.30; the weather is lovely. I got a certificate for a three-day health course I finished today. Slopester said the teacher looked like you. She had a Chinese character tattooed on her leg. She brought a dildo in today and showed us all how to put a condom on. Then we watched an STD slide show. Proper horror show it was! Staring at slides of vaginas with STDs made me queasy.

Poor 'Nancy', an old rambling man, was covered in blood as I peered through 2B's pod window on the way to class. Some guy was beating him up, and the back of his shirt was soaked in blood. I never expected an old crazy man to get beaten. I think he was bleeding from the back of his head. It's a shame. It is a cruel place here at times.

A lot of people got sentenced this week. A paisa in cell 9 got ten years for a DUI in which someone died. Twiggs in cell 11 got nine years for a $20 bag of crack that didn't even have his fingerprints on it. Gigolo Harry finally got sentenced. They are releasing him after three and a half years.

The sewer got blocked somehow and is flooding the pod downstairs. In the chow tonight, another dead rat was served to some poor soul in D pod. How obscene is that? The longer I am here, the more the horrors of this place become apparent. Everyone who ate the slop can now go to sleep with the knowledge that a rat (or rats) was swimming in their food.

Stalker is strung out on his new meds. He had a hissy fit on the doctor and demanded something that wouldn't make him tremble so much. Now he is on Trazodone.

Honduras is gone. What a lucky young man! I miss him already, as we bonded with our little Spanish conversations. I'm guessing how the witnesses in his case disappeared, considering the coyotes work for the Mafia.

I'm reading *Meditations from the Mat*. The yoga way of life is starting to sink in. I'm letting go of my old ways and thought processes and becoming a less fearful and stressed person. It is amazing how much more there is to yoga than just the exercises. It is making me stronger. For example, when there are fights in here, I am no longer hastening to observe them like everyone else, or getting involved in gossip. I'm slowly reinventing myself. The book also mentions how we choose to punish ourselves by reacting to our environment. This particularly applies to jail. Punishment is our teacher teaching us not to punish ourselves. If punishment is my teacher, then this time is a blessing.

The guard just announced that razors are now at 5 a.m. What utter bastards. Trying to save money because they know we are sleeping. They keep finding new ways to torture us.

Love you loads,
Shaun XXX

24

....

For months, I'd been using a laptop Alan Simpson had received permission to establish in the visitation room. Through a headset, I'd listened to the evidence against me: thousands of wiretapped phone calls. Whenever I heard a drug deal between any of the co-defendants, I documented the dollar amount. The total of all of the drug deals among all of the co-defendants was approximately $5,700. The prosecutor had never missed an opportunity to say we were a multi-million-dollar drug ring, so Alan was glad the calls didn't offer any proof of her allegation. He said the total trumped her claim that I was a serious drug offender, which required proof beyond a reasonable doubt of more than $25,000 dollars of drug income received during a calendar year. As no one had yet agreed to cooperate, and the state's own evidence now seemed to be evidence in my favour, Alan said he could file for another bond hearing and for a hearing to enable him to play some of the calls in court, so the judge could hear the extent of the drug dealing.

Stoked by this development, I called Claudia, and she relayed the news to my parents. Alan said it would help the bond hearing if people sent in letters of support. As I had family and friends around the world, the parents of my godchild, the Senns, set up a support website, including the format for writing a letter to the judge. My parents and sister contacted all of their friends – some of whom remembered me as a teenager before I'd left for the States – and hundreds of letters came in. Claudia's family members and my relations in Arizona pledged to attend the hearing and speak on my behalf. Claudia's parents, my second cousin Lorraine, my aunt Ann and her husband, Donny, offered their houses as collateral for my bond. Touched by the outpouring of support, I once again grew excited at the prospect of getting out.

I'd only been asleep for a couple of hours when a bright light startled me awake. Squinting at the source, I saw the flashlight belonged to Mr Big, a six-foot-four hulk of a guard whose outfit barely contained his muscles. He was standing outside my door, easily recognisable by his thick permed hair and old-fashioned square-framed glasses. He looked like he belonged in a 1970s magazine for bodybuilders. 'Attwood, wake up! You've got court!' His voice was as deep as they come.

I felt rough. 'What?' I said. I hated the monthly court appearances – a day in holding cells for a few minutes of the judge's time that always ended with a continuance of the case – but today was different. If the judge reduced my bond, I could be out as soon as tomorrow. The prospect of freedom squashed my reluctance to get up.

'You've got court! Take a shower! Be ready downstairs when you're done. Here's a razor.'

I slipped off my bunk and took the razor. Half asleep, I set off for the shower. The empty day room was quiet except for snoring and the flopping of my sandals. In the shower, I lathered soap on my face and began shaving by touch. No mirrors were allowed in the jail, so I had to feel my face to detect where the hair needed to be removed from. It had taken months to learn to do this without cutting myself too much. The quality of the razor was so poor it took a long time to shave. The water made me feel more awake and excited at the chance of getting out. When I was dried off, dressed and ready, Mr Big activated the sliding door and ordered me to wait in the corridor below the control tower. Other inmates arrived, all of them on the list of those scheduled for transportation to court.

Mr Big descended the control-tower stairs to escort us out of Tower 2. 'Gentlemen, proceed down the corridor in a straight line, one after the other.'

Just as the prisoner at the front set off, a youngster turned to Mr Big and said, 'This is bullshit. I wanna go back to sleep. You can tell the judge I'm refusing to go to court.'

Mr Big walked up to the youngster and inhaled loudly, expanding his massive chest well into the youngster's personal space. He gazed at the youngster for a few seconds, his veins and tendons protruding from his neck like ropes. 'You're going to court!'

The youngster jumped and complied.

'Proceed, gentlemen!' Mr Big followed us out of Tower 2 and along the breezeway where crickets were chirping so intensely they sounded like an English pedestrian crossing. He deposited us with the 100 or so groggy prisoners from various towers congregating at the back of the reception area. The guard at the door was shouting surnames, letting a few inmates at a time into the building and ticking names on his clipboard. Upon hearing him yell Attwood, I stepped forward.

'ID.'

I fished my ID from my top pocket.

'Go on in. Strip down to your boxers.'

I joined the back of the line of men in pink boxers, holding their bee stripes, about to be strip-searched, and removed my filthy clothes.

When I got to the front of the line, a guard said, 'Throw your stripes in that basket and step into that room.' When I was undressed, he said, 'Now hand me your boxers.' Standing naked, I watched him feel the lining of my boxers for contraband. 'Raise yer balls . . . Very good. Pull back yer foreskin . . . OK. Now turn around and spread 'em . . . OK. Put 'em back on,' he said, returning my boxers.

I exited the room and continued down the corridor. A trusty handed me a new set of stripes, which I put on. I turned left and walked down a stretch of corridor with a few cells. The two holding cells were full to capacity, so I joined the inmates collecting in the corridor.

Ten minutes later, a guard appeared. 'What do you stragglers think you're doing out in the walkway? Get into those cells now! Do you hear me? Now!'

The men cussed and groaned.

'Inmates inside move all the way to the back of the cells so these fellas can get in!'

It was a slow process, like trying to squeeze into a mass of bodies at the front of a concert. The stench of sweat, bad breath and cheap deodorant was inescapable.

Spotting me, Wild Man bulldozed in my direction, knocking everyone in front of him out of the way. 'Hello, la'!' His eyebrows had hardly grown back, so he still looked like a monster.

'How do, la'?'

His bear hug and the force of the men pressing against me made it difficult to breathe.

'There's way too many Englishmen in here!' someone yelled. 'That's what the fucking problem is!'

'Wild Man alone's more than enough,' I said, raising a few laughs.

'If you have a fucking problem with the English, come and fight us right now,' Wild Man said, generating more laughter even though he sounded serious.

I was glad of Wild Man's company. He was pleased about the developments in the case and how the calls getting played in the courtroom would help us all. The men around us grew bored and testy.

They stared at the walls, the ceiling, the back of each other's heads. When the cell door opened an hour later, we all cheered.

'When I call your name, step out of the cell with your ID in your hand!' said a guard. Eventually, he called six names, including Wild Man's and mine.

'Stand in a line!' yelled a guard standing with two others jangling leg chains in the corridor. 'Now face the wall!'

A guard came up behind me and said, 'Raise your left foot towards me.' He secured a chain around my ankle. 'Now the right foot.' When all six sets of leg chains were on us, a guard yelled, 'Turn around!' They put handcuffs on us, starting with Wild Man, who was first in our line of six. Then they chained our handcuffs together. I was chained to Wild Man and an old Mexican with boils on his face.

'Bet you never thought we'd end up chained together like this,' Wild Man said, grinning.

'It's my worst nightmare, la',' I said.

'Welcome to my world, la'. You've gone from stockbroker to criminal all within three of my visits to America.'

'Go and wait in that cell!' a guard yelled.

The six of us penguin-shuffled towards a large holding cell at the end of the corridor. The leg chains only permitted half steps, and everyone on the chain gang had to take care to step in sync so we could move as one. We joined the other chain gangs in the holding cell. When all of the prisoners going to court were packed into the cell, the guards locked the door and clustered around a small isolation cell opposite us. In the isolation cell, an irate prisoner with a freckly face and red hair in a ponytail was scowling through the Plexiglas at the guards.

'Are you gonna behave yourself and go to court?'

'Fuck you!' the redhead yelled, narrowing his eyes.

'Looks like he doesn't want to be a good boy.'

The redhead headbutted the window, provoking laughter from the guards. 'Fuck you!'

When the guards laughed even harder, he spat on the window. The thick glob of phlegm crept down the Plexiglas, leaving a trail glistening in its wake.

'We'll just tell the judge you refused to see him then. I'm sure that'll make him happy.' The guards smiled at him mockingly and walked away.

It was another hour before a transportation van parked outside the jail. The exterior door buzzed open, and two transportation guards came in.

'OK. Any chains with green-coloured padlocks on them, get on your way!'

The lead person in every chain gang looked at the colour of his padlock.

'We're green!' Wild Man said, and pushed through the prisoners to get to the door.

We shuffled out and down a ramp to the van.

A guard opened the back doors. 'Get in slowly! One at a time! Watch your heads getting in! Slide all the way down the seat! Squeeze in there!'

The six of us cramped together on a narrow ledge on one side of the van. Six more sat opposite. Two groups of four sat in the space between the driver and us. Plastic mesh separated each group. The van doors slammed shut, and the trapped air stifled us.

'Can you get some air blowing back here?' Wild Man yelled.

A guard in the cabin adjusted one of the vents so it aimed to the back of the van. But the trickle of air struggled to reach the van's hindquarters. Every time the van turned a corner, the six of us slid along the ledge to the back of the van, crushing the man at the end of our chain gang. I took the brunt of Wild Man's 280 pounds. The atmosphere and the swerving of the van made me queasy.

When we arrived at the Madison Street jail, the first rays of the day were illuminating the sky, tingeing the sparse clouds an orangey-red. The van went through a security gate and parked in a lot below the building.

The doors clicked open. 'Get out! Watch your heads!'

Each man stepped down, almost falling over, tugging the men on his chain gang.

'Slow down getting out!' The guard led us through an exterior door into a holding cell, brightly lit, with many security cameras, where we waited for a few minutes.

The interior door opened. 'Proceed to your left!' yelled a large guard with a shaved head.

We exited the cell, turned left and shuffled down the corridor. The babble of many prisoners yelling grew louder.

When we arrived at a space facing four adjacent cells crammed with noisy prisoners, the guard yelled 'Stop here! Line up!'

The prisoners had been transported from various local jails to wait in the Madison Street jail's dungeon before going to court. The guards removed our chains. There was a sound like sandpaper scraping against a wall as a trusty slid a plastic barrel full of Ladmo bags across the concrete towards us.

A guard opened one of the cell doors. 'Get a Ladmo bag, and get in there! Fellas in the cell, make room! Push back against that wall!'

I took a Ladmo bag and followed the ultimate space-maker: Wild Man. The walls in the dungeon cells were some of Sheriff Arpaio's worst. Multiple layers of filth had smothered the original paintwork. The colour now was a dull yellowish-brown, dappled with dark-brown raised patches of God knows what. The floor belonged to the cockroaches. Any we trampled, the living quickly ate. The toilet at the back reeked like a dive-bar's urinal at closing time, a smell that I gagged on as I made my way further in. The area around the toilet was coated in urine from the countless men who'd missed their aim over the years. Wild Man kicked a few pairs of legs out of the way as if they were sticks on a forest path. He power-gazed the men he'd disturbed into conceding his space requirement. We squatted down. Pushing a sleeping man out of the way, Wild Man stretched his legs out.

Waking up, the man yelled, 'What the fuck!'

'So what?' Wild Man leaned his large head towards the man, who flinched and wriggled away.

'It's only fucking six o'clock!' announced an inmate at the front of the cell, looking at the clock in the guards' room.

'Court's not till ten,' I said to Wild Man. We chatted to pass the time, shifting positions when our pins and needles were too uncomfortable, occasionally raising our shirts over our faces to protect ourselves from the stink of inmates defecating. Spotting cockroaches venturing into our neighbours' clothes broke up the monotony.

At 7 a.m., a chain gang arrived outside our cell, 12 men from the maximum-security quarters of the Madison Street jail. They were unchained and ordered to enter our cell.

'There's no fucking room in here!'

'Then make some fucking room!' a guard yelled. 'Push all the way to the back!'

The weary crowd further compressed itself. I was pushed closer to one of the walls at the side. The 12 entered, trampling on the tangle of limbs below them. But no one spoke up because the medium-security prisoners feared the maximum-security prisoners, many of whom were murderers.

Two large Mexican American new arrivals noticed a small Mexican-American leaning against the back wall. The two whispered to each other as if plotting something. After the cell door locked behind them, they acted as if they were heading to the toilet. But the larger one veered towards the man they'd spotted, dragged him kicking and yelling towards the toilet and started cracking his head against the steel. *Thwack-thwack-thwack* . . .

All of the talking, joking, heckling, snoring, laughing and complaining stopped at once. Mesmerised by the violence, the men in the immediate area shuffled out of the way. When the victim's head cracked open, gushing blood, the two Mexican Americans stomped on him, putting their full weight on his joints as if to snap them.

Watching them attempting to murder someone was registering with my adrenalin. It affected my neighbours, too. The men at the back sprang to their feet, and within seconds everyone rose. I scrambled up but had nowhere to go. I felt panic seize the crowd. Fighting started to spread from the back of the cell. The crowd lurched towards the front, taking me with it. I raised my forearms to shield myself from the flailing arms. Wild Man said, 'I've got this one, la',' shoved me against a wall and stood in front of me like a totem pole with prisoners bouncing off him, some of them helped on their way by his big hands.

Guards rushed to the cell. One of them fingered his keys and worked one in. They entered fast, wielding Tasers and fire-extinguisher-sized canisters of pepper spray. The crowd folded out of their way. The fighting stopped. They grabbed the three Mexican Americans – easily identifiable by their blood-soaked bee stripes – and dragged them out. Looking at the victim on the floor, I couldn't see any signs of life. Everyone was staring at him. The guards cuffed the culprits, medical staff stretchered the victim away, and trusties mopped up the blood. Minutes later, the chatter resumed.

At 7.30 a.m., guards congregated outside of the cell and started calling the surnames of the men with the earliest court times. The extracted men lined up and were chained together. The cells became less crowded. Just when we had enough space to stretch our legs, a guard ordered us into the cell next door, where I spotted some of my co-defendants. Pleased to see them, we exchanged hugs. They asked what was going on with the case.

'Alan's trying to get the calls played in court so the judge can hear you guys were only busted doing nickel-and-dime deals.' I handed them copies of the itemised drug deals, showing the $5,700 total. 'This list could change everything!'

After months of no legal developments and their public defenders insisting they sign plea bargains, they were pleased with the news.

At 9 a.m., a guard called my name and those of my co-defendants. We were chained, led down a corridor and ordered to wait outside a holding cell for females. Wild Woman appeared with her hair streaked every colour of the rainbow.

'What happened to your hair, love? It looks like you've been to a gay festival,' Wild Man said.

'How did you do that in jail?' I asked, worrying about the impression it would make on the judge.

'Can't tell you me secrets, now can I?' Wild Woman rasped.

We travelled through a tunnel and waited for an elevator. We packed ourselves in. Wild Man positioned himself so he could rub up against Wild Woman. As the guard pressed the elevator button, the Wild Ones stole kisses.

'I love you,' Wild Man said.

'Love you too,' Wild Woman said.

From the elevator, we were separated into two cells: males and females. When it was close to 10 a.m., the guard escorted us into the courtroom. I panicked when I saw the TV crews, but the guard explained a teacher who'd molested some of his students had been sentenced to more than 100 years. We were ordered to sit on the rows of benches at the side of the courtroom in front of the public gallery. I saw Claudia and my local family members, but I was prohibited from talking to them, so I could only smile and bounce my eyebrows.

My attorney, Alan Simpson, arrived, armed with all kinds of statistics and pie charts on fancy coloured paper and a tape recorder to play some of the calls to the judge. The co-defendants' attorneys mobbed him for information. He responded by whispering in their ears. The look spreading over their faces suggested they were expecting the great Alan Simpson to finally – after almost a year of locking horns with the young prosecutor – demolish the case. The prosecutor greeted Alan with her usual competitive smile, but she and Detective Reid (who attended nearly all of my court hearings) looked a bit daunted. The attorneys were whispering in the ears of my co-defendants, spreading the buzz around the room.

The judge assigned to my case came out, bespectacled, grim and in a wheelchair due to injuries he'd sustained in the Vietnam War. We all rose. Ignoring the judge, the Wild Ones continued to laugh and talk to each other loudly. Judge Watson ordered our escorting guard to remove the Wild Ones from the courtroom for horseplay. Detective Reid smirked as they were escorted out. I couldn't believe they'd misbehaved on such an important day. I feared the impact of their behaviour on the judge and the motions Alan was working on.

Alan told the judge that the total drug deals on the wiretaps amounted to $5,700. He said he'd brought his tape recorder and would like to play some of the calls. The prosecutor objected to the court hearing the calls. Hearing her object to her own evidence pleased me and the co-defendants. We figured we had her. But the judge said now was not the appropriate time for the court to hear any of the calls. The case was continued. My co-defendants were cleared from the courtroom.

Next was my bond hearing. Alan asked for a bond reduction on the basis of the $5,700 list of drug deals. That total did not warrant a $750,000 bond. Members of my family – including my aunt Ann's husband, Donny, an ex-policeman – and Claudia's stood up, vouched for me, offered to take me into their homes and offered their homes for my bond. It was a strong show on my behalf. I enjoyed watching Detective Reid's face tense up. The prosecutor spoke only briefly, raising some mild objections. Then she sat down. She seemed defeated. My supporters' eyes were sparkling as if they were sure the judge would reduce my bond. When it came time for him to rule, he said he was unable to make a decision and he was taking the matter under advisement. I felt a pang of disappointment, but the bond hearing had gone so well I was confident of a positive decision soon. I left the courtroom convinced I'd be out in a week or so. I spent the half-day journey back to Towers indulging in fantasies of freedom.

25

....

Shepherding a group of us back into Tower 2, Officer Noble said to me, 'I need to talk to you.' He looked serious.

'What is it?' I asked.

'Wait down that corridor.'

I walked away, growing alarmed.

After directing the rest of prisoners into their pods, he approached me. 'You've been Page 2d.'

'New charges! How's that possible? I just had a bond hearing. New charges!' I said, frustration rising in my voice.

'If you just had a bond hearing, that's how they stop you getting out: new charges. And another thing–'

Still reeling from the first shock, I braced myself for another.

'–you've got two new cellies.'

I paused for a few seconds. Stunned. 'How did that happen?'

'They're always moving you guys around. We wouldn't want you to get too settled now.'

Walking up the stairs, I felt the full weight of what he'd said. I prayed my new cellmates were the mellower type of criminals.

Big Wood stopped me at the top of the stairs. He told me to step into his cell, so I followed him. 'They've put a black dude in your cell. We're trying to get him moved to an all-black cell. He has a bottom-bunk slip 'cause he has seizures. He's a bit of a loudmouth, but he's all right. We just can't have a black dude celling with two woods.'

I didn't mind living with a black man but not a loudmouth of any race. 'What about my other new celly?'

'He's a youngster. Busted with drugs in prison. Here on new charges.'

I returned to A10, intent on making the most of the situation by greeting my cellmates with all of the congeniality I could muster. I pressed the door open a few inches, and the youngster I didn't see sat on the toilet shoved it back in my face.

'Wait outside a minute,' he said with attitude. 'I'm unpacking my ass. You wanna smoke?'

I'd dodged having to live with a smoker for almost a year. I was in no mood to deal with a smoker on top of everything else. 'No. I don't smoke. This is a smoke-free cell.'

'It *was* a smoke-free cell,' he said. 'OK. You can come in now.'

The cell reeked of his business on the toilet and the rollie he'd just lit. He had numerous pockmarks on his face and the mischievous look of the State-raised. He took another drag.

'Look, I've been here for a year, and I don't appreciate you smoking in my cell,' I said, growing angry.

'What ya gonna do about it?'

His tone brought my stress to its boiling point. 'You wanna handle it like that?' I asked, wagging my finger at him.

He coolly took another drag as if the prospect of fighting me hardly fazed him. He rested the rollie at the base of the window.

We were inching towards each other, fists first, when the door swung open and banged against the wall. I whirled around.

It wasn't the black loudmouth I'd expected but a Bluto of a man almost filling the entire doorway. Wincing in pain, he limped into the cell and said in a gruff voice, 'I guess whoever's on the bottom bunk's moving out and I'm moving in.' He stood there, panting, grimacing at us in a way that said he was in no mood for an argument.

Amusement crept into the youngster's face. 'What the fuck's wrong with you, big dawg?'

Unfurling his mattress on the bottom bunk, the man replied, 'I was Tasered six times. Some kinda high-powered cop Taser.' He collapsed onto the mattress – the bunk barely contained him – and lay there trembling like a beached whale.

Jay, the head of the blacks, rushed in next with two massive torpedoes in tow. 'This guy's gotta go,' he shouted, pointing down at the Tasered man. 'The guy who just moved out is moving back in,' he said, referring to the black loudmouth.

The number of hostile people in my overcrowded cell was tipping my mind.

'Why do you think so?' the youngster asked snidely.

''Cause they just put him in with me, and we both got bottom-bunk slips.' Jay was angry because the black loudmouth had been reassigned to his coveted bottom bunk.

The Tasered man propped himself up. '*I* just got Tasered six times. *I* need a bottom bunk.'

'Do you have a bottom-bunk slip?' Jay yelled, curling his bottom lip at the Tasered man.

'Not yet.'

'Then you gotta move back out! The guy they moved out has epilepsy. He needs this bottom bunk.'

'You ain't no guard! You ain't telling me what to do!'

'You calling me out?' Jay rested his fists on his hips, shaping his arms to his body like the handles of teacups.

'You need to get the fuck out of our cell,' the youngster said, pointing at Jay.

Bouncing his eyes from the blacks to the whites, the Tasered man appeared to be on the verge of springing up to attack the blacks.

Not standing up for your own race in a situation like this was punishable by your own race smashing you. I'd been in jail long enough to be held accountable. Hoping to prevail with reason, I said, 'Obviously he needs a bottom bunk. Look at the state of him.'

'Who the fuck asked you?' Jay yelled. 'This is between me and him.'

I was about to say, 'Hey, I live here too, dawg,' at the risk of irritating Jay more, but my name was called over the speakers. 'Hold up. I think they're calling me.'

'Attwood. Page 2. Turn out for the Madison Street jail. You're going to court.'

Hurrying to abandon my home, I scooped up my property and dashed along the balcony to Nick's. 'All hell's breaking loose in my house. Will you mind my store and stuff while I go to The Horseshoe? Hopefully, I wont be gone for too many days.'

'Sure, bro. What's going on?'

'My new cellies are arguing with the blacks over the bottom bunk. You or Big Wood might want to go over there to try calm things down.'

I descended the stairs, glad to be distancing myself from the quarrel I could hear intensifying. Youngsters were snooping around my cell too, desperate to mooch tobacco from my new cellmate. I hoped things would be less chaotic upon my return.

Officer Noble escorted me to an empty holding cell in the reception building. The focus of my worrying shifted from the situation I'd left behind to the one I was entering. I feared the new charges would affect my case and the judge's pending decision on my bond hearing. It was Thursday evening, and I was concerned about getting stuck in

The Horseshoe's filthy cells with the influx of people who get arrested on the weekend.

Transportation arrived hours later. Shackled by a hick transportation officer, I boarded an old school bus and joined the minimum-security prisoners sitting two to a seat, chained to each other. Being the only medium-custody inmate on the bus, I received some respectful nods. When I sat down, the driver gunned the engine and the bus trundled off. The male prisoners heckled the six females locked in separate Plexiglas cubicles behind the cabin. Voicing what they'd like to do to them, the men worked themselves into a frenzy. The women humoured the men with sly smiles that said the men were brazen idiots. I was glad when the guard blasted the radio, drowning out the commotion. The men gave up on the women and sang along with rock oldies. The heat, noise, fuel smell, cuffs and new charges were annoying me. I took some deep breaths and tried to steel my mind for the challenges ahead. The van parked, and we joined the queue for the jail. The arrestees in street clothes looked warily at us bad men in bee stripes.

Police cars kept pulling up to deliver their fresh captures. Mostly men. Sullen-faced. Wide-eyed. Some beaten-up looking. A minority had to be dragged from the cars to the jail. I was reminded of my arrest and arrival on 16 May 2002. Wait a minute, I thought. 'What's the date?' I asked our group.

'May 16th, dawg.'

May 16th. One-year anniversary of my arrest. Can't be coincidence. Prosecutor's playing mind games! Has it in for me. I'm doomed. Maybe not. This shows a mean but immature streak. Maybe my attorney can exploit that.

A police van parked. Three prostitutes got out. The one in a miniskirt with a dragon tattooed on her thigh set the male prisoners off. They taunted her with obscene remarks, but she lashed back with the panache of a drag queen. Remaining quiet, the other two prostitutes hung their heads.

I relinquished my cuffs inside, and an inmate yelled 'Ain't you that guy–'

I put my finger to my lips too late.

'–that English guy on the cover of the *New Times*?'

I attracted many looks of approval but said nothing, just entered the walk-through metal detector.

A large Mexican American rapped on the window of a cell, and waved me over. 'English Shaun! I'm one of your co-defendants.' Yet another co-defendant I'd never met. I couldn't believe they were still expanding the size of my case.

A guard deposited me in a cell I remembered well. Plexiglas front windows. Walls caked in brown filth. A seatless steel toilet in the corner. About 40 men. Many high and drunk. Some bleeding or with Taser wounds. Everyone keeping a wary eye on everyone else. They were huddled so close on the concrete I tripped over them as I worked my way in. The few men in stripes nodded at me to join them, but I was in no mood for jail chat. Instead, I returned to the spot against the back wall where no one wanted to sit due to the toilet smell. I assumed a half-lotus position and read a yoga meditation book I'd smuggled in with my legal paperwork. It was a futile attempt to settle my mind. Every so often a prisoner was extracted or deposited. It wasn't long before the hot, stale atmosphere began to wear me down.

'I need to take a fucking dump!' a fat man announced. 'Who's got the fucking shit roll?' He spotted a hobo using a toilet roll as a pillow, walked over and snatched it, interrupting the rhythm of the hobo's snores. He shoved past me, dropped his pants and let the toilet have it. His stench permeated the cell. I held my breath. My neighbours gagged and moaned.

When a guard finally extracted me, I plodded to the next cell to savour the air in the corridor.

The next cell was the same. I wasn't there for long before two young Mexican Americans starting quarrelling over who shot who and then one struck the other. We all scrambled to our feet at once. The lightning punches of the taller youngster pummelled his opponent's face, showering those nearest with blood. I'd seen so much violence, I'd become desensitised. A year ago, I would have felt the fear visible in the eyes of the audience. But in comparison to a pack of torpedoes smashing someone, a one-on-one fight seemed trivial. A flurry of blows collapsed the smaller Mexican American. The taller switched to kicks. I visualised the taller one a few days from now: recruited as a torpedo for the Chicanos, proudly employing his fighting skills to do the dirty work of the head of his race.

'Loco got shot. I heard you had somethin' to do with it,' the victor said.

'Nah, I had nuthin' to do with that.'

'Not what I heard. I got the word two weeks ago. I know who smoked

Loco. I'll die for my barrio. My primo tells me you had somethin' to do with it, and you threatened my primo, too.'

'I was locked up then. I'm with Mini Park, ese. I don't know what you're talking about. I'm an original Mini Park gangsta. It's not like that, ese.'

'I represent my barrio. I'll die for my barrio. I'm stickin' by what I heard.'

'It's like that?'

'Yeah, it's like that.'

'We'll handle this, ese.'

The loser crawled to the toilet, pulled himself up and washed the blood from his face in the sink. The door swung open. Everyone looked at the guard as if expecting him to notice there'd been a fight, but he just yelled a name and extracted a man. The guard shut the door, and we all sat down.

The loser ripped his top off. Expanding the canvas of gang tattoos on his chest, he swaggered up to the victor. 'So what the fuck you sayin'?' Blood was leaking from the cuts on his face.

'Loco got smoked, ese. Why you squaring off on me?'

There was a crescendo of gang slang. Two men exchanging saliva motes but not blows. I concluded neither really wanted a rematch. The victor had nothing to gain. The loser had saved face by scraping himself off the floor and showing he was ready for round two. The situation followed the path of least resistance. It reversed. Proclaiming how gladly they'd die for their hoods, they bonded.

'Can I have some love?' the smaller one said. His olive branch led to much hugging and gang-handshaking. It morphed into the surreal. They were now a married couple making up after a spat, sucking up to each other. With toilet paper, the taller cleaned the blood from the other and then massaged the injuries he'd inflicted. Knowing they would smash me to a pulp was the only thing that stopped me from laughing out loud. We all listened, riveted by their drama.

The smaller gangbanger was adept at dealing with eavesdroppers. He jumped up and yelled 'Does anyone in here look at this man any fuckin' differently 'cause of what just happened?'

Silence.

'All right, all right, y'all go back to your business then.'

Everyone resumed talking.

I was extracted for fingerprints and photographs. My charge sheet showed some ambiguous drug charges and a conspiracy charge with another $750,000 bond. How could I bond out now? I would have to wait to see my attorney to interpret the charges. I was ordered into another cell. I figured it was early morning. I wanted to sleep but fought the urge, as it was too dangerous in The Horseshoe. Eventually, a guard called us out for court.

It was the same set-up and judge as last year. The prosecutor wasn't there. This time I was more prepared. When Judge Powischer asked me if I had anything to say, I responded, 'Your Honour, last year I asked you to reduce my bond from $750,000, and the prosecutor told you I was the head of a large drug ring. After listening to all of the thousands of wiretapped phone conversations, my attorney and I totalled the value of all of the drug deals among all of the co-defendants, and it came to less than $6,000. I ask you to reduce this bond to a reasonable level.'

'Less than $6,000!' the judge barked. 'I have nothing showing that! The bond stands at $750,000 cash only.'

Something tightened in my stomach. I should have known better than to expect a bond reduction, but hope is what keeps you going in jail. Even if my regular judge reduced my first $750,000 bond, I now had a second one. The prosecutor had blocked my attorney's attempt to get me out. It was obvious why she hadn't put up any resistance at the bond hearing. I dwelt on having to tell Claudia and our families.

'It's English Shaun!' someone said in the next cell. 'What's Sammy the Bull like?'

'I never met him.'

'We know you guys were kicking it together.'

'I seriously never met the guy.'

The large Mexican American who had noticed me enter the jail introduced himself as my co-defendant Richard. 'I got sentenced to a year. The prosecutor tried to get me to sign some paperwork, Exhibit A, saying I knew you and was getting drugs off you, but I told the judge I didn't know you and Exhibit A wasn't true.'

I thanked him, wondering how many of the co-defendants had been asked to sign Exhibit A.

Time is almost imperceptible in The Horseshoe. I had to check with a guard on the way out to calculate I'd spent almost another day in holding cells. Going on two days of no sleep, the men on the return bus lacked the energy to heckle the women in the glass cubicles. They sat quiet and despondent, their eyelids drooping, dark circles around their eyes. The bus rumbled back to the jail, vibrating me to the core.

At Towers, I wanted to nap, but my cell was full of smokers. They appraised my foul mood and dispersed. I went to Nick's to retrieve my bags. 'I'm outnumbered by the smokers now,' I said.

'If you don't want them smoking in your cell, you're gonna have to settle it the old-fashioned way,' Big Wood said, implying I needed to resolve the issue with my fists. 'It's your cell. You've been there the longest.'

'Why don't you move in here with us?' Nick said.

'How soon can you arrange it?' I asked.

'I'll talk to Noble today.'

I returned to my cell. The Tasered man on the bottom bunk seemed to be in a semi-conscious state of recuperation, so I chanced putting my store bags down next to him. But he reanimated. Rubbing his eyes with the back of his fingers, he leaned up slowly. Sniffing the air, he dropped his legs off the bunk and put his feet on the concrete. He looked like a big dog that wanted to be fed or else. 'Give me a candy bar!'

Exasperated by his demand, I was about to say something impolite, but Officer Noble announced, 'Attwood, roll your shit up.'

The announcement lifted some of the weight of my troubles of the past few days. I snatched my bags and rushed to Nick's cell. 'Thanks, man. How on earth did you get me moved in with you so fast?'

'I didn't.'

'What do you mean you didn't?' I asked, anxiety shooting up from my solar plexus.

'I haven't spoken to anyone yet.'

'Better go ask Noble,' Big Wood said.

Stood on the stairs, I windmilled my arms at Noble in the control tower. He swindowed back an M sign. I shrugged.

'You're being rehoused to the Madison Street jail,' he said over the loudspeaker.

I formed a Y with my arms.

'Admin's reclassed you to max security 'cause your total bonds are showing as one-and-a-half million on the computer.'

'They're separating you from your co-defendants and putting you where the killers are housed,' Slopester said. 'Watch your back, England.' He looked sad to lose me.

The weight of my troubles returned. Only much heavier this time.

26

....

I spent half a day in holding cells before arriving at a small two-man cell on the second floor of the Madison Street jail. It was about 2 a.m. Light was slanting into the dark cell through oblong gaps in the door, illuminating my new cellmate cocooned in a white sheet, snoring lightly on the top bunk about two-thirds of the way up the back wall. As I'd just come from a jail where men were prone to fight over the bottom bunk, I was grateful he'd taken the top.

Delirious from two days' sleep deprivation, I was looking forward to a good rest. I thought my standard of living had improved – two-man cell, bottom bunk – until I noticed movement on the cement-block walls. Putting the movement down to hallucinations, I blinked several times. Still movement. Stepping closer, I saw the wall was alive with insects. I flinched. There were so many I wondered if they were a colony of ants on the move just like you see in documentaries. To get a better look, I put my eyes right up to them. The insects were mostly the size of almonds and had antennae. American cockroaches. I'd seen them downstairs in The Horseshoe, but nothing like this. A chill spread over my body. I backed away from the wall. As my night vision picked up, I spotted more insect shapes circulating on the ceiling, going in and out of the base of the fluorescent strip light. Every so often one dropped onto the concrete and resumed crawling.

Examining the bottom bunk, it dawned on me why my cellmate had opted to sleep at a higher elevation: cockroaches were pouring out of gaps in the wall at the level of the bunk. The area was thick with them. Placing my mattress on the bottom bunk scattered them. I walked towards the toilet, crunching a few of them under my shower sandals. I urinated and grabbed the toilet roll. A cockroach darted from the centre of the roll onto my hand, tickling my fingers. My arm jerked as if it had a mind of its own, losing the cockroach and the toilet roll.

Using a towel, I wiped the bulk of them off the bottom bunk, stopping only to shake the odd one off my hand. I unrolled my mattress. They began to regroup and harass my mattress. My adrenalin was pumping so much, I lost my general fatigue. Nauseous, I sat on the stool contemplating how best to sleep. I wondered how my cellmate was managing to sleep through the infestation and my arrival. I decided to copy his technique. I cocooned myself in a white sheet and lay down, crushing a few more cockroaches. The only way they could get to me now was through the breathing hole I'd left in the sheet by the lower half of my face.

Inhaling their strange musty odour, I closed my eyes. I couldn't sleep. I felt them crawling on the sheet around my feet. Or was I imagining things? Frightened of them infiltrating my breathing hole, I kept opening my eyes. Cramps caused me to shift onto my other side. Facing the wall, I was repulsed by so many of them just inches away. I returned to my original side. The sheet trapped the desert heat to my body, drenching me in sweat. Sweat tickled my body, tricking my mind into thinking the cockroaches had infiltrated and were crawling on me. Every now and then I became so uncomfortable I had to open my cocoon to waft the heat out. It took hours to drift to sleep, and I only managed a few hours. I awoke stuck to the soaked sheet, disgusted by the cockroach carcasses compressed to the mattress.

The cockroaches plagued my new home until dawn appeared at the dots in the protective metal grid over a begrimed strip of four-inch-thick glass at the top of the back wall – the cell's only source of outdoor light. Then they disappeared into the cracks in the walls, like vampire mist retreating from sunlight. But not all of them. There had been so many on the night shift that even their vastly reduced number was still too many to dispose of. And they acted like they knew this. They roamed around my feet with attitude, as if to let me know I was trespassing on their stomping ground.

My next set of challenges, however, I knew would arise not from the insect world but from my neighbours. I was the new arrival again, subject to scrutiny about my charges just like when I'd run into the skinheads on my first day at Towers jail. I hoped my cellmate would wake up, brief me on the mood of the locals and introduce me to the head of the whites. No such luck. Chow was announced, and he didn't even stir.

Everyone except my cellmate emerged into the day room for breakfast. A group of prisoners did something I'd never seen in jail before: they gathered around the trash bin under the metal-grid stairs and emptied insect carcasses from plastic peanut-butter containers they'd used to trap cockroaches during the night. All eyes were on me in the chow line. Watching who sat where, I held my head up, put on a solid stare and tried to seem as at home in that environment as the cockroaches.

It was all an act. I was lonely, afraid and loathed having to explain myself to the head of the whites, who I assumed would be the toughest murderer in the maximum-security pod. I'd been in jail long enough to learn that skulking off to my cell with my Ladmo bag would imply I had something to hide. I'd observed the techniques well-received inmates had used to integrate and seen the bloody consequences of failed attempts. It was time to apply that knowledge. With a self-assured stride, I took my Ladmo bag to the whites' table, giving them the opportunity to question me.

'Mind if I sit with you guys?' I asked, glad exhaustion had deepened my voice.

'These seats are taken, wood. But you can stand at the corner of the table.'

Assuming the man who'd answered was likely to be the head, I sized him up. Cropped brown hair. A dangerous glint in his Nordic-blue eyes. Weightlifter-type veins bulging from his sturdy neck. Political ink and serious scars on his arms. About the same age as me, he was the end result for a man embracing the prison gangs.

'Thanks, dawg. I'm Shaun from England.' I volunteered my country of origin to reveal I was different from them but not different for any of the reasons that get you smashed.

'I'm Bullet, the head of the whites.' He offered me his fist to bump. 'Where you roll in from, wood?'

'Towers, dawg.' The bond story had mollified the skinheads who'd smashed David. It was time to use it again. 'They increased my bond and reclassed me to max.'

'What's your bond at?' The skinheads at Towers seemed less threatening than Bullet.

'I've got two $750,000 bonds,' I said in a monotone. This was no place to brag about bonds.

'How many people you kill, br-r-rother?' He pronounced the R as if he were Tony the Tiger saying, 'They're gr-r-reat!' His eyes drilled into mine, trying to determine whether my body language lent credence to my story. I knew my body language so far was spot on.

'None. I threw raves. They got us talking about drugs on wiretaps.' Discussing drugs on the phone did not warrant a $1.5 million bond, I knew, and beat him to his next question. 'Here's my charges.' I pulled out the sheet I'd kept handy in my shirt pocket.

Bullet took the paper. Scrutinised it. Attempting to pre-empt his verdict, the other whites studied his face. On edge, I waited for him to respond. Whatever he said next would determine whether I would be accepted or victimised by them.

'Are you some kind of jailhouse attorney?' Bullet asked. 'I want someone to read through my case paperwork.' During our few minutes of conversation, Bullet had seen through my act and concluded I was an educated man – a possible resource to him.

I appreciated his quid pro quo. He would accept me if I took the time to read his case. 'I'm no jailhouse attorney, but I'll look through it and help you however I can.'

'Good. I'll stop by your cell later on, dawg.'

After breakfast, I sealed as many of the cracks in the walls as I could with toothpaste. The cell smelled minty. But the cockroaches still found their way in. Their day shift was gathering information on the brown paper bags storing my commissary. Bags I'd tied off with old rubber bands I'd squirrelled away. Relentlessly, the cockroaches explored the bags for entry points, pausing over and probing the most worn and vulnerable regions. I read all morning, wondering if my cellmate were dead in his cocoon, his occasional breathing sounds reassuring me.

Bullet stopped by late afternoon and dropped his case paperwork off. He'd been charged with Class 3 felonies and less – not serious crimes, but he was facing a double-digit sentence because of his prior convictions and Security Threat Group status in the prison system. The proposed sentencing range seemed disproportionate, so I decided to advise him to reject the plea bargain – on the assumption he already knew to do so but was just seeking the comfort of a second opinion, as so many unsentenced inmates did. When he returned for his paperwork, our conversation disturbed my sleeping cellmate – the white cocoon was shuffling – so we went upstairs to his cell. I told him what I thought. He was excitable, a different man from earlier. His pupils were almost pinheads, as if he were lit up on heroin.

'This case ain't shit, dawg. But my prosecutor knows I done other shit, heavy shit, all kinds of heavy shit, but can't prove it. I'd do anything to get that sorry bitch off my fucking ass. She's asking for something bad to happen to her. Man, if I was ever bonded out, I'd chop the bitch into pieces. Kill her slowly, though, first. Like to work her over with a blowtorch.'

Such talk could get us both charged with conspiring to murder a prosecutor, so I tried to steer him elsewhere. 'It's crazy how they can catch you doing one thing yet try to sentence you for all of the things they think you've ever done. They didn't catch me doing much–'

'Done plenty. Shot some dude in the stomach once. Rolled his body up in a blanket and threw him in a dumpster.'

I found the subject of his past murders as unsettling as his future ones. 'So what's all your tats mean anyway, Bullet? Like that eagle on your chest?'

'Why you wanna know?' Bullet's eyes probed mine.

My eyes held their ground. 'Just curious. I've never been to prison.'

'It's a war bird. The AB patch.'

'AB patch?' I asked.

'What the Aryan Brotherhood gives you when you've put enough work in.'

'How long does it take to earn a patch?'

'Depends how quickly you put your work in. You have to earn your lightning bolts first.'

'Why you got red and black lightning bolts?'

'You get SS bolts for beating someone down or being an enforcer for the family. Red lightning bolts for killing someone. I was sent down as a youngster. They gave me steel and told me who to handle, and I handled it. You don't ask questions. You just get blood on your steel. Dudes who get these tats without putting work in are told to cover it up or leave the yard.'

'What if they refuse?'

'They're held down, and we carve the ink off them.'

Imagining them carving a chunk of flesh to remove the tattoo, I cringed. He was really enjoying telling me this now, and I was thinking he'd accepted me too much. That he was trying to impress me before making demands. His presence made me uneasy. I was beginning to understand his volatile nature and that frightened me.

I was unable to sleep properly that night. Cocooned in heat, surrounded by cockroaches, I listened to the swamp cooler hissing out tepid air. I gave up on sleep and put my earphones on. I tuned into classical music on National Public Radio. Relaxing into a Vivaldi violin concerto, I closed my eyes and pressed my tailbone down to straighten my back as if I were doing a yogic meditation. The playful allegro thrilled me, lifting my battered spirits, but the wistful adagio brought sad emotions to the surface, and I finally cried.

27

....

A giant Bosnian guard deposited me in a visitation cubicle – a bare room, two plastic seats, a small table – assigned for legal visits.

'How're you doing?' Alan Simpson shook my hand, jangling my handcuffs. He wasn't smiling today.

'Not very well,' I said, and sat down.

Shocked to see my eye partially closed due to an infection, he shook his head.

'Pink eye. Cockroaches from hell. New charges. Doubled bond. I don't know where to begin. You said the case would take a year. Well, it's been a year! And it's deteriorating. What the bloody hell's going on?' I'd never raised my voice at him like that before. Mentally, I was at an all-time low and needed to vent.

Taken aback, he said, 'What's going on is this.' He slapped down some papers. 'Take a look at your new grand jury indictment real quick and tell me who you think the other two co-defendants are. Their names are crossed out.'

I read the few pages. 'It says I'm charged jointly with one of the co-defendants for possessing some prescription pills on 16 May 2002, so that can only mean Claudia. Holy shit! They've indicted Claudia! Does this mean they'll arrest her?' I asked, panicking at the prospect of her ending up in Arpaio's jail. On the day of the raid, the police had found two prescription pills in my medicine cabinet. I'd had them for so long, I was unable to remember what they were for. The find had not resulted in any charges a year ago, and I had never expected it would.

'I doubt she'll be arrested. I'll try to get her indicted by mail. What about the other person?'

'It says I used her name to deposit checks in a stockbrokerage account at E*TRADE. That can only be my ex-wife in Tucson, Amy.'

'Are you sure?'

'That's my best guess. How can they suddenly indict these people after a year?'

'These charges were prepared before your bond hearing.'

'So I could have been rearrested if I'd bonded out?'

'Exactly.'

'Isn't it illegal to punish someone for having a bond hearing?'

'Yes.'

'Anything we can do about that?'

'Not really. We can't prove these charges were brought up as a response to the bond hearing. They'll just say these things were discovered during the ongoing investigation. Besides, the judge has denied the bond reduction anyway.'

'Unbelievable!' I felt the legal system closing in on me from all sides. 'But those few prescription pills were found on day one. Claudia has nothing to do with them. How can they stick them on her like this?'

'They haven't found what they've been looking for in the past year, so they've resorted to measures like this. If you're right, and Claudia is indeed your co-defendant, then they're likely to stop her from visiting you. Co-defendants cannot visit co-defendants.'

My face flushed with anger. Had the prosecutor indicted Claudia to stop her visits, to sever my lifeline? It made sense. It wasn't about Claudia; it was about breaking me down. How could I tell Claudia?

'When is my case ever going to be resolved?' I asked brusquely.

'I don't know. Let me call the AG's office and find out what's going on. Give me a call towards the end of the week.' He zipped his briefcase.

Yearning for reassurance, I resented his eagerness to leave. 'I don't know how much longer I can take this for.'

'Just hang in there. Remember to call my office,' Alan said. Drops of sweat were glistening on his forehead. We shook hands, and he was gone.

May 2003

Claudia love,

I am so sorry I called you this morning and I was too upset to talk. I shouldn't have called you immediately after calling my parents. I didn't want the inmates to see I was upset in here. I was beginning to cry and didn't want to break down in front of people. It was so hard to listen to my dad's upset voice and tell him the news of my move and the loss of your visits. Karen didn't even speak. She was flabbergasted. It is torture to hear my parents get distressed about my situation. It seems unending the agony everyone is going through.

I am OK, love, but I'm suffering mentally. I was seeing roaches that weren't there, and I heard voices again like when I first got to Towers. Don't tell anyone. I didn't want to say anything on the phone because if they find out here they strap you into the torture chair for six hours 'for your own protection'. I probably just need a few nights of good sleep. If I didn't have you keeping me sane, I would have lost my mind by now. I have a goal that's getting me through this. It is to wake up every day safely and to open my eyes and to see you.

It's tricky here having commissary, saying no to people. I did break some bread, but I finally said enough is enough, and I got called a 'Jew'. I haven't even got my stereo on display except on lockdown. I tell people who ask me that I don't even have one. These people are a lot tougher than at Towers.

I called the embassy, and then I got nervous and hung up. I need to calm down before I call them again. I'm losing my mind. Maybe I should just tell the Medical here about my mental health. I should request meds, Valium or something. What do you think? I don't know what to do. There is nothing I can do. They want to destroy me and take my life away. I'm a first-time offender. This is insane. I am so confused, love. I fear I'll have a nervous breakdown. I miss your visits, and it's really upsetting me. I can't imagine how you are feeling. I think I'd better go look at your pictures again.

I just looked at your pictures. You seem so far away. It's like you are a dream and I am in hell.

This is certainly a creepy place. It's a different form of torture here. The roaches, the open shower and toilet, it's much creepier than Towers. When I went to the shower this morning, roaches were just running wild all over the day-room floor. I've never seen so many. It's obscene! I can't toothpaste-seal the whole pod, and they just come straight in from the day room under my door. It's tricky when you're trying to sleep and they are running across the walls inches away from your head. There's a strange scratching noise at nights in the walls as well. I suspect it's rats or mice. There is nowhere to hang my towels and undies to dry. I have no extra blanket to do yoga with. At nights, they turn the lights on at weird hours during the walks. On the latest walk, they came in and checked if my light or vent had been loosened. At least if the experience and suffering of Towers actually did me some good, then this will probably do the same. That's my positive outlook on the situation.

My celly is quiet. He has slept constantly. Who knows what ails him?

I told the fellas at the chow table about the rat parts in the red death at Towers. They responded with, 'Oh, we'd just eat 'em.'

'Chew 'em right up.'

Not the responses I expected. They get much less bread with dinner here, I noticed.

Thanks for the photos, love. You look as beautiful and radiant as ever.

Love,

Shaun XXX

Dear Mum, Dad and Karen,

I hope everyone is doing good despite the bad news on the bond hearing. It was rather disappointing after it was presented so well in court. Alan said I may be here up to a year longer now while they try to gather evidence against me and find witnesses. I've already done a one-year sentence, so another shouldn't be a problem.

I've been here so long I have a better understanding of the legal system. I feel the judge was told not to drop the bond during the advisement period. Time after time I've seen him drop bonds for people with more charges than me, with higher bonds than me and from foreign countries. The whole thing is being dragged out so that witnesses can be paid off and deals struck to testify against me in court. I have a trial date, but I expect if they have no witnesses it will just be postponed. The Black case, a conspiracy wiretap case tried by my prosecutor's boss, was postponed continuously for three years until nine witnesses were found, and then they were all successfully prosecuted, and the leaders got sentenced to decades. If Alan's motions are unable to get the case kicked out, I will ultimately have to plead guilty to whatever they want and accept the punishment. The amount of money they spent on the investigation is flabbergasting, and they must be vindicated at the end of the day. There's still hope. I don't think Alan Simpson will do much worse than getting me five years. If my jail time amounts to 2+ years by the time they're done, I'll be halfway through that scenario. I have one of the best legal minds in town on my side, so it is still quite possible that things will end not too bad. Maybe prison is something I need to go through to make me grow up.

Since I've been locked up, I have seen an increase in the jail population from my number, 815,706, to 910,000. This means that the state of Arizona alone has arrested almost 100,000 people from a population of less than 2 million. They've locked so many people up that they've started sending inmates to Texas. But a riot by the Arizona inmates in Texas last month put a halt on that. The people running the prisons are crying out for more money from the federal government or else 'murderers will go free and the streets won't be safe', when really, from what I've seen, the prisons are being packed with mostly petty drug offenders. That's how the system stays in business. Enough said.

Love,

Shaun

Dear Karen,

My current conditions will provide good storytelling material. I get to kill roaches all day in between listening to one of my new murderer friends tell me whose fingers and toes he's going to chop off and exactly why. He sounds convincing and doesn't flinch as he vividly describes his future plans to me. Why me? Why does everyone want to tell me their life stories? I would rather be in a cell on my own, but then I wouldn't be helping my fellow men like a true yogi is supposed to do.

There are a lot of Aryan Brothers in maximum security. I've questioned them (politely) about their beliefs. Alan's Mexican Mafia clients are a few floors above me. They are all charged with murders for hire, lots of murders, including police officers, public officials and witnesses.

Yep, it's quite a creepy place here. My visits with Ann are through plastic screens with phones. Rather like when Hannibal Lecter first met Clarice.

There's a vivid assortment of characters. Violent offenders and repeat-offender drug criminals. There are a few chemists (methamphetamine) and an individual whose victim apparently lost her spleen. Most of them have done 10+ years already. I have no access to the outdoors any more. I've spent a fortune on toothpaste sealing cracks where the roaches get in.

So what do you think of the new charges and the dragging of Claudia unnecessarily into the mix? Don't you think it is beyond a joke now?

Love,

Shaun

28

··········

My cellmate, Joe, stayed cocooned in a white sheet for almost a month.
He'd been going through a terrible drug withdrawal that prevented him
from talking to anyone. He only got up to allow food and fluids in
and out. During his journeys to the toilet, he generally acknowledged
me with his eyes – big, hazel and bloodshot – and if I were lucky, I
might get a grunt out of him. Other than missing a front tooth, he
had the handsome look of Barry Gibb during the heyday of the Bee
Gees. I amused myself by imagining him singing 'Staying Alive' in a
high-pitched voice. He was beyond the ideal quiet cellmate. It was like
living with a corpse, and I made the most of the uninterrupted reading.
Another advantage of his condition was it prevented the mooches from
staying too long in our cell. The inmate code required not disturbing
sleeping prisoners. Junkies trying to get commissary to buy a hit of
heroin were constantly doing the rounds. Whenever one pushed our
door open and popped his head in, I'd simply point at Joe asleep above
me. It worked fast. The junkie would act ill at ease, as if afflicted by
sorcery, and move on to his next victim.

The day finally came when Joe didn't return to his cocoon after
breakfast. He finished his sandwiches and said, 'I gotta catch up on my
workouts.' He gave me a parting nod and did lengthy sets of push-ups,
tricep dips and squats in the day room. The prisoners didn't mess with
him, and I was glad to see them show him respect. The more people he
got along with, the less chance of violence spilling into our cell.

Resting on his bunk after working out, Joe turned to me. 'Did you
hear about the attempted escape?'

'Escape!' I said, sitting on the stool. Escaping from maximum security
seemed impossible.

'Right before you got here, they rolled the whole pod up for trying
to escape.'

'This pod?'

'Yup. They were digging the window frame out. Trying to pull the
window out. But they fucked up. As soon as they got so far, they started
bringing in bottles of whiskey, cell phones and drugs.'

'How?'

'They made a big rope with sheets and lowered it down to the street level so they could fish-in their contraband. Trust dope fiends to fuck up their own escape attempt. Bringing in all that shit got them busted.'

That the prisoners had chosen drugs over freedom didn't surprise me. I told Joe about my drug charges and mounting legal problems so he would know I didn't have the types of crimes that invite trouble.

'Man, they're going after you hardcore,' Joe said. 'I hope for your sake you have a good paid attorney.'

'Alan Simpson.'

'I've heard of him,' Joe said, nodding. 'When I was 21, I got busted by the Organised Crime Bureau. I took it to trial and beat it.'

'How much time were you facing?' I asked, amazed to hear someone had actually gone to trial and won.

'Ten years. It wasn't so much time 'cause it was so long ago.'

'Hope you don't mind me asking,' I said politely. 'What're you in for?'

'Manufacturing methamphetamine. Possession of equipment and chemicals for manufacturing dangerous drugs. Possession of dangerous drugs. Possession of a weapon in a drug offence.'

'How much time you looking at?'

'Twenty years.'

Shocked, I guessed why. 'Because of your priors?'

'Yeah.'

'How did you get busted?'

'After we got done cooking up the meth – I did the cook in a partner of mine's house, Outcast – me, my buddy Jim and his girlfriend Laura were sitting around, and Jim tells me, "You know Outcast got busted in this house three days ago. The SWAT team had to extract him outta this house, and he got busted for prohibited possessor of a firearm and drug paraphernalia." I said, "I had no idea that happened otherwise I would never have done the cook here. Call up Outcast. He shoulda told me he got busted. I wanna talk to him face to face." So Jim calls up Outcast, and Outcast says he's too busy to come over. Jim hangs up, and Jim and I know something's wrong. I got a bad feeling about getting busted. So we split up the meth lab and the finished product. Jim's gonna take the finished product in one car, and I'm gonna take the lab, so we don't get busted with everything. It kind of worked. I got busted, and Jim got away. The police did a felony stop on me. They found a meth lab, a gun in my trunk and a little bit – an eight ball – of finished product.'

'So you done with drugs now?'

'Look at the hell I just went through since getting arrested coming down off meth. Getting high's a sucker's game. They're building prisons all over America for people like you and me. We're the ones keeping these bastards in business. And even if the cops don't get you, the dope will get you in the long run. One way or another, it'll catch up with you. Guaranteed. See my foot.' He dangled his foot off the bunk. It had massive scars. 'The day I got my foot shot off, I shoulda been killed.'

'Your foot was shot off?'

'Yup.'

'I've got to hear this one.'

'Here's what went down. I was on a payphone, and my dope-cooking partner, Spike, was in the car. I'm decked out – Italian designer suit, gold chains, the whole nine yards – and some youngster asks me if I wanna buy some dope. The kid won't go away, so I figure I'll teach him a lesson. I say, "Yeah, I'll buy some dope. Get me two pounds of meth." The kid says, "No problem," and asks me to meet him at some street corner later on. We pick up a .45 to rob the kid with and go to the spot. The kid shows up with his girlfriend and a car full of Mexicans. I discuss the price with the head Mexican. It's a good price, so I tell Spike it's not good robbery potential, but the guys look legit and it may be worth actually purchasing the meth. He agrees, so I go back to the Mexicans to discuss the details. The head Mexican pulls out a duffel bag full of half-pounds of meth cling-wrapped. I unwrap one of them, spilling some on their car. This irritates the head Mexican, so I open the door, so if any more spills, it spills outside. I put both of my feet out of the car onto the asphalt. Meanwhile, Spike – high on meth and paranoid after robbing some Mexican dealers for cash – figured I was being kidnapped by the Mexicans and trying to get out of their car. I'm just calmly doing business with them, and he leaps in front of the car and opens up with the .45, hitting none of them but blasting my foot. I try to run but fall 'cause my foot's hanging off. The Mexicans start unloading their guns on Spike, who goes down. I'm trying to get away to get to the donut shop to get rid of the ephedrine I've got on me. I'm crawling away, and I see the head Mexican walk up to Spike, take aim at his spine and fire point-blank. He then put the half-pound of meth I'd opened into Spike's top pocket. He walks back to the car, sees the trail of blood I've left crawling away and starts to follow it. I'm thinking my number's up. There's no way I can get away from him. By now, people are gathering, and the car full of Mexicans motion to the head guy that they're leaving. The head Mexican's halfway to me. He stops walking, looks at me, looks at the car, pauses like he's deciding what to do, then heads back to the car.'

'Man, you're bloody lucky! I can't imagine being in a situation like that. Did the cops bust you with the ephedrine?'

'No. I booked into a hospital under an alias. They put plates and screws into my calf and foot. I escaped from the hospital and took out the screws with a power drill.'

'Ouch! What about Spike?'

'He survived, but he's a quadriplegic now. Lives in a wheelchair with a colostomy bag. After hospital, I went right back to doing dope. How fucked up is that? And now I'm looking at another 20 years.'

I saw parallels: we'd both devastated our lives by choosing to do drugs and making one bad decision after another. Joe revealed he'd booked into the jail as a Sikh to get a vegetarian diet. 'In prison, they used to make us go to Sikh classes and chant and meditate in order to get the Sikh diet. When I see you doing your yoga and meditation, you remind me of that.'

'I'm down as a Hindu.'

'The things we do to avoid red death.'

'I am really into yoga, though. But the jail won't recognise yoga as a religion. I've been getting more into meditation lately. I'm doing it every day.'

'Meditation is powerful stuff. Nelson Mandela told Winnie to do 15 minutes a night when she was in prison. And look at the positive brainwave changes they've recorded in Buddhist monks during meditation. I just meditate lying down.'

In the weeks that followed, Joe and I grew close. He schooled me on prison etiquette, and I came to trust him in a brotherly way. We shared and discussed self-help books. Surrounded by maniacs, I felt blessed to have a cellmate focused on improving himself.

Some of the whites resented Joe and me minding our own business. They made a sport of spilling the drama of the day room into our cell. We'd humour them, and when they were gone, we'd laugh and chant *Ommmm* . . . Unable to get a rise out of us, they resorted to intimidation.

Larry, a torpedo for the Aryans, swaggered into our cell. I stopped writing at the table, and Joe put his book down on his bunk.

'Check this out, me and a couple of the guys just cleaned up the pod for you. It's your clean-up day.' Waiting for our reaction, he stood tall, lean, topless, tattooed from the neck down.

I wanted to point out that it wasn't our clean-up day, but I had a hunch Larry disliked me and would be more inclined to listen to Joe.

Nettled by the interruption to his reading, Joe dangled his legs off the bunk and sat bolt upright. 'Check this out, dude. Number one: it's not our clean-up day. Number two: you can take that shit down the run to somebody who's gonna listen to you who cares.'

'What?' Larry shrieked. 'We'll see about that!' He shot out of our cell.

I looked at Joe for guidance.

'Get on your bunk, celly,' Joe said, implying danger.

My heartbeat accelerated. 'What do you think's going to happen?' I asked.

'He can't fight his own battles,' Joe said in a low voice. 'So he's gonna—'

Larry rushed in with two Aryans: Bullet and Ace. Ace was 50-something, an old boxer long past his sell-by date. He had a broad face, pocked and scarred, and a crushed nose. He had unnaturally white skin, as if he'd spent most of his life in cells deprived of sunlight. He had severe diabetes, and decades of drug use had not been kind to his health. He shuffled into our cell with the gait of a cripple and tried to intimidate Joe with a voice so gravelly it made me wince. 'Hey, Joe, you need to apologise to Larry for disrespecting him.'

Bullet just stood there like Ace's goon, as if ready to pounce on Joe or me if one of us said the wrong thing.

'I'm not gonna apologise to anybody 'cause I didn't disrespect anybody,' Joe said. 'In fact, Larry disrespected me.'

'Between all three of us,' Ace said, taking stock of his comrades, 'we've got seventy-five years in the prison system. Larry told me that you told him to take that shit down the run to someone who cares – and we're the ones down the run who care! So you need to fucking apologise to Larry!'

Out of all of my cellmates, I trusted Joe the most. He had an indescribable quality – some kind of inner peace – that I warmed to. I felt safe living with him, and I knew he'd spring to my defence if anyone threatened me. Recent events had elevated my tension. My new indictment. My failure to get bonded out. The move from Towers jail. The meeting with my attorney. Claudia losing her visits. The last thing I needed was three lunatics in my cell venting on Joe, who'd done nothing wrong. The sense of injustice I felt made me snap. So far in the jail, I hadn't sunk down to the level of violence that was the norm. I was using jail as a learning experience. I didn't want to go to lockdown for fighting or to affect my case with bad behaviour. But the more I listened to them, the angrier I grew. The situation seemed to be heading for violence anyway, so I began calculating our chances of winning a fight. Joe had been doing 500 push-ups a day and looked stronger than the three of them, except for perhaps Bullet with his powerful build. Ace was all bluster and could easily be shoved to the ground. Larry lacked build but could move fast: a reasonable match for me. If a fight broke out, Ace would be on the floor gasping for an inhaler, leaving Joe fighting Bullet, and me Larry. Two other reasons were pushing me in this direction. I wanted to show Joe I'd stand up for him, and I wanted to show them they couldn't bulldog us. I had something to say, and I knew as soon as I opened my mouth I was committed to a certain course of action. I would have to back my words up physically if it came down to it.

Taking them by surprise, I spoke up from the bottom bunk. 'Hold on a minute. Larry came charging in here saying it was our clean-up day when it's not even our clean-up day. Whoever told Larry it's our clean-up day has caused this trouble, and I think that person needs to be dealt with.'

Ace's face puckered as if a cockroach had crawled into his mouth. They recoiled in shock for a few seconds, as if they couldn't believe I'd dared to speak up.

'You need to keep the fuck out of it,' Bullet said, slanting towards me, dangling his fists at the height of my head.

But there was no stopping me now. Intoxicated by my own audacity, I pressed on. 'Whoever told Larry it's our clean-up day needs to be dealt with, not Joe. We were just in here minding our own business before all this drama came into our cell.'

'You're really starting to piss me off,' Ace said, his head trembling as if an alarm clock were going off inside it.

'Keep your fucking mouth shut,' Bullet said, thinning his lips. 'You've got nothing to do with this.'

'Yeah, I do! Joe's my celly, and what's going on here is wrong. I know you guys would back your cellies up if you felt the same way,' I said, citing their own code.

Bullet crouched near enough to thump me and raised his eyebrows. Staring back, I could tell from the way he was looking at me that he was after Joe, not me.

Addressing Joe and me as a common enemy, the other two yelled: 'Who the fuck you think you two are?'

'You fucking guys know it's your fucking clean-up day!'

'What're you fucking thinking, going disrespecting Larry like that?'

'You need to fucking apologise!'

They were working themselves up to do us harm.

'But it's not our clean-up day!' I yelled. 'Whoever told Larry it was our clean-up day has caused all of this!'

'Shut the fuck up, England!' Bullet yelled.

'That person needs to apologise!' I said, about to spring up.

'I won't tell you again!' Bullet yelled.

Just when it seemed they were about to pounce on us, Joe said, 'Look, there was a misunderstanding. I apologise, Larry.'

The apology stunned them. They gawked at each other, not knowing what to do.

The atmosphere in the room remained combustible until Larry said, 'All right, fellas. Let's go.' He led them out.

As Bullet left, he turned and shot Joe a look that said, *I'll get you one of these days.*

When they were out of earshot, Joe rested his back against the cement-block wall, and crossed his legs. 'Bullet and Larry can fight, but that loudmouth Ace ain't shit. My partner, Otis, shot him one time in a car.'

'Shot him! How come?' I wiped the sweat off my brow with my hand.

'Ace was in the back seat. Otis was in the passenger seat. My buddy, Mike, was driving. Ace says to Otis, "Well, don't you know who the fuck I am?" Otis says, "Man, why don't you just shut the fuck up," grabs Mike's .38, and points it back to the back seat at Ace's leg. Mike tells Otis, "Don't ever point a gun at someone if you're not gonna shoot them." So Otis shot Ace in the knee. Ace screamed like a little girl and said, "Take me to the hospital." Otis said, "Fuck this dude. Take me to go get my stolen car." Mike tripped out, kicked Otis out and took Ace to a hospital.'

* * *

The next morning, I was on my bunk reading the *Financial Times* when Bullet stopped outside of the cell.

'Can you trade this stamp for an envelope?' he yelled through the oblong gaps in the door.

'I don't need a stamp, Bullet. But I'll give you an envelope for a milk.' A milk was considered a fair price for a stamp or an envelope.

'Keep your fucking envelope! Take my state milk from me! Motherfucker!' He punched the door and walked away ranting. He'd left without an opportunity for me to calm him down or to negotiate a different trade. I spent the rest of the day braced for his return. But he never came.

June 2003

Dear Mum, Dad and Karen,

Thanks for the books. I read the Paul Fleischman one and I'm halfway through *Meditation Now* by Goenka. I like the idea of getting to the root of our problems in the mind. I have been chipping away at stuff with yoga and it has benefited me. Getting rid of the worry voice is my problem. No matter what I do it creeps in with what-ifs. What if they hold me for years? What if they send me to prison? What if I lose at trial? What if the judge has taken a dislike to me and gives me ten years or more?

Before my arrest, I never really analysed my mind and compartmentalised it. I never had the need. I'm sure slight worries came in, but I was relatively happy-go-lucky. My yoga meditation helps me push worrying thoughts away. But recent traumatic experiences strengthened the worry voice. It constantly creeps up through the day no matter what I am doing. When I am reading, I absorb some paragraphs and then suddenly I'll find I just read the last few sentences and I can't even remember them as I am now focused on a worry.

I am living as Godly as possible and applying all the yoga yamas (five moral restraints) and niyamas (five observances), and I'm trying to minimise the five afflictions (spiritual ignorance, pride, desire, aversion and fear of death). I apply yoga breathing throughout the day, and sometimes visualisation. I've done quite a lot to fight stress. More than most people. I can't imagine how I would be coping without yoga and spirituality.

To indict Claudia to sabotage my visits is to torture me further. What manner of justice is this? I've led a raving lifestyle and I can understand that I must suffer for my sins, but to charge Claudia, who has done absolutely nothing wrong, clearly illustrates that this is a far cry from any normal process of justice. Thomas More the judge said that the justice system should be tempered with mercy and not be all about punishment. Inmates keep coming and going and some even going and coming back, but I just remain here, month after month.

See how easy it is to get back to negativity and worry. I switched from the wonders of meditation to my usual worry, my grim situation. If only I had a technique to address the constant surfacing of garbage in my mind. I must try to feel no anger or resentment to those torturing me. I pray for their ways to be amended. It is negative thoughts about what is going to happen to me that are drowning me. Where do these thoughts come from? Goenka says they come from very deep down.

Love,

Shaun XXX

Dear Mum, Dad and Karen,

Thank you very much for the book *Please Understand Me II*. Oddly enough, it caused a chain reaction with the inmates, and I'm now everybody's resident psychological test analyst. The inmates observed me on the phone asking Claudia the test questions and started prying into what I was up to. So now they're lining up requesting I do the test for them and help them analyse the test results for their loved ones. I already did two alleged murderers today. One came out as the performer ESFP and the other as the champion ENFP. So many people are asking me to do the test with them that I'm exhausted and having to schedule them for later in the week. This book has caused quite a ripple in the pod.

I'm sure you have all done these tests before, so I am anxious as to what results you all obtained.

I find psychology fascinating, and I'm very grateful for the book. It has helped me interrelate with people, to understand people and to help remove some of my misconceptions, especially about the alleged murderers. This must be a criminal psychologist's dream to have such candidates approaching me (a non-authority figure therefore guaranteed honesty on their answers), demanding I do these tests on them. This must remove inaccuracy, as inmates boast about lying to their doctors all the time in here; maybe I should keep the results.

Anyway, it's enabled me to learn a lot and have some fun. As I write this, I'm watching one alleged murderer tell another inmate (of unknown criminal origin) about the test, waving his test results in his face. Maybe you should contact a professor and tell him/her about the existence of such raw data.

Madison houses the courts, so they wake you up at 5 a.m. here for court, and they immediately bring you back when you are finished. This will make all the difference in the world IF it goes to trial, from turning me into a sleep-deprived nervous wreck into actually being able to rest.

It's still 'nuthin' nice' here. I feel like I am being slowly cooked alive by constant unbearable heat. It's quieter, though, and more conducive to yoga, studies and book-writing.

It's terrible what they have done to Claudia and clearly illustrates what they will do to destroy me.

Thanks v. much for the books, love, support etc.

Love,

Shaun

Dear Mum, Dad and Kags,

Ann and Donny came in earlier today, and that visit went well. I'm glad that you got my email about all the unnecessary civil-rights violations. I'm not asking for freedom, I'm just asking for a prompt resolution to the case.

I started month six in yoga today. It takes about one and a half hours. I think I'm getting very flexible, because during the back body stretch I previously strained to touch my toes whereas now I can touch over them to the middle of my feet, legs not bent, for a few minutes. It's nice to feel the advancements. New exercises this month include the bridge and the tree. It's hard to do the tree with one's eyes closed.

Recent conversations with the fellas here include how one inmate decided to remove someone from his house. He shot him in the arm, removing it, then proceeded to kick him out of his house while the guy was bleeding profusely from the stump. He then called his friend and said, 'I shot X.' The friend asked, 'Is he alive?' He replied, 'Sure he is, I just kicked him out of the house.'

I've got to see massive scars from various biker accidents and to hear tales pertaining to biker accidents and shootings. An Aryan Brother showed us a 12-inch scar covering his calf muscle and described a biker accident after which he found his leg stuck over his shoulder with his calf hanging over his face. He was completely unable to move, stuck watching the contents of his calf dribble out.

Love everyone,

Shaun xxxx

Mum, Dad and Karabus,

It was nice to speak to D and K today. Sorry I missed you, Mum. Happy Birthday and Anniversary and stuff! I'm glad you got the card.

People from prison state that county jail time is the hardest time to do, so I'm through the worst. I'm over the shock, pain barrier, etc. and I've adapted to my new surroundings. No worries!

It's quieter here, so I can concentrate on writing. In the psychology book it said my type is good at writing fiction books. With all the stories I am hearing, I will write a book revolving around criminals, crime, etc. Maybe I can write pulp fiction.

Claudia has sent me tons of pics from her stay in England. I'm well pleased that she had such a good time. I've got pics of everyone in here now, including Nan, Sue, Karen, friends, etc. I look at them most nights before I go to bed. You seem planets away, but I know eventually, hopefully soon, I'll be home celebrating with everyone.

I've been reading quotes from Gandhi (when he was a lawyer) about the purpose of the legal system. Gandhi said it should be used to change men's hearts. My heart is most certainly in the right place now. I hope I get a positive break in the next few months.

Yoga month six is going good. I pulled some hand exercises from future months into the mix that include the tripod. I can only do the tripod for about one minute.

Claudia is such a love, and she has kept me in the best of moods regardless of what has happened. If I can survive this, I'll be able to survive anything for the rest of my life.

Thanks for all the books, love, continued support.

Love,

Shaun

29

....

'Get the fuck out of our room with all that hair on you!' Joe said to Bullet, who'd just come from the inmate barber. 'I've just finished cleaning the room.'

'Check this out, motherfucker, I'll kick you out of your own fucking room!' Bullet said. 'You don't ever tell me that!'

Larry strutted in behind Bullet.

'Well, get to kicking then, you bad motherfucker,' Joe said.

'I'll be right back, 'cause I'm gonna put on my tennies.' Bullet left.

'Shaun, Larry, you fellas mind stepping outside while I handle my business?' Joe said. For one-on-one disputes, the routine was for everyone to leave the cell so the two men could fight.

I brushed past Larry hovering in the doorway. 'C'mon, Larry,' I said, not wanting him to remain near enough to intervene on Bullet's behalf. 'If you stand there, the guards will wonder what's going on.' Reluctantly, he followed me to the nearest table in the day room. We were about ten feet from the cell door, almost ringside for the fight, which we could watch through the oblong gaps.

When Bullet returned, Larry said, 'Hey, Bullet, it ain't worth going to the hole over. Forget it.'

'Shut the fuck up!' Bullet snarled.

Joe and Bullet squared off. Gazes locked.

'You shouldn't have disrespected me like that,' Joe said, shuffling forward.

'You ain't telling me what to do, motherfucker,' Bullet said.

'You'll feel differently in about 30 seconds,' Joe said. 'I'm about to teach you to respect me.'

Shuffling from side to side like heavyweights, they probed each other with jabs. Bullet feinted a jab and walloped Joe's ear with a right hook. Joe stumbled and only just yanked his pelvis back in time to dodge a kick. But he leaned forward, exposing his head. Bullet punched Joe in the temple. The inner peace always shining in Joe's big hazel eyes disappeared – replaced by fierce concentration. Joe shook the pain from his head and let loose a series of jabs as if swatting a fly. But Bullet dodged the jabs, dropped into a crouch and tried to grab Joe. A kick to the hip propelled Bullet backwards, and he snagged his leg against the toilet, losing his balance. Joe moved in with a perfectly timed punch to the jaw that sent Bullet against the wall. Bullet's legs went out, and he clanged the steel toilet as he fell. Larry shot into the room, and I followed. Blood was trickling from Bullet's mouth.

Larry urged Bullet to get up. 'Let's get back to your cell before the guard walks.' Larry locked his elbows under Bullet's armpits and forklifted him onto his feet. They walked out unsteadily.

I could barely contain myself. 'That was fucking brilliant! I thought he had you, but you turned it around just like that,' I said, clicking my fingers. 'Where'd you learn to fight like that?'

'It was nothing,' Joe said, panting. 'Two grown men trying to hurt each other over dumb shit.'

'So what'll happen now? Does this make you the head of the whites?'

'Nah. I ain't into all that. I earned a reputation in prison as an independent. That's why most of the guys in here know not to fuck with me.' Joe splashed water on his face, took a few big breaths and rested on his bunk.

'What's an independent?' I asked, taking the stool.

'A guy who keeps himself to himself, but'll throw down if disrespected.'

'So how come Bullet messed with you?'

'Bad chemistry. I've never liked that dude since he's been coming in here asking you about his case while I was trying to sleep. He thinks he's something he's not. That's usually the case when someone's always running their mouth, acting tough.'

'Will he still have an issue with you after this?'

'The fight should squash the beef. He knows better than to come back with a shank.'

'I hope so.' Swelling with pride for Joe, questions poured out of me that I'd been dying to ask. 'What's your deal with the Aryan Brotherhood? It's like some of these guys are itching to fight you, but they're wary of you at the same time.'

'I do a few things on the streets to make money. The Aryan Brotherhood knows about these things and think they're entitled to a part of my action. But here's the rule: if I was doing something on the yard to make money, then, yes, they would be entitled to 25 per cent of the action, but since my action is done all on the streets, they got no stake to claim. So yeah, they get a little upset, but those are the rules. They respect me 'cause I've always stood my ground and don't let nobody punk me out. That's why they're wary of me: they know I play for keeps just like they do. I know a lot of them inside and on the streets, and they know I don't play no games. I know the guy who schooled the Aryan Brotherhood about the Aryan race when the High Wall Jammers changed to the Aryan Brotherhood.'

'High Wall Jammers?'

'I'll explain it to you in a nutshell. Back in the '50s and '60s, the blacks in the Arizona Department of Corrections used to rape vulnerable white guys all the time, so the whites started a prison gang called the High Wall Jammers, and they started killing the blacks that were involved in these rapes. This was all going on in Central Unit, also known as The Walls, and in 1970 the High Wall Jammers changed their name to the Aryan Brotherhood, the gang that started in San Quentin prison back in the '60s and spread across America. I've done almost 20 years, and I've met a lot of gang members: ABs, Mexican Mafia, Warrior Society, Mau Maus, skinheads. There's very little I haven't seen or been through.'

'I bet you've got some good stories.'

'Check this one out. Back in '94, I was at Cimarron Unit in Tucson, serving eight for armed robberies on illegal-alien drug dealers. In Building 1, I knew three Aryan Brotherhood probates: Roy, Henry and Nate. All youngsters.'

'What's a probate?'

'Someone aspiring to join the Aryan Brotherhood who hasn't put enough work in – killing, shanking – to get patched up.'

'OK.'

'There was 800 on the yard. Three hundred whites. Thirteen Aryan Brothers. So, Roy and Nate are stepbrothers. Nate found out his celly was a chomo, and he figured killing a sex offender would help him earn his AB patch. The Brothers didn't give him the green light on the kill. Instead they said, "Beat the crap out of him so he has to roll up from this yard." Roy and Henry kept point at the cell door while Nate punched the chomo in the back of the head two times. The chomo collapsed and died. They decided to put him back on his bunk like he was asleep, cover him up and ride it out. It worked for three days: the guards thought he was asleep. But when he didn't show up for chow, they got suspicious. They lifted the sheet up and found a stinking bloated corpse. They locked the yard down. Someone snitched, and the 13 Aryan Brothers and Henry, Roy and Nate were sent to lockdown pending an investigation. Facing the death penalty, Roy and Henry cut a deal with the prosecutor against Nate. The prosecutor offered Nate a deal: 25 to life. Nate said no and asked for a trial. They put Henry and Roy in protective custody. The rest, they put in supermax, SMU1 in Florence. The trial went ahead and Nate was acquitted. They rehoused him at The Walls, also in Florence. The 13 Aryan Brothers were sent back to Cimarron, and they offered Nate the AB patch for going the distance. Nate said, "Fuck you guys and your patch." So Nate was eating at the chow hall, and he chewed something in his food that turned out to be a hypodermic needle. He got hepatitis C and successfully sued the prison for 200 grand. The Aryan Brotherhood would have killed him, so they put him in protective custody. So the Aryan Brotherhood couldn't get Henry and Roy, they sent them out of state. Youngsters come in thinking it's cool to get in with the gangs, and this is what happens. The gangs just use them and often kill them when they try to quit that lifestyle. It's blood in, blood out.'

30

....

Three out of thirty inmates collapsed from heatstroke in July. An emergency medical team extracted each person. In the day room, we wandered around dizzy, gagging on the hot foul air, clutching our chests, the worried looks on our faces reflecting our struggle to stay alert so as not to be hospitalised next.

On top of the heat, I was lovesick for Claudia. We were both depressed about losing our visits, and she was brooding over her charges. She turned to alcohol. She was difficult to talk to on the phone, as if she were a different person. For the first time, I wondered whether our relationship would survive my incarceration. She also revealed she had a stalker. She hadn't told me previously because she thought I had enough to worry about. Her stalker had read the article about me in the *New Times*. He'd threatened to shoot her and to visit me at the jail. He'd also threatened Claudia's mother, who'd called the police. Claudia was terrified. Trapped inside the jail, I felt helpless to protect her. Initially, I hoped he'd be arrested and end up in the jail with me. But when my anger subsided, I realised Claudia only had a stalker due to the crimes I'd committed. I felt responsible.

The heat and stress made it difficult to sleep, write and concentrate. Then chest pains began, accompanied by a tingling in my extremities. I submitted a request to Medical, not expecting to be seen but to document the condition in case I was hospitalised. The pains usually came on when I was reading. I'd have to put my book down and take deep breaths while clutching my chest until they went away.

Every day, I took multiple showers just to cool down for a few minutes. So did everyone else. The wait for the lone shower stretched to over an hour. Rather than stand in line, we placed our towels and boxers in a row on the metal privacy divide separating the shower area from the day room. Whoever's boxers and towel were at the front went next. With the shower running all of the time, the tiny black flies that lived on the pond of scum and semen took to our towels. A quick belt of the towel against the wall got rid of them. We had one towel each, which we illegally hung out to dry on string ripped from clothing and sheets. But the guards enjoyed pulling our clotheslines down and threatened to ticket us for destroying county property. So our towels never dried. After each shower, I'd dry myself off as much as possible with a half-wet towel. I'd stink afterwards, as my towel used over and never allowed to dry was cultivating a fungus with an offensive mildewy odour. In our pod, the smell of mildew came on slowly at first, blending in with the usual smells. Smoke. Body odour. Bowel movements. Urine. The smell of mop water heavy on bleach. But by the time we were all taking showers every few hours, the mildewy smell dominated. After a few days of everyone complaining, the smell went away. But not really. We were just so used to it, it was less noticeable. I figured this out when I left the pod and returned. Upon re-entering the day room, the smell assaulted me. It faded over the next few days as I reacclimatised to it. After showering and towelling, the smell of my body repulsed me. Multiply that by 30 men and add it to the smell of the drying towels and all of the other smells and you can understand why the guards were reluctant to leave the control tower to do security walks. One guard said we smelled like a health hazard.

Our skin did not take kindly to being treated in this fashion. There was the worst outbreak of skin infections I ever saw in the jail. It looked like chickenpox until the bleeding started. Nearly everyone had it. After dotting my body, it attacked my chest with a cluster of purple-red rashes. It travelled, too. Not so much on my chest but clusters shifted on my limbs, and I'd wake up amazed by their overnight migrations. It itched like crazy. I scratched my limbs constantly but learned not to scratch my chest, as the scabs there detached and bled too much.

'It's just a heat rash. There's nothing we can do about it,' the guards kept telling us, ignoring our demands for cooler air.

Adding to Joe's discomfort was an inguinal hernia extending into his scrotum, trapping fluid in his scrotal pouch. Even though an inmate had died in the past year from a strangulated hernia, the medical staff declined Joe's request for an operation. The condition made Joe urinate every few hours, disrupting his sleep and mine. Whenever the roar of the toilet flushing woke me up, I had to battle the heat and itchy skin to get back to sleep. I'd tell myself, *Don't itch. You'll only make it worse. Give yourself a good scratching when you wake up in the morning.* I actually looked forward to scratching in the morning. The first scratch of the day was always the best.

Joe taught me how to get seen by Medical. Most inmates put in one medical request and waited for the outcome. But Joe likened a medical request to a lottery ticket. The more lottery tickets you entered, the greater your chances of winning. He was putting in a medical request every day. I copied him. We soon ran out of forms. To get more we had to cajole our neighbours into requesting them from the guards during security walks. I started to receive daily rejections from Medical, but then one of my requests proved Joe's theory.

A guard extracted me and escorted me up several flights of stairs to Medical, where the air blew mildew-free and much cooler than in the bowels of the jail.

I was weighed and asked a few questions by Nurse Shavonne, a jovial African American about the size of a blimp. 'I really dig your accent. Will you say something for me?'

Amused by her request, I searched through my repertoire of English phrases. 'The rain in Spain falls mainly on the plain.'

'No! Not that. Will you say, "Do you think I'm sexy, baby?"'

I giggled and did my best impression: 'Do you think I'm sexy, baby?'

Nurse Shavonne laughed so hard I feared for my safety. Not realising I'd just passed some kind of audition, I hoped she was done with me. But she insisted on us taking a tour of the Medical Unit. In each room, she said, 'Listen, everybody! Go on. Go on, Attwood.'

'Do you think I'm sexy, baby?' I responded for about the sixth time, bracing my ears for Nurse Shavonne's laughter.

She couldn't get enough of my English accent. I was glad when she ran out of staff members to exhibit me to and deposited me in the Plexiglas holding tank for sick prisoners.

I waited two hours to see the man the inmates called Gay Dr Jean. All of the previous doctors I'd dealt with were abrupt and discourteous, and I'd been told that Dr Jean was different, a frisky individual. I found a thin man wearing rectangular glasses. He had short blond hair. Smiling at me, he was holding a stack of my medical-request forms in a three-ring binder.

'So you've been having a variety of medical issues?' he said in a chirpy voice.

I told him about the bedsores, the skin infection, the persistent itching, the chest pains, my insomnia. He complimented me on my English accent. I half-expected him to ask me to recite some Austin

Powers lines, but he didn't. He asked me to remove my top. I showed him the rash on my chest. My torso was all protruding ribs and hair matted with sweat.

'These things happen while it's hot,' Dr Jean said, examining the rash. He grabbed a tube off a shelf. 'Here's some hydrocortisone cream to relieve the itching and some Benadryl to help you sleep. I'll put you in for an EKG for the chest pains. Let's take a look at the bedsores, shall we?'

I dropped my pants and pink boxers, embarrassed by the smell, and turned around.

Dr Jean crouched to inspect the bedsores. 'Heat, sweating, sitting around. Nothing we can really do,' he said with pity. 'I bet you wish you were in the cooler climes of England.'

I pulled up my pants and turned around. 'Yes, it's much cooler. But it rains too much. Kind of like Seattle weather.'

'Whenever I see it on the TV it looks so green and wonderful. All those castles and countryside.'

'We've got loads of castles. Especially in North Wales, close to where I'm from . . . ' I elaborated on the scenery of my motherland to extend my stay in the cool air. Before I left, he surprised me by offering a handshake.

Back in my cell, I was applying antifungal cream to my buttocks when Joe rushed in. 'Hat Trick's collapsed in the shower!' Hat Trick – a crystal-meth chemist in his late 50s – was a friend of Joe's. He was podgy, had a wizard's beard and friendly piggy eyes. He loved animals and told me many stories about his unusual pets.

I pulled my pants up and rushed down the run with Joe. We joined the group of whites standing over Hat Trick.

'It's my lungs,' Hat Trick wheezed, his face corpse pale. 'I ain't got much longer to live.'

'You wannus to yell "Man down"?' Larry asked.

'It's probably the only way I'm ever gonna get to Medical,' Hat Trick said.

Half of the whites pounded on the Plexiglas at the front of the day room, yelling 'Man down!' at the control guards. Inmates all over the pod joined in yelling 'Man down!' Prisoners in neighbouring pods flocked to their windows to watch us. 'Man down! Man down!' It was like a chant at a soccer match and good to see everyone working together to help Hat Trick.

'Lockdown!' a guard announced. Guards from neighbouring housing units dashed down the corridor and into our pod. They swarmed around Hat Trick, quickly joined by medical staff who extracted him on a stretcher.

An hour later, they took us off lockdown, and an old-timer suffering from heat exhaustion collapsed on the toilet. They locked us down again. As they stretchered him out, the prisoners yelled: 'How many more of us have to fall out before you get us some fresh air in here?'

'Turn the fucking air up!'

'It's gotta be cheaper to give us some air than put us all in hospital!'

'It's not hot enough in here! Could you please turn the heat up?'

'Where's our ice cream?'

Hat Trick returned, disorientated, with a heat-exhaustion diagnosis and a pink slip of paper. 'They gave me a ticket for passing out in the shower!'

None of us believed he had been ticketed for being ill. We assumed he was delirious until he showed us the paperwork.

DISCIPLINARY ACTION REPORT

ON 7 24 03 AT APPROXIMATELY 1647 HOURS AT 225 W. MADISON STREET JAIL, PHOENIX, AZ 85003 2-3 D-2 INMATE A927117 WAS TAKEN BY WHEELCHAIR TO MEDICAL WHERE R.N.B. DIAGNOSED HIM WITH HEAT EXHAUSTION DUE TO TOO MUCH ACTIVITY. THIS DISRUPTED THE OPERATION OF THIS INSTITUTION BY HAVING TO COVER (3) SECURITY WALKS AND DELAYING MEDICAL PILL CALL.

For collapsing in the shower, Hat Trick received 30 days' full restriction. No commissary, visits, phone calls, recreation.

July 03

Dear Love,

I'm writing this in the dark, so I really can't see it. Apologies for the handwriting. I'm trying to dry off (sweat) before I put my antifungal cream on and go to bed. I ate my Benadryl and I'm sleepy.

I've been thinking a lot about your depression and drinking. It must be hard, waiting for me. Drinking vodka almost every night may make you feel good temporarily, but eventually it will turn into a problem. Balance is the key! Go out and have fun on the weekends, but don't throw away your goals and plans. Be strong, and try to do positive things.

I did another mammoth yoga session. Three hours. Medical sent me an extra blanket, and I was happy to start doing my yoga with it. I now do the bridge and the tree. Month six is a long workout: one and a half hours because there are so many exercises to do. It feels absolutely fantastic, though. It's pretty strenuous. I'm holding all these positions for minutes now.

I'm tired but still sweaty, so I'm just going to have to mix the antifungal cream into my sweat.

I think about you constantly. You drive me wild with your amazing beauty.

Goodnight, sexy arse!

Shaun

In August, one of the regular outbreaks of food poisoning affected dozens of men. As converts to vegetarianism, Joe and I avoided it. The prisoners blamed the green baloney for their diarrhoea and dizzy spells. They used up their toilet-paper rations, and the guards refused to provide any more. The prisoners asking me, 'Are you done with your *Financial Times* yet, dawg?' were not checking up on the stock market.

Another hazard of our environment was all the filthy rusty metal. I was unaware of its potential for harm until Bullet, in the act of extorting Hat Trick, nicked his thumb on the cell door. His thumb ballooned to twice its size, but the guards refused to take him to Medical. When it turned black and fungal, the guards assured him he'd be seen by Dr Jean, but still no one came for him. The stretched skin eventually split open and leaked pus. Only then did the guards escort him to Dr Jean, who hospitalised him. The hospital doctor cut Bullet's thumb down the middle to drain the pus out, and the inmates made bets as to whether he would lose it.

'That's called boomerang karma,' Joe explained.

Bullet returned from hospital angrier than usual. The thumb incident had really got to him.

'This motherfucking bread's way too fucking mouldy to eat!' he yelled at the guard serving Ladmo bags at the foot of the metal-grid stairs.

'What do you want me to do about it?' the guard said.

'You try eating this shit! Would you feed your family this fucking crap?'

To denounce the food or a guard even was one thing, but it was never a good idea to bring a guard's family into it. The guard snatched the Ladmo bag from Bullet. Bullet grabbed a fresh Ladmo bag from the guard and rushed away. The guard gave chase, caught up with Bullet halfway up the stairs and seized the Ladmo bag. Bullet threw his carton of milk at the guard. It hit the guard's neck and splattered open.

'Lockdown!' announced the guard in the control tower.

About ten minutes later, four massive goon-squad guards marched to Bullet's cell. I heard a key open his door, then boots sliding and a body getting walloped. Bullet appeared with a brown leather harness around his body and arms. There was a chain attached to the back of the harness, held by a guard walking him down the stairs like a dog. He never returned.

Guards escorted me to Medical for the EKG Dr Jean had ordered. Nurse Shavonne attached the EKG sensors to my legs, and her eyes bulged when she saw the reading.

'What is it?'

'The reading,' was all she volunteered.

Convinced the jail had finally done me in, I expected to have a heart attack on the spot.

She disconnected the sensors and retried but got the same reading. 'I'd better go get the doctor!' She rushed from the room as fast as she could carry her great mass, as if any delay might be fatal to my health.

The prospect of there being something wrong with my heart was making it beat much faster.

Nurse Shavonne burst into the room, eclipsing the doctor behind her.

Dr Jean worked his way around her and stared at my legs. 'They're not supposed to go on his legs. Put them on his chest.'

'Thank goodness! You had me worried there,' I said.

'With that sexy English accent, you're my favourite inmate.' Dr Jean winked at me.

The next EKG reading was fine. I returned to the holding cell, where two men were comparing spider-bite wounds so infected Medical had actually agreed to see them. Looking at their wounds leaking pus – raised reddened areas threatening to erupt – the bleeding rash on my chest seemed trivial. Yes, my chest was itchier than ever, and a splinter group of pox-like sores had been travelling up my legs recently as if it were a living thing with a consciousness homing it in on my groin, but I wouldn't have traded my rash in for their zombie-movie wounds. No thanks.

August 2003

Oh Claudia,

I just spoke to Alan Simpson, and he said Wild Man got eight years, almost the maximum sentence, and that doesn't bode well for me. I'm very nervous. This is such an awful bloody never-ending mess! He didn't give me the impression that I'll be getting out anytime soon, so that leaves marriage as the only way of getting our visits back.

We've had constant lockdowns. It's excellent suffering. No showers for days on end. I itch all day now like a wild animal. We've had no toilet paper for over 24 hours, so we're using the *Financial Times*! I'm hanging out in my pink boxers all day to try to minimise the heat.

I told you that I help the whites out with cookies if they get no store. It costs me nothing, keeps me in their good books and puts me at less of a risk of violence. How do I do it? I lend out 2 for 1 commissary items to the Chicanos. For example, if I lend them $4 worth of store then they pay me back $8. I use the entire profit to pay for cookies for the whites who get no store (and sometimes Chief – the lone Indian). Most people greedily eat all of their store within days, so it's easy getting the Chicanos to do 2-for-1 deals. I've also allowed some people to put money on my books for them to spend. If you're getting money on your books from people, you stand less chance of getting attacked, because if you get attacked, you end up getting moved, taking their money with you.

There are some heavy-hitting criminals in here now. My new next-door neighbour in cell 5 is a bigger than Wild Man-looking man in his 40s. His name is Mayhem. Another new guy in cell 7 is about 6 ft 4 in. and 300 pounds, he has a big scar on his face and looks like a classic con. This morning an Aryan Brother threw his milk at the DO, and we were all locked down. I think he is now on the loaf programme.

Chow is in the house. I'll write more later.

Yours always,

Shaun XXX

Dearest Claudia,

I am itchy and waiting for the shower as I'm writing this. 'Tis very early in the morning, and chow is in the house. I am going to have one granola bar, one pack of mixed nuts and two milks. That's as healthy as I can get it.

It was nice to do yoga after the three-day lockdown. My body feels liberated, and it helps me cope with the stress. I love doing exercises standing on my head. I can't wait to show you what I am now capable of. I am officially Plastic Man, as I can bend in so many different ways.

They turn our lights out at 10.30 now. I guess they're trying to save on the electricity bill, so I listen to my radio from 10.30 till about 11.30 or 12, then I try to get to sleep. I listen to Radio Unica (Dr Isabel's problem page in Spanish) or Coast to Coast with Art Bell. I like the political stuff.

I jokingly asked Big O to jump in the shower with me, and he said that they don't shag Englishmen in 'the place'. The blacks call the joint 'the place'. Big O is the biggest black. He must be over 300 pounds. It was Big O, Money and Godzuki that were all arguing over the flavours of 'motherfuckin' SoBe drinks' the other night. I think that would make a good play. A bunch of inmates locked down, depressed, and then suddenly the blacks argue over SoBes. It lasted for about 30 minutes.

I'm going to try to get back to sleep now that our mopped floor has dried.

Have a good weekend.

I L U

Shaun XXX

In September, I read a book by Arnaud Desjardins, a student of Eastern spiritual traditions. I learned about monks who, from time to time, do horrible things such as eat their own faeces as a show of mental stamina. According to Arnaud, 'To appreciate a painful situation is to be at one with it, to be at one with the suffering. It is only in this way that we can learn something.' Thanks to books like Arnaud's, I made further progress on how I viewed my own suffering. I'd put myself in jail, yes, and was doing my utmost to accept my karma cheerfully, but these books really helped me stay focused on learning as much as I could from the situation. Although the conditions had crushed my spirit over the summer, I was bouncing back. I stopped taking the Benadryl that helped me sleep and instead meditated for up to an hour before bedtime. Meditating, I tuned in to the rhythms of my body, from my heartbeat and breathing to the anxiety rippling through me. When worries intruded into my mind, I'd push them out. This approach took the edge off my tension.

Lying down after meditation, I questioned my propensity for crime. Were there any criminals in my family? Definitely not my parents. But my aunt Sue was a master of operating in grey areas of the law. Some of the genes on my father's side were definitely suspect. As far as nurture was concerned, my sister had turned out well, and I had had all of the advantages in life not afforded to most of my neighbours, which made me all the more blameworthy. I put my crimes down to sheer hedonism. The selfish pursuit of pleasure by a man with more money than common sense.

In a cell upstairs, I started an English class for the Mexicans. If the jail didn't want to educate prisoners, then maybe I could make a small difference. Most of them could barely write at all, so I helped them compose letters in Spanish for their loved ones. I had five students: four murderers and one charged with attempted murder. One of the murderers was a midget with a thick beard and a boyish happy face. Mid class, he'd stand up, flex his muscles like a strongman and chuckle. Some of the whites disapproved of me helping another race, which worried me because a female guard was smuggling drugs in, and the men had been up for days and were looking for someone to smash. But Joe intervened with the whites and told me to continue.

I incorporated some new yoga postures into my routine. Triangle. Bow. Boat. Lion. I was in the canoe pose – belly down, alternate arms and legs slightly raised – when Lloyd, a member of the notorious Lindo Park Crip gang who expected to be sentenced to death by the end of the year, came in and said, 'You look like one of my victims trying to crawl away.'

I didn't know what to say.

'Lloyd's all right when he's not murdering people,' Joe said. 'I get along good with him.'

Through his friend, a chief justice court clerk, Lloyd had tracked down the witness to one of his armed robberies. While she held her four-year-old son up to shield herself from him, he shot her in the face.

Shortly after that murder, a second witness was found floating in a canal. The *New Times* did a cover story on Lloyd. He liked me because we'd both made the cover of the *New Times*.

September 2003

Dearest Claudia,

You asked how I am feeling. Sick. I feel sick because we have no visits and deep inside a voice says you are slowly forgetting about me. I have spent hours writing you letters and you have not responded to any of them. I get no mail from you, and I can feel you drifting . . . drifting . . . drifting away from me. And when I call you, I hear so much pain in your voice I wonder if my happy Claudia will ever come back to me. I know it's hard for you, and this mess is all my fault, and that is making me feel even worse.

We're suffering lockdown after lockdown. This lockdown run has no amount of days on the notice, and the reason given is 'INVESTIGATION'. They have paraded us out of our cells twice and searched the whole pod. This morning they strip-searched all of us. The goon squad did it. I took the pictures of you down just in time before the goon squad came. In the pits of hell I am, but I am constantly thinking about you. As you have stopped writing to me, I reread your old letters during these nasty lockdowns.

You are my world, and my biggest fear now is losing you. We have been through so much, it would be such a shame. If you continue to not write to me, then I shall be forced to write enough for the two of us combined.

Devotedly,

Shaun

Dearest Claudia,

Sorry about the previous sad letter. It's so hard being separated from you. Please try to understand how hard it is to be in jail. The kinds of thoughts, worries and stresses that run through my mind, and how helplessly, hopelessly trapped I am in here. I apologise to you for sounding down on the phone. You are feeling depressed and that explains your behaviour. I love you so much, I just want it all to end and for us to begin our family. We should be snuggling, spooning and having unprotected baby-making sex!

I've been trying to read Karl Marx, but others keep coming into the cell and distracting my concentration. In cell 5 is an attempted-murder-charged skinhead called Little Wood, and in between shooting up drugs he stumbles into my cell and natters with my celly Joe. Joe humours everyone. He says it is good 'giving', and it will help his karma for sentencing.

In cell 7 is South Carolina, who we've awarded 'sufferer of the year'. He is diagnosed with one to two years to live because of stomach cancer, and he also has syphilis, hepatitis C, herpes, metal screws coming loose in the steel rod in his leg and other ailments. He's another attempted murderer, as he stabbed the lady who gave him the syphilis after he found out he had it. He stuck her a bunch of times in the belly with a one-foot-long knife. He is in agony peeing, and he hasn't pooped a solid stool in over three years. It hurts him more to poop than to urinate. He speaks in a creepy South Carolina accent and says, 'If I'd a wanted ta kill da bitch I woulda.' I'm surrounded by lunatics, love. I'm so lucky to have my karma-book-reading celly Joe.

Please be strong for us. Your strength is my strength.

Shaun XXX

Darling Claudia,

It is the morning after I just listened to your sweet voice. Talking to you is the highlight of my day, and I appreciate you taking my calls even if you are not up to writing.

I did my yoga workout, and now I'm waiting for the shower. South Carolina 'sufferer of the year' is in the shower right now. He takes about seven showers a day to soothe his ailments. They gave him little cups to poop in today so they can check his stool. This morning he asked me if yoga would help him, so I showed him month one in the yoga book.

Chow has been rotten spuds and carrots every single night! I'm getting fed up with spud-carrot sandwiches three months in a row. My only meal of the day!

Luv yer loads!

Shaun XXX

31

··········

I was in a packed court holding cell when two Tempe transportation guards stopped outside. They kept glancing at me, rousing my suspicion since Tempe Police Department had initiated my case.

'Which one's the snitch in this cell?' one asked.

'Attwood's the snitch,' the other said.

'Attwood's the snitch. OK.' When they knew everyone had overheard, they walked away. They'd 'jacketed' me. In the '60s, federal agents jacketed the leaders of radical student groups. By giving the impression that the leaders were cooperating with the authorities, they could turn the group against their leader or at least flip those members who fell for the ploy.

I felt the hair on my arms rise. If the men in the cell believed the guards and figured out I was Attwood, then I could be smashed or possibly killed. In the jail, snitches were as hated as child molesters.

'They're just trying to cause trouble for Attwood,' one inmate said.

His words relieved me. I was about to volunteer my name and explain that Tempe police were out to get me because they didn't have much of a case, but a much larger prisoner said, 'If we've got a snitch in here, we need to handle it.'

As if to prevent me from speaking up, the muscles in my face tightened. Now what? I thought. Other prisoners sided with the larger prisoner, clamming me up even more. All eyes were roaming the room in a mad search for Attwood. I pretended to look for Attwood, too, but my face blushed. Thinking about it blushing made it blush even more, and I feared it would give me away. The more vocal prisoners debated what to do, mainly expressing enthusiasm for smashing Attwood. I figured I was about to pay the price for all of the violence I'd dodged since my arrest. I assumed the guards who'd started it wouldn't be in a hurry to stop it either. I remained motionless, saying nothing, convinced opening my mouth would invite disaster.

About five minutes later, a guard yelled, 'Attwood, come out!'

Everyone looked at everyone else, as if ready to pounce on Attwood. I stayed still until the door opened, then walked out.

'You're not going to believe this,' I said to my attorney. 'Two Tempe cops just told the inmates in the holding cell I'm a snitch.'

'You cannot be serious,' Alan Simpson said.

I described what had happened. He told the prosecutor. The prosecutor guaranteed a full investigation. The inmates in the cell would all be interviewed. I'd have to identify the officers in a line-up, and they'd be reprimanded.

In a holding cell afterwards, dwelling on what had happened, I could only think of one person capable and motivated enough to jacket me – Detective Reid – but of course I had no evidence to back up my hunch. He'd led the investigation, said some things he probably shouldn't while arresting me and attended nearly all of my court appearances with the air of a stalker. I remembered his emotional reaction when no drugs were found at my apartment, and how he'd threatened me over the keys to the safe.

When I returned to my floor at the Madison Street jail, the guard in the control tower said, 'Attwood, you've been rehoused upstairs for your own protection.' He wouldn't even let me go back to my cell to collect my property. A porter brought it out in plastic bags packed by Joe. My books and stacks of legal paperwork slowly tore the bags open as I followed the guard to the elevator.

'Where we going?' I asked.

'Wherever I take you,' he said.

The elevator stopped at the fifth floor. I followed the guard down a series of corridors. We arrived at a control tower overlooking four pods. All of the prisoners were locked down except in one pod. The men out in the one pod were watching me, some smiling. Many of them were older men, clean cut, a breed apart from the prisoners I'd seen so far. The guard in the control tower instructed me to a cell in a pod that was locked down, and activated the sliding door. As I approached the cell, one of the rips in the bags containing my property expanded and shed a few golf pencils, which clinked as they hit the floor. The control guard hit the button to open the cell door. The door slid open with a mechanical groan. I went in.

Inside the cell, a startled black man in street clothes was hiding a glass pipe in the toilet. 'What the fuck!' he said. The trapped crystal-meth smoke reeked like cat urine with a twist of lemon.

Anything can happen in the jail, but I hadn't expected this. 'Who're you?' I asked, putting my bags down. The door slid closed behind me.

'Who the fuck are you, coming in here making me flush my motherfuckin' dope?'

'They just moved me up here.' I didn't appreciate him talking to me as if I were new to the jail. 'I've been in jail for almost a year and a half.'

'A year and a half! What the fuck for?' he asked.

'Drugs. It's a complex case.'

'Mine's a complex case, too.' His eyes found my commissary bag. 'Got anything to eat, wood?' Addressing me as wood meant he assumed I was a gang member.

'Not much. Just enough for me. Why the street clothes?'

'Getting released at midnight. Girlfriend's bonded me out.'

I was glad I'd be rid of him soon. He was not someone I could sleep safely around.

'Gimme something to eat, wood.'

I didn't mind giving him a store item as he wouldn't be around long enough to demand more, but I felt disrespected by his tone. Knowing he was testing me, I tried to establish some boundaries. 'Where's your manners at? If you ask politely, I'll consider it.' I knew if we were going to fight, it would most likely happen now. I stared at him as if I were crazy from starvation and willing to fight to the death to defend my food. He had about a 50-pound weight advantage, but I'd been working out fanatically all year. He had sneakers on, but I had on deck shoes I'd acquired from a diabetic, not slippery shower sandals. Tense from being moved, I had no patience left for diplomacy. I figured showing him I'd fight was the best way to get him to back down. Without realising it, I'd adopted the prison mentality.

'All right, man, can you at least hook your celly up with a little somethin'-somethin'?' He'd switched from intimidation to playing on the rule that cellmates look out for each other.

Knowing what he was up to gave me a sense of control over the situation. 'I've got Snickers, MoonPies. I ain't giving up any of my peanut butter.'

'Oo, a MoonPie.'

His response pleased me. A MoonPie was half the price of a Snickers. I'd only bought them for trading purposes. Giving one away would not cut into the commissary I'd allocated to eat. I handed him a MoonPie. He flushed its wrapper down the toilet and crammed the whole thing in his mouth.

Realising the top bunk didn't have a mattress, I fumed, 'No mattress!'

He stopped chewing loudly to say, 'You got mine when I leave.'

'I ain't lying on that steel. I'll flag a guard down when he walks.'

'He ain't gonna give you no motherfuckin' mattress. They just ignore you up in this motherfucker.'

'What is this pod anyway?'

'Temporary lockdown housing.'

'What the bloody hell's that?'

'They put people here they don't know what to do with till they decide what to do with them.'

'So you saying I won't be here long?'

'No one's here long.'

I hated being in transit. Having nowhere to settle. Uncertain where I'd end up next. 'What's our neighbours like?'

'Got none. This pod's mostly empty.'

'How about that pod over there with all those guys hanging out?'

'Them's all chomos and rapos.'

'What?' I asked, shocked. Having never seen a pod full of sex offenders before, I pressed myself to the cell door's narrow window to get a better look. None of the men had tattoos. Many were old or middle-aged, fat, bespectacled, meek-looking. I didn't want to imagine what they'd done.

'Some high-profile Catholic-priest motherfuckers over there,' he said, shaking his head.

I didn't doubt it, as Catholic priests had been on the news recently. I put my commissary bag on the top bunk to use as a pillow and to prevent him from stealing out of it. I climbed up and read. The metal really punished my back. I heard the day-room door slide open. I jumped down, banged on the window at the guard and yelled for a mattress. The guard walked by as if I didn't exist. My cellmate laughed. I cursed the guard, returned to my bunk and read for hours, unable to absorb much or let my guard down in case my cellmate tried to pull a fast one.

Come midnight, I wanted to sleep, but my cellmate hadn't left. By 1 a.m. I assumed he'd lied about getting released and I was stuck with him and no mattress. I was wallowing in disappointment until 2 a.m. when the guards collected him. When the door shut behind him, I finally started to unwind. I jumped down to watch him go, convinced watching him go would prevent him from ever coming back. When he was out of sight, I basked in the sensation of being completely alone for the first time in ages. My mind was briefly happy, but my body ached all over from the steel. I moved to the bottom bunk. His mattress smelled of his sweat and the lemony-urinous odour of the crystal meth he'd been smoking. Drifting into sleep, I wondered what kind of person the jail had turned me into.

32

··········

The following afternoon, the noise *step-squeak-slide, step-squeak-slide* interrupted my reading. It was coming from the day room. I thought I was familiar with all of the sounds in the jail until I heard that one. The *step-squeak-slide* grew louder, so I rolled off my mattress and went to the cell-door's narrow window. Someone was approaching. I backed away so as not to get caught staring.

A tall frail young man in bee stripes limped past. He had cropped copper hair, a gaunt freckled face and a shrivelled left arm sticking up uselessly in the air. I waited for him to circle the day room again and then moved closer to the window to get a better look. As he neared my door, I saw how sad his eyes were and the rivulets of perspiration on his face. Dragging his lame left leg behind his strong right step, he passed by. Watching him do laps, I put my face closer and closer to the window. Eventually he saw me and gave me an uncertain smile. I smiled back but also felt guilty for watching him. I returned to my bunk and tried to read, but my mind kept wondering about the man I'd watched and how hard it must be for the handicapped in jail. Wanting to know more, I planned to talk to him at his cell window when I was allowed out for a shower. By law, prisoners in lockdown had to be let out for one hour each day to take a shower, make a phone call and walk around the day room. But inmates in lockdown were prohibited from loitering outside each other's cells. He was housed in cell 1 next to the shower, so my best bet was to talk to him by hovering near the entrance to the shower, which wouldn't be so obvious to the guard in the control tower.

Every day, my hour out was an hour later than the previous day's. For the next three days – commencing at 6.30 a.m., 7.30 a.m. and 8.30 a.m. – I was disappointed to see him asleep in the foetal position. But at 9.30 a.m. on the fourth day, I caught him awake but forgot all the things I wanted to ask him.

'Hi, I'm Shaun,' I shouted at his window.

'Hi,' he said, sitting on the bottom bunk, barely audible behind the Plexiglas. 'I'm Chicken Wing.'

'Do you have any deodorant?' I asked, assuming he was indigent.

'No.'

'Need some?'

'Er, yeah, yeah, sure.' He seemed confused.

'I'll be right back then.' I fetched him a deodorant from my cell and pushed it through the gap below the bottom of his door.

He scrambled from his bunk, crouched down and grabbed it. 'Thanks,' he said in a weak voice, staring at the deodorant as if he didn't know what to do with it. 'Got any crackers? I'm hungry!' he yelled, his face shaking with excitement now.

'Sorry,' I said, disappointed I had none. 'Haven't any left.'

'Oh, well. Never mind. Thanks for the deodorant,' he said, and about-faced, ending my plan to learn more about him.

The next day an announcement was made: 'Attwood! Cell 4! Roll up!'

Nervous about being moved, I starting gathering my property together.

A few minutes later, a second announcement: 'Hernandez! Cell 12! Roll up!' And then a third: 'Miller! Cell 1! Roll up!' The only person in cell 1 was Chicken Wing.

Glad Chicken Wing was rolling up, I hoped to get another chance to talk to him. I coiled my mattress, placed my collection of books onto a bed sheet and made a carrying sack. When the sliding door opened, I followed the control guard's instructions to wait in the corridor next to the guard tower. A guard came down the corridor, handcuffed me and left. Hernandez and Chicken Wing were called out but not handcuffed. The three of us stood together, awaiting further instructions.

'How're you?' I asked Chicken Wing.

'I dunno. OK, I guess,' he said.

'Pleased to meet you again,' I said, offering him my handcuffed hands.

The guard-tower door clicked open and a Mexican American emerged.

'Where we going?' Hernandez asked the guard.

'Dunno. It's up to the guards in 5-4,' the guard said, handcuffing Hernandez.

Chicken Wing couldn't be handcuffed in the usual fashion. It was impossible to cuff his good arm to his handicapped arm, but security protocol demanded he be cuffed somehow. The guard strapped a thick brown belt around Chicken Wing's waist, and handcuffed his good right arm to the belt buckle, rendering him unable to carry his mattress. Reluctantly, the guard carried it. Shackled and carrying our heavy belongings, we struggled to 5-4. Instructed to wait at the foot of the control tower, we sat on our mattresses.

'What's your accent?' Chicken Wing asked with a curious smile.

'English. I'm from England.'

'England! You Scottishman, Englishman, Londonman you!' Growing excited, he started to stutter. 'S-S-S-S-So t-t-tell me, wh-what's it like in England?'

'Cold and wet most of the time. Very green 'cause of all the rain. The people are friendly. I think you'd like it.'

'I-I d-d-don't like the cold. W-W-Well d-d-do they have car races in England?'

I paused to think. 'I don't follow that. They have the Grand Prix in Europe. A lot of it goes on in France, which is next to England. There's some motorbike race on the Isle of Man, a small island off the coast of England, and people are always getting killed.'

'D-D-Did you see them get k-k-killed?'

'No, I never went. I only saw bits on the news. But I had a nice little Japanese sports car before my arrest.'

'D-D-Did it have gears?'

'Yes. Up to fifth and a twin-turbo engine.'

'I-I-It went fast! It went faster! It went fastest!' Chicken Wing yelped. He made a low rasping sound, mimicking the roar of an engine revving, while shifting gears with his good arm. As his euphoria grew, he turned up the rasping noises and began rocking. Perched hazardously on his rolled-up mattress, he lost his balance. Hernandez and I were riveted as Chicken Wing toppled backwards and banged his head against the wall.

'B-B-Blood?' he asked, touching his head. 'Am I bleeding?' Rubbing the back of his head, he howled, 'Will I die?'

We were assuring Chicken Wing he was neither bleeding nor about to die when a guard emerged from the control tower. 'You lot are going to B pod. Miller, cell 1. Hernandez, 9. Attwood, 14.'

Glad to be housed in the same pod as Chicken Wing, I resolved to get to know him better. I watched him approach cell 1. His new cellmate, a tattooed youngster, fetched his mattress.

33

··········

In the *Twilight Zone* episode 'Nightmare at 20,000 Feet', William Shatner spots a gremlin damaging the nacelle on the wing of the plane he is aboard. The gremlin has the wide eyes of a zombie and a weatherworn animal-like face: a face like that of my new cellmate in lockdown, Squeegee, who was in the throes of heroin withdrawal. Forty-one-year-old Squeegee had scraggy shoulder-length hair and abscesses the size of emu eggs on his tattooed arms, some of which were hatching into open sores.

'I was arrested on October the third for the seventy-seventh time,' Squeegee said in a soft-spoken Texan accent.

'How can you be arrested that many times?' I asked.

'Forty-seven of them were misdemeanours. I've been in prisons and jails across Arizona and Texas, and I can honestly tell you this place is the worst. Sheriff Joe's jail's hard time, dawg. It's even worse than death row.'

'What did they charge you with this time?'

'Weed. But it's a bullshit case. The cops pulled us over for a traffic violation. I was in the passenger seat. The cops became suspicious and searched the vehicle. They found a roach with a tiny bit of weed in it.'

I explained my charges and asked about his drug history.

'I lived in Tyler for 20 years. At nine, I started smoking weed, boozing and burglaring. I dropped 20 hits of acid at 14. I was 21 when I moved to Phoenix and got into crystal meth. Five years later, I was slamming it. I was 38 when I got into heroin. In '98, I shot up some coke and fell in the bathroom. My dad found me and called the paramedics. In June of 2000, I shot a dime of heroin, went outside and collapsed on some bushes. My sister found me and called the paramedics, who revived me. Up until this arrest, I was shooting a gram of heroin a day. That's three hits a day for three and a half years. Three times a week, I treated myself to a special high. I'd cook a quarter gram of heroin, melt a quarter gram of coke into it and add half a gram of speed. It all dissolves nicely in the spoon. There's nothing like it. It's the best high there is. It makes your body warm, gives you an instant erection and makes your asshole tingle.'

I laughed at his candour. 'When were you last employed?'

'I worked construction – roofing, cement, clean-up – for 15 years. My girlfriend of nine years broke up with me in 1990 'cause of my habits. Since then I've hung out on the streets.'

Squeegee passed the time wriggling around on his bunk, his eyeballs rolling around inside his head as if they were tracing figure eights and loop-de-loops on the cell walls. Sometimes I caught him gnawing on the abscesses on his arms. When he attempted to eat, he suffered chronic flatulence. He filled out a medical request form: 'I need to see a doctor. I have been here 10 days, and my heart just keeps raising [sic]. I can't sleep. I toss & turn every 30 seconds. I need to see someone.'

The lack of human contact in lockdown can send prisoners crazy. But I viewed it as an opportunity for uninterrupted thinking. I read like never before, and my mind began to skirt around the big questions in philosophy. What are we? Where are we? Why are we here? My father sent me *On the Origin of Species*. Reading the book that had shaken the foundations of many religions raised even more questions. I wondered why Darwinism and creationism couldn't be reconciled. What if our creator made a species that evolved? What if our creator was some kind of cosmic scientist to whom we were like a strain of bacteria in a Petri dish? But then who created the scientist? Or God?

Boggled by how insignificant humans seem to be in relation to the vastness of the universe, I strained my mind on these questions, only to conclude I'd never know the answers. On religion, I decided most people need some form of spirituality to flourish as well-balanced beings – especially during difficult times – and that's why I'd turned to yoga. After Adam Smith's *The Wealth of Nations*, I finished Karl Marx's *Capital*. I learned that at the height of the cotton industry, the people living in the region of my hometown were worked so hard they didn't last long. Maybe 30 to 40 years. The chapters on child labour and ailments appalled me. Obsessed by history books, I ranged from the Second World War back to the Sumerians. Fascinated to learn how much knowledge they had in areas such as astronomy, geometry and trigonometry as far back as 6000 BC, I wondered why I'd been taught Westerners had discovered most of these things in recent centuries. Reading was transforming my world view. I read for over 14 hours a day, until my brain and eyes ached so much I couldn't take it any more. Every word I didn't understand I looked up in my dictionary: metaphysics, inchoate, caprice, solipsism, empiricism, acrimony, abstruse, irascible, phlegmatic . . .

'How're you liking the fifth floor, English Shaun?' asked a tall, grinning 20-something with a handsome Hawaiian-looking face and a snake tattooed on the side of his neck. He was standing outside my cell door, yelling at the narrow window.

'How do you know who I am?' I asked, approaching the window.

'I've been to your raves. Name's Mack. You gave me some Ecstasy one night at DJ Steel Rok's apartment. Tempe cops even offered to cut me a deal if I could provide information on you, but I told them to fuck off.'

'They did?' I said, surprised, until I thought of Detective Reid.

'Yeah, we both know a lot of the same people. Glad you finally made it upstairs. I read the *New Times* article on you. They've got a few high-profile cases up here.'

'Like who?'

'Let's start with the Indian living next door to you: Chris Cleland. Remember the Rodeo fire up by Show Low and Heber that was on CNN every day?'

'Yes. It was all over the news. The biggest fire ever in Arizona.'

'Your neighbour in 15 is the Rodeo Arsonist.'

'No way!'

'Don't get too excited. He's just some brain-damaged Indian the Feds found for a fall guy.'

'You saying he didn't do it?'

'Who knows? But if you talk to him, you'll see what I mean.'

'Who else is up here?'

'The 101 Slayer.'

I'd heard a news report on the 101 Slayer. He'd run some people off the Interstate 101. The police had thought only two cars were involved, but a third car was found three days later with more dead people in it. 'What's he like?'

'He's cool, man. He's from a rich family. He used to go to raves, too.'

'Any more up here on the news?'

'In 11 is the skinhead who made the news for spray-painting a swastika on a mosque. The guys in that pod over there only get the loaf to eat. It's a disciplinary-segregation pod. They just moved two guys from the Mexican Mafia in there for soaping off the American flags painted on their cell walls. That was on the news. Arpaio made PR out of it. In that pod over there is the abortionist, Dr Ross, who the *New Times* ran a whole series on. They say he molested his patients.'

'He's all over the news. He's got no chance.'

'He says he didn't do it, and I kind of believe him 'cause he refused to sign a plea bargain and he's taking it to trial. If he loses, he's gonna get a lotta years. My celly was on the news, too. His girlfriend dumped him, so he figured he'd commit suicide by doing a bunch of robberies and getting shot by the cops. He did the armed robberies, but they just ended up arresting his dumb ass. That guy yelling to you down the vent from the sixth floor is some maniac who killed a bunch of people.'

'How do you know what all these people are accused of?'

'You find out when you go to court with them and see them on TV. The last time I went to court, some chomo teacher was sentenced to 400 years: 50 for each victim. All the news channels were there filming us spitting on him. Some soldier got four years for statutory rape. The 17-year-old daughter of his colonel seduced him at his barracks, but he goes to prison 'cause she's underage.'

'I just saw they gave the death penalty to that guy who killed the Sikh right after 9/11. The Sikh was the uncle of two of my friends who own an Indian restaurant. How much time you facing?'

'For ever. When the prosecutor brought up how much time I'm facing, I told her, "I'm going to fuck your dad in the shower and then have a little snack afterwards." She said, "I'm gonna see to it that you never see the light of day again." The goon squad escort me to court now in all kinds of shackles and chains.'

Later on, an inmate shoved a note under my door:

Shaun,

This is Mack in B12 again. This pod is cool. Every day we get a comedy hour when certain inmates are on their hour out. It's some pretty hilarious shit. So have some laughs. Tell me, do you have a radio? I have two, if you need to borrow one let me know.

I am in here on 54 felony 2's. Shitty deal. I have a real good lawyer though. I am lookin' at 540–775 yrs. However, I am innocent, and I will only be convicted on one Attempted Murder from 2001. I gave

255

my lawyer $40,000, so hopefully I won't serve more than 8–40 yrs.
If there is anything you need, let me know.
Mack

Oh yeah, here's a list of shit you might hear people yell at nite.
Who shit in the shower?
There's roaches in the ice.
I'm going home tomorrow.
Take a fucking shower.
Ya got any oranges?
What are ya gonna do for me?
You ain't gotta lie to kick it.
I was teabagged in the army.
I've seen so many balls.
Hook me up with your sister.
Your sister's got a pretty mouth.
Why don't you look at some balls, ballgazer?
Sweet.
We're gonna shank that little fuck.
Shut the fuck up, Leprechaun.
If I was in Durango, I'd smash your ass.
I wanna go home.
I would fuck the shit out of your grandma.
Last call for alcohol.
I'm not supposed to be here.
This is all a big mistake.
Does anyone have a Honey Bun for Ramon?
Do that shit in the shower.
You shit-eating pole smoker.
Gentlemen, time's up, time's up, your hour has expired. You need
to go back to your cell and lock down.
Look at these haters surrounding me every day.
Don't smile at court tomorrow, you'll get another charge.

At a legal visit, Alan Simpson said four of my co-defendants had
agreed to testify against me: Wild Woman, DJ Spinelli, Melissa, Boo.
Due to these witnesses, I was now looking at a minimum of nine years
if I plea bargained and the judge didn't aggravate my sentence, and
a maximum of hundreds of years if I lost at trial and the judge gave

me the aggravated sentence for each count and ran the sentences consecutively. If I held out for much longer on signing a plea bargain, Alan warned, each additional witness found would add at least another year to my sentence. The news shell-shocked me.

Wild Woman had signed a cooperation agreement with a sentence ranging from four to eight years – far better than the decades she was facing on more than 150 felony charges. Unbeknown to me, her public defender – who had barely done anything for her throughout her incarceration – had frightened her into cooperating by stating that Wild Man and I were setting her up to take the fall for our crimes, and that most of the evidence would go against her. He told her she would get anywhere from 25 to 99 years if she didn't cooperate. After agreeing to cooperate, Wild Woman was told that her life was in danger from me. She was whisked off to Payson jail, where the police booked her in as 'Missy' and prohibited her from writing to anybody, including her dying mother.

Wild Man wrote, urging me to sign a plea bargain so Wild Woman wouldn't have to testify in court. Angry and unable to stomach even the nine-year prospective minimum sentence, I refused to sign a plea bargain. Against Alan's advice, I demanded a trial. Months later, Wild Woman sent an apology.

Hey now! Hi Shaun,

I hope this letter has found you in good health and that you are doing OK. I have wrote and re-wrote I don't know how many letters to you, but no matter how I write it I just can't find the right words to tell you how sorry I am about everything and all the trouble I might have caused you. I never meant to do you any harm. I really didn't. I am so sorry, Shaun, and I mean that from the bottom of my heart. I am sorry for being weak and letting everything get to me. I should have stood by you and I didn't and I hate myself for that. It's something that I have got to live with for the rest of my life. I feel I got pushed into doing something that was against all that I believe in and I was at a low point in my life. I was not thinking straight. I had been told that my mum did not have long to live, sad to say she passed away, and I was told that it was getting pinned on me and if I did not stand up for myself then I would lose. They also said it would get me home to my mum, but it didn't.

To tell the truth, la', I was scared shitless and I didn't know what to do and I was in a mess for the longest time. I could not sleep, eat or anything. I was so upset and confused by it all. I just kept thinking that I had to get home to care for my mum and that I had to put our friendship on the line. It was the most horrible choice I have ever had to make. If I could turn back time, I would. I never meant to hurt you or make a mess of things for you. Please believe me that I love you with all my heart and it hurt me so bad knowing what I was supposed to do, it all made me so ill. I only hope that you will forgive me one day. You are a great guy, you were a great friend to me, and I thank you for being there when things went crazy with Wild Man.

I received your article last week. It made me cry. I hate the thought of you going through that shit and believe me I know what it was like. I am not doing too badly now. I tried to kill myself twice, stupid I know but I was in a bad way for a while. I have since become Muslim and I started to study Islam. It has changed my way of life. I meditate every night. It helps me to focus and it takes me to another level, a higher state of mind, and I feel more at peace with myself. I would love to do yoga but I don't know if I can do it as I still have a lot of back pain. I used to read my Koran a lot, but I don't have one now and I am trying to get one. I don't smoke any more. I don't curse and I pray to God as often as I can. I don't eat pork or ham. I hope I can be a better person.

Anyways, la', I will close this letter for now, please forgive me for all the trouble I may have caused you, you are always in my heart. I hope to hear from you soon.

Please take care and stay safe. I worry about you.

Stay strong. Peace. All my love always,

Wild Woman

October 2003

Dear Claudia,

Now I've been moved upstairs, it didn't take long to be recognised. Just like at Towers when I met Billy the Hippy who I'd taken really good care of one night, well, Mack in cell 12 here was at some apartment in Tempe when I brought my party friends over. I was v. nice to Mack, and he's offering to help me however he can. He already sent me a tub of peanut butter, which is good because I'm now five days without the veggie diet. They've been trying to give me a white sliced cheese with grey speckles in it, and it is yuck. We've been getting stale pitta bread lately and genetically modified plums that went to the size of grapefruits and suddenly stopped. Now we're getting two slightly rotten oranges in the mornings.

Last night, Chicken Wing was walking around on his hour out, and someone asked him to go to cell 7. Chicken Wing stumbled over there and then went hysterical and started running around the pod shouting in a spastic voice, 'They're fucking sucking! They're fucking sucking! He's eating sperm! He's eating sperm! He's eating sperm! Fucking sucking! Fucking sucking!' for about ten minutes and cackling like a possessed Rain Man. It was pretty funny. Maybe #7 is a gay cell! I've saved my dessert, a donut, for Chicken Wing. I'll stick it under his door on my hour out. Good 'giving'. I feel so sorry for him because he is in here and handicapped.

The maniac above me is losing his voice from shouting: 'Shut the fuck up, punk!'

'Punk ass, bitch!'

'Get away from my door, punk ass!'

He also makes noises that sound like he's digging through the ceiling, which is of concern as he's supposed to have murdered a bunch of people.

In the next pod is David, a nice all-American lad with a good job, no drugs and a beautiful young Spanish wife. He got sentenced to a flat 21 years. He came home from work one day and his wife was having sex with another man in his bed. David told the man to quickly leave, and then he went to the bedroom closet, pulled out a fully loaded shotgun and blasted his wife in the head. The shot removed most of her head, killing her. Yikes!

I drew a picture of the view from our cell's skinny window located above the top bunk near the ceiling. Looking east, I can see the stadium directly in front of me. Looking down, I see the parking lot roof and street. I think it's Jackson, because I can see a grey building which looks like the Jackson Hole bar where I threw the rave Mechanism. I can view it at any time, so it's easy for me to see you on the street. I just need a time.

That's my update. I'll write more later on.

Love you,

Shaun XXX

P.S. I discovered that I had brought the roaches upstairs with me. They had nested in one of my brown envelopes. I wondered where they were coming from. Hopefully that was the last of my run-ins with them.

Love,

Today's gone pretty fast. I read all day. Chicken Wing ran around making fake orgasm noises and shouting 'runny poop' over and over again. Someone left 'duky' stained pink boxers in the shower. I suspect my celly. He sneezes and itches all day, and his long hair is falling out and decorating the room. He's ill from the heroin come down. At least he's quiet, though. He naps with his eyes open. Quite odd, eh?

I've started talking to two Arab fellows downstairs, and they are both a good laugh. They sneak upstairs on their hour out to talk to me.

I did get to meet some interesting people at the weekend. On Saturday, a downstairs neighbour, Leprechaun, went to Visitation, and I finally got to meet him at close range. He is short but stocky. He looks like he is in his mid-40s and he has long straggly hair and a beard. He has Irish features and long nails on his hands and feet. His toenails curl down over his toes. So upon closer examination, he fits all of the leprechaun criteria, but I guessed that his leprechaunness probably ended there, he was probably a nice guy to talk to and probably didn't act like a leprechaun. The DO escorting us to the elevator was 6 ft 4 in., ginger-haired with Elvis-style sideburns. We got to the elevator and Leprechaun talked:

'I was on TV. I pulled me pants down. I was all right. She thought I was attractive. She called me mother.' He grunted.

The DO shook his head and looked at Leprechaun like he was crazy.

Then Leprechaun yelled at the DO, 'You've never smoked!'

At this point I concluded that he was a genuine leprechaun. The DO couldn't believe what he was hearing. The angry Leprechaun continued:

'She saw me on TV and called me mother. She said I was very handsome. I said I didn't want anything to do with her. I was trying to light a cigarette and my pants dropped. Then there was a big light. It was all on the TV.'

I've finally met a leprechaun!

Then on Sunday I went out for a hair trim and the tall skinny Chicano/Italian inmate barber starts cutting my hair and telling me that he had been peeping at me in the shower from the pod opposite. He said he saw me with an erection, and he was wondering if I needed a new cellmate. Yikes! He'd done eight years in a prison which was 'nuthin' nice' and he was now bisexual. I told him that I threw raves and that most of my friends were bisexual but I was a max inmate (he was medium) so that he couldn't move to my room. It doesn't matter where I am, I always seem to attract the freaks somehow!

I love you more than garlic naan,

X Shaun X

November 2003

Dearest Claudia,

It's chilly in here now. Last night I slept in my full clothing with a skinny sheet over me. The chow was yellow rice last night, and my celly didn't want his so I purchased it for a bag of Gardettos.

I've also been writing some exposé-style stuff for my jail book, and yesterday I wrote a big chapter on the food. Squeegee used to work in the kitchen in '99, so he told me about what goes on in there. Some of the food he helped cook (boil) was 15 years past its sell-by date. It was canned vegetables. Squeegee gets sentenced soon, and he is stressed out about whether the judge will give him 1 year or 1½ years. I wish I could trade places with him, but I wouldn't like to swap teeth with him. He's another bugger-the-fillings-until-the-teeth-hurt-type person. Now they are hurting and can't be filled. He had two pulled today and gets two more pulled in two weeks' time. All back ones.

The inmates say the madman in the cell above me is James, a mass murderer. He is growling and yelling at the people in his pod. His voice travels quite loudly through the vent:

'Punk   arrrggghhhhhh!   Punk   snitch   hideout   bitch arrrghhhhhhhh!'

I talked to him through the vent the other day. I pretended to be Mike, one of the 9/11 detainee Arabs downstairs who was in the shower, and James proceeded to tell me about stabbing someone

60 times, and then he gave me some names that he wanted killing. 'Kill all of 'em and take care,' were his parting words. He thinks he's getting 75 years and claims to have murdered his own daughter.

Leprechaun is hassling people downstairs and telling the young gay lad in cell 7 that he knows that he 'hangs out in the streets with his ass in the air,' and 'he should try fuckin' his mom cos she hasn't had any dick in 20 years'. He's being a crude little leprechaun this weekend.

It'll be almost two years of jaildom soon. Unbelievable! Even Alan Simpson said the case would take less than a year to resolve. It's so unreal. I just woke up one day and, boom, I was taken away. I can handle doing this time, but it kills me to be putting the people I love most through it as well.

See you in court,
Shaun XXX

Hello precious,

It's almost lights out time, and I'm pretty exhausted. The philosophy and thinking books that I've been reading have sapped my brainpower. I'm back to writing again, and I'm currently writing about my first month at Towers.

Thank you for taking three calls this evening. I imagine I sounded pretty mental on the phone. You made me feel a lot better. I was worried about a number of things. When Alan talked to me in court, I was doolally nervous and I did not fully understand what he said to me. I did hear him say ten years, and then my mind started worrying. I figured the Tempe cop who lied to the inmates that I was snitching and tried to get me smashed was part of a bigger picture of them just wanting me to die or to be locked up for ever. Plus, with Wild Woman cooperating against me, everything at once has just hit me again when I expected the madness to end. It just gets madder.

I dreamt that I got many years and that for you to wait would ruin your life, so I ate a gram of heroin and killed myself so you could go on with your life. As I did it, I knew how much it would hurt my mum and it made me hysterical but I knew that I had to do it and I did it anyway. It's hard to get these negative thoughts under control recently. I hate being weak like this, and I don't like to burden you.

Sometimes I feel like I am going mental in here, and I try to disguise it by being positive all the time, but it's so hard. Getting deeper into yoga and meditation certainly helps. My usual worries are trial, sentencing and what is going to happen. I can be sat reading and then a silly little thought will just pop into my head and then my mind goes and I'll have to reread what I just read. Not knowing what is going to happen to me for this long is utter torture. Squeegee says anyone else would be on meds or mental by now for being in jail for so long. My efforts to stay sane are exhausting me. I miss simple stuff like us buying smoothies and going grocery shopping at nights.

I am sorry for putting you through this, and I constantly feel guilty for letting my family down. I can't believe they are trying to give you a felony for a few prescription pills. Squeegee is an expert on misdemeanours, he has 40+, and he thinks that they'll end up offering you a misdemeanour to avoid trial. He said a felony will really hurt when it comes to job applications and stuff like that.

Tonight's been a wacky night. Mack intercepted a love letter from a gay in another pod to Macho Sean in cell 8. It was news to everyone, and now the whole pod is singing YMCA. I joined in on my hour out and sang a little bit of 'I'm too sexy for the jail . . . too sexy for the jail' and some 'Relax' by Frankie Goes To Hollywood. All of the excitement gets me going, and then I feel sad because I wish I were enjoying life with you.

All my love,
Shaun XXX

December 2003

Dear Love,

It's all so terrible. Today the judge said that I would get life if I lose at trial. I would definitely kill myself if that happened. Nobody here has ever heard of a first-time drug offender getting such a high plea. I am getting so screwed if I sign this deal now.

I have often thought about slashing my wrists at night and dying slowly in a pool of my own blood whilst on my rack. I have thought about hanging myself also, BUT I think about all of the people that love me, especially you, and it stops such thoughts from becoming actions.

I've had to increase my meditation time. I've started meditating first thing in the morning to begin my day on a positive note. I visualise large triangles spinning around me and a beautiful sphere of light. I think about the people I love, including you and my family members.

Love you loads,
Shaun XXX

Claudia's public defender refused to prepare a defence and urged her to sign a plea bargain for three years of probation, two years of drug counselling costing $50 dollars a month, and a $5,000 fine. She didn't have the money to pay the fine and feared a felony would ruin her career prospects.

Claudia went to see her attorney to tell him no. The meeting snapped her out of a depression. He said we'd get our visits back if she signed for a Class 6 felony – conspiracy to sell or transfer prescription drugs – and paid a $200 fine. She happily agreed, and her sentencing hearing was set for 23 December. She said getting our visits back was going to be the best Christmas gift she could possibly ask for.

Out of love for me, Claudia went to court and pled guilty to a crime she hadn't committed. When I rang her, she was the happiest I'd heard in months as she said she was coming to see me. When the visit we were so looking forward to wasn't announced, I worried something was wrong and called her.

Claudia answered, and started sobbing right away.

I braced myself for a nasty development. 'What's wrong? What's the matter?'

'They . . . wouldn't . . . let . . . me . . . in.'

'Calm down. Try to tell me.'

'I . . . I . . . again, I just lost the one thing I used to look forward to three times a week, which is coming to see you. I just signed my life away 'cause I was lied to.' Her voice was growing angry now. 'I stood in front of a judge and said yes, yes, yes, all because my public pretender, that Dick Tosso, that motherfucker–'

'Try to calm down,' I said, outraged but eager to hear more.

'He was never nice to me. He was always trying to get me to turn and talk against you. The first thing I asked him was, "What can I do to be able to get visits back?" He called me, and he was shouting, implying I was being an idiot for not taking a misdemeanour and up to three years' probation. But if you're on probation, you can't visit the jail. He said if I pled guilty to a felony, I'd get visits back. The judge said, "A felony will impact you for life. It will impact your right to vote and any civil rights that you have. Certain jobs you'll never be able to get." And just at that moment and with a confident smile I said yes 'cause all that was important to me at that moment was getting our visits back.'

'I can't believe this!' I said, furious with her public defender. 'I didn't know an attorney can just lie to you like that. You need to put a complaint in to the Arizona Bar Association.'

'That's not gonna get our visits back!'

'Maybe I can get Alan Simpson on it.'

'When? What are we gonna do in the meantime? I'm so sad.' She sobbed. 'I don't think I'm ever gonna be able to see you again until you're out. They haven't even tried you. They're moving so slow.'

'We've come this far, and it hasn't been easy. We can make it through all the dirty games these attorneys are playing. Look, I love you. We can get through this.'

'You're always so positive. Maybe too positive.'

Without the visits, I feared for our relationship. That Claudia was the victim of a mess I'd made receded into the background as my anger erupted at the prosecutor and Claudia's public defender for subjecting her to more injustice than she could bear.

34

....

'How're you doing, Million Dollar Bond Guy?' asked Dr Ross – a $600,000-a-year abortionist accused of molesting his patients – as we were escorted to court in chains. During the '90s, Dr Ross had become famous on TV for criticising the escalating violence against abortionists and their clients. He'd patrolled his clinic in a bullet-proof vest, armed with a gun. He was a strapping man, greying at the sides, with a wolfish shape to his face.

'Holding up,' I said. 'I've been hearing about your case on the radio all week. Is it true you may get a new trial?'

'I didn't even hear the news this week. What did they say?'

'They said one of your alleged victims was arrested soliciting two undercover vice cops, that she lied on the stand, hid her true occupation as a prostitute and that your attorney is asking for a new trial.'

'Oh yeah, it's all true. The Attorney General's office must have known she was a prostitute before the trial. Most of my alleged victims were highly sexually active drug users who were using abortion as a form of birth control. Some were up to their fourth abortion. I'd tell them, "Protect your vagina! Use a condom!" But, no, they didn't like to use condoms. They'd rather get pregnant and pay me $360 for a fucking abortion.'

'Why didn't they just take birth control?' I said.

'Because they were too fucking high and stupid to remember to take their pills. You know all about trial by media, Million Dollar Bond Guy, but it's much more corrupt than you can imagine.'

'How so?'

'Let me tell you what's really going on here. Most bastard DAs are seeking higher office and would run over their own mother to get a higher appointment. To make it look like they're getting tougher on crime, they arrest several people and take their cases straight to the media. They're probably all at it, contributing to press articles and news reports claiming they're "from sources close to the investigators and prosecution".'

'In my *New Times* article, there were quotes from sources close to the investigators and prosecution, and a quote from the prosecutor.'

'Exactly. That's how they begin their game. I suggest you go to the *New Times*, and search under David Ross, abortionist, and pull my whole series. How does it feel to have your civil liberties denied by these bastards taking their cases to the press?'

'They've trampled on your right to a fair trial. What they did to me was nothing compared to you.'

'Justice – ha! Look at my charges. I allegedly molested my patients. Do you know what that means?'

'No.'

'It means that I put my fingers into their vaginas. What do they expect? I'm an abortion doctor! Some of the women had rectal examinations and now they are screaming abuse.'

'So are these women motivated by money here?'

'Maybe it's the guilt. Some of them are on their third and fourth abortions and they want to take their anger out on someone else. I hope to God that none of them get awarded compensation.'

'I'm writing a book about my experience; maybe you should do the same.'

'Someone needs to write about this and let the world know what's going on in Arizona's justice system.'

The inmates told Dr Ross he'd get a life sentence if he didn't sign the plea bargain offered to him. He said his conscience prohibited him from admitting guilt when he was innocent. To take a life sentence when you could sign for much less, you have to either be crazy . . . or innocent. My gut told me he was the latter and that his foul mouth had contributed to his demise.

On 2 January 2004, Dr Ross, who'd lost at trial and was facing anywhere from probation to 74 years, went for sentencing. Seventeen supporters wrote to the judge that he was a skilful surgeon who'd battled for women's rights to have abortions. His wife said the alleged victims were 'strangers who enter your life uninvited and pluck you out of your existence in one beat of the heart'. Even a female judge who'd known him for 20 years wrote, 'Dr Ross's manners at times raise hackles, but he . . . would not use his position to harm defenceless women.' But continuing to protest his innocence only aggravated his sentence. The judge chastised him for being remorseless and sentenced him to 35 years. On my radio, I heard the alleged victims rejoicing at the judge's decision. One said, 'I hope he dies in prison.'

'I was sliding soap under the doors in the next pod, and Dr Ross was crying. I gave him shit for breaking down,' Mack said.

The next day, Dr Ross was at Visitation with his mother-in-law, who he called Big Bertha.

'How does it feel to stand up for yourself and have your life taken away?' I asked.

'In this justice system, if an innocent man doesn't kowtow to the court and proclaim his guilt, heaven help him. There's nothing I can do now except start my appeal.'

'How long does an appeal take?'

'Five years if I'm lucky.'

Terrified of ending up like Dr Ross, I began to contemplate what to say to the judge at my sentencing hearing.

35

....

For the first time, I did a ten-minute headstand. I discovered Greek philosophy and became obsessed with Plato's *Republic*. Biographies took up much of my time: Timothy Leary, Howard Hughes, Aldous Huxley . . . Meditating, I visualised being inside various shapes: spheres, tetrahedrons, spinning Platonic solids . . . I imagined light running down my spine, grounding me with the earth. I sat in the lotus position for 20 minutes staring at a mandala, and then when I closed my eyes, the glowing image of the mandala remained. I discovered higher states of consciousness without poisoning my body with drugs. I longed to visit an ashram and to read Sanskrit texts. I rambled in letters home about parallel universes, sunspots, supervolcanoes and the Illuminati. I moved on to an advanced Spanish text. Attempting to learn Mandarin, I sketched Chinese characters. All of these things were helping me take my mind off the time I was facing.

Some of the inmates in the upper-tier cells thought it would be fun to coax Chicken Wing into climbing the metal-grid stairs that rose from the front of the day room up to the balcony.

'I've got crackers! Come and get them!' a prisoner yelled as if talking to a dog.

'Cookies for you over here, Chicken Wing!'

'You can do it, Chicken Wing!'

Chicken Wing looked around for his cellmate to get the food, but his cellmate was in the shower. Chicken Wing attempted the first stair but stopped when he almost fell over.

I got on my hands and knees and yelled through the gap under my door, 'Don't do it, Chicken Wing!'

'I can't come up the stairs!' Chicken Wing yelled.

'Come on, climb the stairs!'

'*Cookies,*' a man shouted in the Cookie Monster voice, shaking a rack of cookies.

Egged on by their shouting, Chicken Wing tried again. The inmates stood at their doors and cheered. He made it to the second step, swaying, hanging onto the railing with his good hand, and they cheered again. He almost fell forward onto the third, but he righted himself to more cheering. Pausing to consolidate his gains, he looked over his shoulder at the distance he'd travelled and grew scared.

'Don't give up now, Chicken Wing!'

'You can do it, homey!'

'You better get your ass up here if you want these cookies, dawg!'

'*Cookies*,' came the Cookie Monster voice.

Using the railing, he pulled himself forward but fell to one side and collapsed on the stairs. The inmates booed, laughed and rained abuse down on him.

Emerging from the shower in his pink boxers, his cellmate found Chicken Wing sprawled on the stairs. 'You shouldn't fuck with a cripple like that!' he yelled at the men upstairs. 'I'll be right up there when I get dressed to get those cookies from y'all!' He helped Chicken Wing up, got dressed, charged up the stairs and demanded the cookies.

Chicken Wing's cellmate was sentenced and rolled up a few days later. The guards celled Chicken Wing with a schizophrenic old man who urinated on the walls. Chicken Wing spent most of his time on the bottom bunk at exactly the height the old man urinated at. Living in constant fear of the old man urinating on him sent Chicken Wing into a depression. He stopped badgering us for crackers.

On my hour out, I watched the old man accost a guard. He was standing at his cell door, gazing at the Mexican American female through the window. 'Why I am here?'

'What do you mean: why am I here?' she replied.

'Why am I here?'

''Cause you've got charges.'

'I'm not here for the good of my health, you know! Why am I here?'

'You have charges,' she said in a sympathetic way.

The old man danced around the cell, twisting his head from side to side as if seeking something. He stopped as suddenly as he'd started and looked at the guard with a crazy expression. 'I don't see my charges! I definitely don't see them! My charges aren't in here! Why am I here?' It was more than she could take. She abandoned him still ranting about not seeing his charges.

The old man's behaviour took a worse toll on Chicken Wing. He stopped speaking to us and barely left his cell during his hour out.

Whenever I peered into his cell, he was on his bunk rocking dementedly, his face blank.

After taking a shower, I paid him a visit. 'Come and talk to me, Chicken Wing.'

'No! Go away!'

'Look, if you tell me what's wrong, maybe I can help you.'

He ignored me.

'I'll get you anything you want off the store list.'

'Anything?' he asked, his remote expression fading.

'Anything.'

'Cookies?' He grinned like a child, and I knew I had him.

'Lots of cookies.'

He raised himself awkwardly and stumbled to the window.

'What's the matter?'

He looked over his shoulder at the old man asleep on the top bunk. 'He's gonna pee on me. He already peed on my mattress.'

'How about I fill out an inmate request form, asking they move you to another cell, and you sign it?'

'I'll do it! I'll do it! I'll do it!'

The guards moved him all right, but in with Leprechaun. Chicken Wing's mood improved for a few weeks, until Leprechaun leaked to us that Chicken Wing had been wetting the bed. This led to many cruel jokes during Chicken Wing's hour out. On the grounds that their cell reeked of urine, Leprechaun requested to move out.

Squeegee's public defender duped him into signing a plea bargain stipulating a minimum sentence of four months, a presumptive sentence of one year and a maximum sentence of two years. Reviewing the police reports, Squeegee decided the police had conducted an illegal search and had no case against him. His attorney refused to prepare for a trial and insisted he stick to the plea bargain. After consulting his family, he petitioned the court to revoke the plea bargain and replace his attorney. The judge denied both requests and sentenced him to a slightly mitigated sentence of nine months.

During his last week with me, Squeegee mentioned Bonzai.

'Throughout the jail, I've heard so many people talk about Bonzai,' I said. 'Is he the bogeyman of the Arizona prison system or what?'

'I served time with Bonzai at Florence,' Squeegee said.

'You knew him?'

· ·

'Yeah. Robert Wayne Vickers.'

'What's his story?'

'He was just some tall skinny kid arrested for doing burglaries in Tempe. He was only sentenced to do a few years. He came in in the late '70s. He was real quiet, not considered a threat at all at that time, so they housed him with the general population at CB4, all two-man cells. He snapped 'cause his celly drank his Kool-Aid and didn't wake him up for chow. He waited for his celly to go sleep and killed him with a shank made from a toothbrush. He carved the word Bonzai – misspelled with a Z – on his celly's back. To show the guards his celly was really dead, he put a cigarette out on the corpse's foot. After that they called him Bonzai or Bonzai Bob.

'They charged him with murder and moved him to a single cell in CB6 – super-max housing for death row, gang leaders and the most violent prisoners. In CB6 they were locked-down all day except to come out for showers. They said you couldn't escape from it, but Bonzai managed to get up on the roof.

'Another time, he picked his cell-door lock, waited for one of his neighbours to come out for a shower, came out and almost shanked the guy to death, but the guards stopped it. So he got attempted-murder charges for that one.

'Back then, the cells had power outlets, and you could heat up food in your cell, like plug-in hotpots from the store. In '82, Bonzai boiled up some Vitalis hair gel and took it with him when they let him out of his cell. He told his neighbour to come to the front of the cell and threw it on him. Then he used toilet paper to set him on fire. His neighbour died and a bunch more nearly died from the smoke.'

'Why'd he kill that guy?'

'He'd talked some shit about Bonzai's niece. They transported him to Florence for a court appearance. In the holding cell, he picked the lock on his handcuffs but made it look like he was still cuffed when they took him into the courtroom. He waited for the judge to start, then jumped up and attacked the people in the gallery. It was on the news. When the guards were about to cuff him for another court appearance, he pulled out a shank and stabbed one in the stomach and the other in the shoulder and the armpit. He was so dangerous, the warden had a shower installed in Bonzai's cell and had the door welded shut. They considered him the most dangerous inmate ever in Arizona's prison system. In '99, they finally let him out of his cell – to give him a lethal injection. The guards said in his last years his crazy eyes made him look like he was possessed by the devil.'

January 04

Dear Mum and Dad,

I am sorry about recent stressful events in court. I suspect, as usual, there will be no March trial. No hearings to listen to the calls have been set, and I'm expecting a better plea bargain. The current plea was tinsel-wrapped to entice me. When in reality the judge could sentence me to 12 years, of which the Department of Corrections would make me serve 85%, and I calculated I'd be 44 when I got out! Nothing is as it seems in this insidious game that the prosecutor and Detective Reid play with people's minds and lives. In my 20 months in jail, I have never witnessed a first-time offender with like charges get offered so much time. They are hell-bent on making an example out of me. Look how they took it to the media immediately to make a splash and to get public opinion against me. People with more serious charges than me generally get probation or less than five years if it's their first time in trouble.

I am deeply sorry that by prolonging my legal fight I am also prolonging your agony. Sometimes I feel like I should just give in and sign the plea and let them do what they want to me. Just to end the uncertainty and stress and costs. It's a horrible situation I've put myself in. Sometimes I cannot concentrate on my studies because I fear I am about to lose the prime years of my life. This is the end phase of extremely high-stake negotiations, and that's why our stress levels are peaking. I honestly think that things shouldn't be dragged out too much longer. My goal is to be in prison before the summer heat starts to cook us alive.

All my love,
Shaun

Darling Claudia,

Oh love, it's so boring and lonely in here. It's like I'm just forgotten, packed away, frozen in time.

There is a Rule 11 in cell 8 called Ed who sleeps on his cell floor and is sometimes observed crouched under his little table or crouched below the TV in the day room. Ed sometimes comes to our door and tells us that his friend in Sedona is selling puppies and wondering if we want to buy any. I went to court with Ed and another Rule 11 last week, and they just shared bizarre stories that didn't even match each other's conversations. Anyway, Ed keeps his plastic water bottle cold by sticking it in his toilet so it is wedged below water in the flush hole. Last night Ed woke up to take a pee and forgot to remove his water bottle. Ed peed on his water bottle and then proceeded to flush the toilet and flooded his whole cell. This happened in the middle of the night. Ed was upset and asked my celly, Squeegee, as to why Squeegee hadn't told him to take his water bottle out of the toilet. Quite bizarre, eh?

Anyway, they are about to turn the lights out.

Love you,

Shaun

Darling Claudia,

Today was weird. We have been on security override since last night because of a riot on the second floor, and our water was turned off all day for repairs. The riot happened because two pods got out of their pod doors and fought a bloody battle. We heard reports of an inmate smashing a fire extinguisher into other inmates' heads. It sounds like the jail nearly lost control.

They took my celly, Squeegee, to Alhambra, which is the processing centre on 24th St and Van Buren where we all go before going to prison. Then they gave me a new celly from the second floor. He was a Chicano caught with a needle, and he was quite a thug. They moved him out pretty quickly. Then the female guard said that she was moving some crazy old crackhead up to my room from room 3. I pleaded with her not to, and Jack, one of my neighbours, pleaded with her and now he is my new celly. Jack is nice. We've played chess, and he likes my books.

They took Ed to mental hospital (finally), so I won't be seeing him again. The other Rule 11 in the pod, Mr Sleepers, is a chubby guy with bugged eyes that comes to our door and tries to sell us psych meds. 'I'll trade you these sleepers for an item of candy.' He showed me a booger (called crows in England). 'Do you think this is a big one?' I'll never forget those words. Mr Sleepers is here for arson.

Leprechaun has a new celly again after his old celly rolled up within a few days claiming to the guards that Leprechaun had put a curse on him.

Ed's old room was pounced on by a wood from cell 3, but now he's complaining that the toilet is broken and that Ed smeared poop on the bunk and walls. Ed's neighbours previously described seeing Ed smearing poop. I guess they were telling the truth.

Some poor sod in cell 2 called Randy got sentenced to 26 years today. Randy is the '101 Slayer's' cellmate. He was convicted of armed robberies and had priors. Ouch! Twenty-six bloomin years! Yikes!

Sorry I am unable to call you because of the security override. I hope to hear your sweet voice soon.

All my love for ever,

Shaun

36

....

'How does Arpaio get away with these jail conditions?' I asked a guard.

His reply, 'The world has no idea what really goes on in here,' made me want to tell the world. But how? I was limited to describing the conditions in the letters I wrote to my family and friends.

My mother wrote to a Member of Parliament about the conditions, requesting he demand a resolution to my case. He said that if you commit a crime in another country, you have to abide by their rules. She wrote to Amnesty International, who said they were documenting the human-rights abuses but powerless to do anything about my situation.

Around the same time, my father read *The Clandestine Diary of an Ordinary Iraqi* by Salam Pax. It contained the blog entries Pax wrote as the bombs rained down on Baghdad and described what it was like during the early days of the war. My father thought it would be a good idea to post my descriptions on the Internet as a blog. He sent me a copy of Pax's book. I read it and agreed to the idea. (The prisoner who read the book next was an ex-pilot of Saddam Hussein's who lived below me.) Prior to my arrest, my knowledge of blogs was limited to one written by Claudia's friend Samantha. Blogging had seemed trivial, but Pax proved it could be newsworthy.

My mother had seen some of the news stories about Arpaio's guards being responsible for the deaths of Charles Agster and Scott Norberg, so she was worried about reprisals against me for exposing the conditions. With things deteriorating for me on the legal front, I didn't want to put anything online that might hurt my case either. My father suggested we start the blog under a pseudonym. He googled for prison blogs and discovered there was only one in existence – also set up anonymously. My parents – brainstorming in the computer room that was my old bedroom – came up with the title 'Jon's Jail Journal'. Jon because the Irish spelling of Shaun means John. And Jail Journal tacked on for alliteration.

The riskiest part for me was getting what I wrote out of the jail undetected. If the mail officer opened my letters, I would be discovered. My aunt Ann was still visiting every weekend, so I figured I could stash my blogs in the personal property I released to her. A few sheets of paper among many would probably get through unnoticed. After sharpening my golf pencil on the wall, I started writing.

19 Feb 04

The toilet I sleep next to is full of sewage. We've had no running water for three days. Yesterday, I knew we were in trouble when the mound in our steel throne peaked above sea level.

Inmates often display remarkable ingenuity during difficult occasions and this crisis has resulted in a number of my neighbours defecating in the plastic bags the mouldy breakfast bread is served in. For hours they kept those bags in their cells, then disposed of them downstairs when allowed out for showers. As I write, inmates brandishing plastic bags are going from cell door to door proudly displaying their accomplishments.

The whole building reeks like a giant Portaloo. Putting a towel over the toilet in our tiny cell offers little reprieve. My neighbour, Eduardo, is suffering diarrhoea. I can't imagine how bad his cell stinks.

I am hearing that the local Health Department has been contacted. Hopefully they will come to our rescue soon.

I received a card from Claudia saying she is going to stick with me no matter what happens. Through her brother, Jay, I was able to coordinate a delivery of roses for her on Valentine's Day.

20 Feb 04

My cellmate couldn't hold his in any longer. He pinched his nose and lifted the towel from the toilet. Repulsed by the mound, he said, 'There's way too much crap to crap on, dawg. I'm gonna use a bag.' So, as jail etiquette demands in these situations, I rolled over on my bunk and faced the wall. I heard something hit the rim of the seatless toilet and him say, 'Damn! I missed some!' When he was done, he put the finished product by the door and the stink doubled. He had no water to clean where the errant piece had fallen on the toilet, so it remained, forming a crustation on the rim. We were hoping to be allowed out to dispose of the bag until a guard announced, 'There will be no one coming out for showers and phone calls, as we have to get 120 inmates water from an emergency container!'

The water came back on in stages. In our toilet, its level slowly rose.

'Oh no,' I said. 'It's about to overflow, and we'll be stuck in here with sewage all over the floor.'

'One of us needs to stick his hand in the crap to let the water through,' my cellmate said. 'And you're the closest.'

The brown soup was threatening to spill from the bowl, so I put a sandwich bag on my hand. 'I can't believe I'm doing this,' I said, plunging my hand into the mound. The mound took the bag from my hand. Almost up to my elbow in sewage, I dug until the water level sank.

'I owe you one, dawg,' my cellmate said.

'It's your turn next time,' I said.

Because the tap water hadn't come back on, I couldn't wash my arm. Not wanting to contaminate anything in the cell, I sat on the stool until a guard let us out for showers hours later.

26 Feb 04

At 7 a.m., I awoke to a cockroach tickling the palm of my hand. Like everyone else in the jail except for the staff, it was probably hungry. I flicked it towards the door. It took the hint and headed west.

The excursion of the week was to the Medical Unit for a 'general wellness check-up'. Four of us were summoned from our pod. At the nurse's desk, we were interviewed one after the other:

'I slept with a woman from a trailer park just before I was arrested,' said one of my embarrassed neighbours as the nurse diagnosed him with scabies.

Next up was our chow server. I was shocked to overhear that he has had infectious tuberculosis for the duration of his stay.

The third inmate complained that he had gone two days without his seizure medication and as a result was unable to sleep.

When it was my turn, the nurse insisted I should take a TB test. I protested that I had been tested twice already. She looked at my medical history, and snarled, 'Well, you'll have to take another test before June, so you might as well have it now.'

At least our water is flowing again. Inmates are still trading stories about defecating in plastic bags and urinating in pop bottles. The inmate the media has dubbed the '101 Slayer' boasted he was able to hold his business in for the entire three-day outage. It was also his mum that called the Health Department and got the jail in trouble. Hopefully, our toilets will continue to function normally at least until we are moved to the new jail facility, which should be this summer.

I stashed these first few blog entries into a manila envelope containing mail I'd received. I sandwiched the manila envelope in-between more manila envelopes containing legal papers. Then I put five books onto the pile. I arrived at Visitation holding my property.

'You gotta form approving that property release?' the visitation guard barked.

'Sure do,' I said, waving the form at him.

He examined the form and took my property. He looked in each of the manila envelopes, pulling pieces of paper out here and there. The prospect of him discovering my blog entries made my heart beat irregularly. When he'd finished looking at my property, he put it on his desk.

The visit was from behind a Plexiglas screen, with me chained to a table speaking into a phone. While the guard kept my property, I talked to my aunt Ann for 30 minutes, the whole time worried the guard might go through my property again and find my blog entries. I was glad when he called the end of the visit. I reminded him about my property release. He met my aunt at a security door and handed her everything. She winked at me and left. Getting escorted back to my cell, I couldn't stop smiling to myself as I imagined my aunt leaving the jail with my blog entries. I was full of excitement from getting one over on the system, and looking forward to exposing what was going on.

When Ann got home, she typed up the blog entries and emailed them to my parents. My parents posted them to 'Jon's Jail Journal', which didn't get many hits at the time as it was only read by family and friends.

Sadly, my aunt Ann died a few years later. She was alive, however, when *The Guardian* published excerpts from 'Jon's Jail Journal'. The blogs they chose were the early entries she'd smuggled out of the jail, which detailed my relations with the cockroaches.

37
··········

The hardest part of being unsentenced is not knowing how many years you're going to get. It is a stress like no other. It gnaws at you constantly, haunts your dreams and overwhelms you during moments of weakness to the point where you contemplate suicide as a quick exit from the situation. And there's not much you can do about it. It's not like work stress where you can change your job, or relationship stress where you can dump your partner. The decisions you made that put you in jail are irreversible, and now your fate is in the hands of people vested with the power to put you away for a long time. That so few people hold this power over you makes it all the more terrifying.

The prosecutor wanted me to get as much time as possible to advance her career. As did Detective Reid. All the better for them if I got a 100-year headline-making sentence. I was struggling to hold myself together mentally before the prosecutor obtained witnesses, but now the stakes were so high my mind was starting to snap.

In a courtroom conversation with her boss loud enough for me to overhear, the prosecutor rubbed in how much time I was facing.

'Judge Watson just gave that Tucson drug dealer I prosecuted 200 years,' her boss said, referring to my regular judge.

'Why so many?' the prosecutor asked.

'He thought he was being a smart aleck taking it to trial. He lost at trial, and the judge stacked his charges.' Meaning Judge Watson had sentenced him to consecutive terms for every single drug crime.

'Attwood's refusing to sign a plea bargain and demanding a trial,' the prosecutor said.

'How many charges?' her boss asked.

'Twenty-three, I believe.'

'If he loses at trial and Judge Watson aggravates his sentence and stacks his charges, Attwood could easily get 200 years.'

Even though it was obvious they'd staged the conversation, I knew Judge Watson had sentenced that defendant to 200 years. It was a wire-tap case like mine. The conversation rammed the possibility of never getting out to the forefront of my mind. By the time I got back to my cell, I wanted to smash my head against the cement-block wall until I could no longer think about it. For weeks, I fretted over the man sentenced to 200 years. I imagined him in a bare suicide-watch cell – the next stop for all prisoners after receiving such big sentences. I wondered what was going through his mind, the devastation he was feeling, and that of his loved ones. I feared that amount of pressure would surely kill me.

March 2004

Dear Love,

I can't take it in here any more and I can't take the uncertainty any more, so I told Alan I'll probably sign a plea bargain. I am loath to slit my throat with my own hand, but it is my only option. If I get the nine-year minimum sentence stipulated, I'll be out in just over three years' time. My mum and dad and Alan do not want me to risk trial and a possible 25-year+ sentence.

I was moved. I am in hell again. No air is blowing. I keep passing out while reading and have to take a nap. The 101 Slayer grieved it, and the jail said they are not going to fix it! Cockroaches are everywhere. We are unable to hold them at bay. This pod is the worst yet. There are all kinds of freaks in this pod, including a white inmate with a heavily tattooed face. It looks like war paint.

Did my family send you my Internet journal info? I am not allowed to talk about it on the phone. It has all been created anonymously, so that I do not suffer any retribution.

I spoke to Cody, and I am happy that he got probation. He didn't buy into the BS and obviously they had no case against him. I found out that Wild Woman's mum recently died. I guess I must forgive her even though her agreement to testify added years to my sentence. It's all my own fault for associating with a bunch of drug addicts. What was I thinking?

My new celly, Mark, is nice. He has conspiracy-to-murder charges. It sounds like BS, though. He has two red poodles and his mum has two.

Please write to me just one time.

Love 'n' spoonage,

Shaun XXX

April 2004

Claudia,

When I call you and ask you how you feel or try to get some small talk out of you, you make me feel like I am trying to pull your teeth out. I just don't get it. I understand what misery it must be to have a fiancé in jail and I sympathise with you deeply, but look at how hard it is for me as well, love. Please read my blog and you will understand more about the conditions I am in. I make every effort to be positive when talking to you because you have done so much for me. Our calls used to be the highlight of my day, and now they just seem to make me sad. I realise how stressed out you are, and that is why I never ask you for anything any more. I am a capable person, and my family have helped me out a lot recently. I've tried so desperately hard to understand you, but no matter what I've done it just seems so difficult these days. I am a prisoner, but you have put yourself in a mental prison. I love you more than anything, and we can have a good life together, and children as we planned, but if you still want that, you're going to have to pull yourself together. For almost two years, we have had our heads above water holding each other up, but I feel that your head is slipping below water and because I am where I am I can't rescue you.

Love,

Shaun X

P.S. I've had a good response to the blog, and I've received letters congratulating me on a writing ability I never knew I had.

In May, I went to court in two minds over whether to sign a plea bargain. Alan Simpson was one of the strongest trial attorneys in town, up against a much less experienced prosecutor, and the police still had little evidence against me. If I took the case to trial and won, I'd be released right away. On the other hand, if I lost at trial, I could get up to 200 years. As much as I believed in Alan Simpson, the chance of getting 200 years was making me sweat more at nights.

In the courtroom, my attorney presented the plea bargain to me long before the judge was due to show up.

'I don't know what to do, Alan. I've fought it this long, maybe if I continue to hold out, I'll get a better plea bargain.'

Alan looked disappointed – he wanted my case done with. 'It's your decision. The prosecutor has indicated she will be preparing for trial if you don't sign this plea bargain, and I believe she's serious.'

'If it goes to trial, what will the cost be to my parents?' I asked, half hoping for a large number to put me off the idea.

'It's not about money. I'm defending you, so I have to represent you at trial whether they can pay me or not.'

'Good. They've got no savings left 'cause of me.'

'In that case, I'd have to do it for free.'

His answer drew me away from wanting to sign a plea bargain. I figured I could gesture that I wanted to take it to trial in the hope of getting a better plea bargain, and if that gamble ended up in a trial, there would be no financial burden on my parents.

'I don't think I want to sign the plea,' I said.

Alan furrowed his brow. 'You're taking a very big risk at this stage of the game. If the judge sentences you to somewhere around ten years, which is near the minimum stipulated in this plea bargain, with the loophole for foreign citizens, you'd be out in just over three-and-a-half. If you lose at trial, you might never get out.'

The prospect of never getting out pulled me back towards signing a plea bargain. But I was still unsure. For the rest of my life, I would have to live with the consequences of what I decided today. The decision was so hard to make, I couldn't make it at all. But I knew I had to do something. I was filled with a sense that my case was drawing to a conclusion whether I signed a plea bargain or not. A conclusion I wouldn't like.

Just then, Ray, the attorney I'd relied on prior to my arrest, showed up. 'What's going on?' he asked.

'He doesn't want to sign the plea bargain,' Alan said.

'Why?' Ray asked, shaking his head.

'I don't think they have much of a case or they would have taken me to trial already,' I said. 'I don't see the prosecutor wanting to go up against Alan at trial. They've got to come at me with a better plea bargain.'

'No, they don't!' Ray yelled. 'Look, you've got one of the best legal minds in town, why don't you just listen to him?'

'He won't listen to me,' Alan said.

'Fucking listen to him, or you'll be sorry!' Ray threw his hands up in the air and marched out.

My mind was so suspicious of anything involving attorneys that I assumed Alan had arranged that little charade with Ray. But what Ray had said rang true, and the forceful way he'd said it convinced me to go with the plea bargain. After signing an unknown chunk of my life away, my focus shifted to getting the minimum sentence of nine years. I knew I had to put on a good show with the help of my family at the sentencing hearing. I also feared that somehow I wouldn't be eligible for the loophole Alan had mentioned.

May 2004

Dear Claudia,

I signed a plea bargain! If all goes well at my sentencing, I'll be out of prison in late 2007. I'm sure the time will go fast, plus we'll have a visitation relationship again. I am to be sentenced in the last week of June. I'll be meeting the pre-sentence reporter in one week.

I feel that we kind of saved each other from ourselves when we first met, but unfortunately I couldn't quite kick my old lifestyle and friends. A very expensive mistake indeed! I have learnt a lot, and I will never make such mistakes again.

Sorry that I don't write to you more often, but I am trying to live off $10 a week, and I also used up all the postcards I bought from Chicken Wing. I hope that you don't think I love you any less because I am not sending you daily letters. I am also starting to feel lovesick because we haven't spoken in so long.

Forever yours,
Shaun

Mum and Dad,

I am very excited about your visit and can't wait to see everyone. I am very nervous about speaking to the judge at the sentencing hearing, and I am currently bandying ideas around about what to say. A fellow in here recently returned from his sentencing. He'd fully expected two years' probation, and the judge gave him fifteen years' prison time because of an allegation by the prosecutor that his family members jeered at the victim in his case in the courtroom. The judge said that neither he nor his family had shown any REMORSE! The remorseless ones, especially people protesting their innocence like Dr Ross, get hung. I also fully expect the prosecutor to paint me out to be a demon and Detective Reid to be pushing for a harsh sentence.

Ann said that the blog about inmate sexual gratification was quite shocking and sickening, but she appreciated I was just 'telling it like it is'. Karen wrote that she and her friends like the more disturbing stuff. I had that in mind when I wrote about Yum-Yum. Yum-Yum brought half of the pod out of the closet. Even my anti-gay cellmate said, 'I guess if I was to sleep with a guy, I'd at least want him to look like Yum-Yum.' This place has a strange effect on people. The abnormal slowly seems normal. Frankie, a Mexican Mafia hit man, is leading the pack and desperately trying to get the guards to move Yum-Yum into his cell. Frankie is the greatest thing to happen to my chess game, as he is the best opponent I've ever played.

Claudia said that Karen is more than welcome to stay with her if there is overcrowding at Ann's. I'm hoping Claudia will tough it out till I'm moved to the prison system. The visits there are contact, one hug and kiss are allowed, and they are hours long. I think that will make a world of difference. Right now, I'm just a voice on the phone to her or a letter here and there. She told me she has to drink to get to sleep and has uncontrollable trembling and anxiety. I feel so helpless in that I can't comfort her and help her.

I have enjoyed the Hemingway stories that I have read thus far. I was quite pleased at his ability to put someone at ease and then for something particularly nasty to happen. His short, monotonous sentences lead up to enjoyable unexpected twists. It's a good style. I am guessing he was a strange man, but I know nothing about him.

Love you loads! See you soon!

Shaun

38

··········

I thought the imminent resolution of my case had saved my relationship with Claudia. I called her, expecting her to be overjoyed at the prospect of our visits resuming in the prison system.

'Hey now! How're you?' I asked in my chirpiest voice.

'Hi. How're you?' she replied in a monotone.

'Your voice sounds funny, are you OK?' I asked, disappointed.

'Not really.'

Regaining my enthusiasm, I said, 'Why? This is going to be over soon. We'll have visits back. Visits are much longer in prison, and they let us hug and kiss.'

Her humphing knocked my mood back down. 'I don't think I can do this any more.'

'Do what? What're you talking about?' I asked, fearing her response.

'Like this . . . like this relationship.'

I was too shocked to speak. I could have been shanked at that moment and felt less pain than the hurt exploding in my brain. Tears tumbled out. For a while, neither of us spoke.

'It's just so . . . ' Claudia started sobbing. 'It's just been too hard without being able to see you for a year. And you think you're getting closer to the end, but what if they keep postponing?'

I was unable to think clearly but determined to win her back. 'I can understand this – you know – how you're feeling,' I said quietly, so the prisoners in the cells wouldn't hear me crying on the phone in the empty day room. 'I'll accept whatever decision you want to make, but do you think it's a good idea to throw away our relationship after everything we've been through?'

'I don't. This is so hard for me, too. It's been two years of me going to sleep every night thinking either you're gonna be home the next day or that this is a bad dream. And I'll wake up, and I'll be here alone, and now it's been two years, and there's not ever an end. You don't even know how long they might send you to prison for.'

What she said was true, and I was too emotional to counter her.

'But Claudia, I love you. I love you so much.'

'Shaun, I love you too. It's just hard. I think . . . what it is, I need to get my life back.'

'I know you do, but this is tearing me apart.'

'It's totally tearing me apart, too.'

The female computerised voice came on the line: 'You have 30 seconds remaining.'

'Does this mean you don't want me to call you any more?'

'Maybe it's best not for a while.'

'But what about—'

The line went dead. I didn't even want to breathe any more. I walked back to my cell with all of the dazed what-just-happened? confusion of someone getting out of a car after a collision. There was so much pressure in my head, my vision kept blurring. During the times I'd feared the break-up was coming, it never had. Now it had finally arrived, I couldn't see how I'd ever get over it. The anguish was too much for me to bear. I rushed back to my cell and curled up on the bottom bunk. Facing the wall, I pretended to read so my cellmate couldn't see me crying. Loudly turning a page every now and then that I hadn't read, I tortured myself even further by replaying images of the times we'd spent together. I barely slept that night and couldn't eat for days. I told my cellmate I was fasting. I didn't expect the pain to go away anytime soon.

June 2004

Dearest Claudia,

Thank you for being brave enough to tell me how you feel on the phone. You are going through a lot, and my situation is too much to deal with. I am sorry so many bad things have happened because of my wrongdoing. I wish things were different, but they are not. For some reason it seems I must lose everything, and I've expected our relationship to unravel for quite some time now. I do not begrudge your decision. I'll always be your friend no matter what. I'll always remember how happy you made me for the brief time we were together. Even though I have been reduced to living like an animal, they can't take away the precious times we shared. I'll always remember singing to myself and dancing in my SUV, happy as can be, driving from Tucson to see you on Bell Road. I'll always remember your pink and zebra apartment and our trips to Indian buffets and LA Fitness, and how we'd sit and drink smoothies after working out. I'm just so sad that I can't even give you a kiss goodbye. My emotional self wants me to fight to keep you. But what can I do from a jail cell? Nothing. I can't even see you. As you can gather, I am going in and out of feeling very sad as the reality of what you said sinks in. I can't even call you. There is no privacy here. I do not want to cry in front of 30 people. I don't want it to end this way. I am still the man that you fell in love with.

Shaun X

I loved Claudia so much I wanted to keep our relationship going, while knowing full well I had to let her go because loving her meant doing what was best for her.

39

....

The night before my sentencing hearing, I couldn't sleep. I lay on my bunk, stuck to the towel I'd put down to absorb my sweat, worrying about the effect of the hearing on my parents, sister and Aunt Sue, who'd flown from England. (Aunt Sue had moved back there in 1992.) Over the past two years, I'd put my family through so much, and I hated the idea of them grovelling for leniency in the sterile atmosphere of the courtroom. I also wondered if Claudia and her family would show up. I'd stopped calling her since the break-up, but her father, Barry, had assured me he'd be there even though he'd had brain surgery and was having regular seizures. Watching the cockroaches climb the walls, I prayed the judge would give me the minimum sentence stipulated in my plea bargain: nine years. It was hard to believe I'd be out of the jail and on my way to the prison system in a few weeks.

Daybreak: retreating cockroaches.

'Get up for court, Attwood!'

I was too nervous to defecate. The cheap plastic shaver cut my chin as my trembling hand rushed to remove a week's stubble in the ten minutes permitted to shave. I showered fast and put on the laundered set of clothes provided by the guard. Each act I completed reminded me I was a step closer to court. Leaving the day room, I again prayed for nine years.

Hours later, sitting alone in cuffs and leg chains in a holding cell outside the courtroom, I thought of my family in the public gallery. What are they thinking? Are they as nervous as me? By the time I heard the jingling keys and boot steps of the guard coming to fetch me, my hunched shoulders were aching from the build-up of tension. Standing up, I felt the blood drain from my face. In the corridor, I had a sense of disembodiment, as if I were floating alongside the guard like a spectre.

We entered the courtroom. The stenographer was a young woman, around 30, my sister's age. She appeared passive. The clerk of the court was a stern-faced woman, around 50. No judge. I passed the prosecutor, who looked the smartest I'd ever seen her in a light-coloured suit. Today was obviously important to her. She hoped to make her name on the back of my case. Detective Reid, with his thick dark hair trimmed and slicked back for the occasion, had an intense look on his face as if he were waiting to find out if a family member were dead or alive. The guard instructed me to sit on one of the benches at the side of the room and not so much as even smile at my family and Claudia's, who were about 20-strong. Two rows of sombre faces. I was pleased to see them all and relieved Claudia and her family were there. But I was too nervous to smile. My jaw was trembling, my face contorting of its own accord.

Alan Simpson walked over to me. 'How're you feeling?'

'Terrified,' I replied.

The sentencing judge entered, a narrow-faced man with greying hair and large protruding eyes. Everyone rose. When we were all seated again, he announced my case number. 'Is the state ready for sentencing?'

'Yes, Judge,' the prosecutor said. 'Gloria Olivia Davis on behalf of the Attorney General's Office.'

'Alan Simpson on behalf of Mr Attwood, who is present in custody, and we are ready to proceed.'

'It is my understanding that several family members would like to speak on behalf of Mr Attwood before I pronounce sentence . . . '

By now, my body's involuntary movements were most noticeable in my legs. They wouldn't stop shaking. As if my mind wanted to extricate me from the situation, it kept going blank and then snapping back to the courtroom.

The first to speak on my behalf was my mother, wearing a black shift dress and jacket. Funeral clothes. As she started to speak, the knowledge that my actions had brought her to the podium made it all the more humiliating. 'Shaun is my son and I love him very much. I know he has done wrong, and we are sorry for that, but there's so much good in him. It's been so difficult living so far away and not being able to visit him. Without Ann, my husband's sister who visits him every week, I don't know what we would have done.'

Crushed by the shame in my mother's trembling voice, I almost cried.

'Shaun's a very special person. He's a kind, loving and generous person who always wanted to help people. He naively believed that by making loads of money you could make things right for people. He was a beautiful baby and an energetic child. Shaun has always had this amazing energy bordering on manic, but I somehow managed to channel that energy into his studies. All through his childhood there were never any complaints about fighting or aggression, and he was successful, eventually getting a place at university and an honours degree.' She looked proud, and I dwelled on how much my behaviour had let her down. 'Shaun has a charismatic personality, and from an early age he has always attracted people. Sometimes the wrong people.' She paused. 'Your Honour, can I say something about Shaun's relationship with Peter?' she asked, referring to Wild Man. In previous court hearings, the prosecutor had portrayed Wild Man as a Frankenstein's monster I'd let loose on American society, so my mother wanted to provide some background.

Detective Reid was shaking his head. The judge nodded sympathetically, encouraging her to continue.

'Shaun has a bond with Peter I never understood. Peter was a problem child that grew into an aggressive teenager. At 16, he tried to commit suicide, but instead of contacting his parents, he asked Shaun for help. That shows the strength of the bond between them. Shaun had a tree, which he and his friends called the wishing tree. It overlooked a deep quarry in a woodland near us where the boys used to play. Shaun would sit in the wishing tree, and he knew then that he would be successful, and he promised his friends, including Peter, he would make everything right for them. Shaun used to believe that Peter would make good if given the chance. It was in keeping this promise he brought Peter to America.'

She said I hadn't meant to hurt people but had tried to make them happy in a misguided way. 'He became very successful as a stockbroker, and later on as a day trader, and we visited him regularly. When he told us about promoting rave parties, we didn't worry. Perhaps we were naive. Shaun's a natural entrepreneur. But I think it all just escalated. He gained a kind of rock-star status and attracted a following of young women.

'I don't know about the drug-taking – perhaps it was his way of self-medicating his depressions. I feel guilty in a way. Perhaps I should have got him anti-depressants in England. I've suffered from depression myself over the years but have always been reluctant to take medication,' she paused, 'until now. That's what's helping me get through this without crying. I just want to take him home with me.'

The pleading in her voice increased my sadness. 'I love him so much, and it's so difficult living so far away. I know that's not possible, but I know once he's back in England with the support of our family, which is very close and loving, nothing like this will ever happen again.' She emphasised the last line as if it were her final plea to convince him. She returned to her seat next to my father, who put his arm around her shoulder, hugging her tightly.

Detective Reid – who'd been shifting in his seat throughout her speech – looked agitated. The prosecutor had her ready-to-do-battle face on.

My aunt Ann was up next. In contrast with my mother, she wore casual American clothes. She hadn't written anything down in advance as she felt that she'd somehow find the right words to say when the time came. Speaking from the heart, she told of how she'd visited me without fail, every Saturday, and of the changes she'd witnessed and the subtlety of those changes that others who didn't know me like she did might not have noticed. She'd been so kind to me, I was really grateful.

Alan called Karen up next. My tall, elegant sister took to the podium, forcing a smile that betrayed how nervous she was. She'd stood by me in spite of all of our childhood squabbles, and I admired that. Gulping for breath, she told the judge how proud she'd always been of her big brother. How proud she was of me now. She started to cry but still managed to make herself heard as she recounted childhood anecdotes. Hearing Karen's words, I again had to fight back tears to remain composed.

My aunt Sue, the smartly suited business woman who'd help launch my stockbroking career, stood next. Nervous, she charged into her speech. The judge asked her to slow down and start again. Taking deep breaths, she spoke about the strong bond we'd always had. She also apologised as she felt she'd failed me, her godson, in some way, and must bear some responsibility. She concluded that she and all of our family would always provide a strong platform of support for me. She sat down, looking relieved to have got through it.

My father got up next, the pressure visible in the lines on his face. 'Your Honour, it is true to say that my family and I have been in a state of shock since Shaun's arrest in May 2002. The situation has seemed so unreal, compounded by the 5,000-mile distance between us and our son. But of course the situation is very real, and frightening, and here I am today talking to a superior-court judge just a few yards from the son that I love who is attired in jail stripes and shackles.' He glanced over at me. 'A son who I played with and introduced, along with his sister, Karen, to the beauties of the English countryside, to the birds and the wild flowers and trees. Shaun developed a passion for ornithology, and I remember him when he was aged around ten or eleven dragging a young ten-foot elderberry, complete with roots, into our back garden, which he insisted on planting in order to attract wild birds, which he could watch from his bedroom window.'

As my father reminisced about my childhood, I broke down. His gentle loving voice penetrated my soul. I was appalled at myself for letting him down, for letting them all down. I cursed my existence and felt deep regret for what I'd done. The tears started. As much as I tried to fight them back, they gushed. I could only cry. I was all tears and heartbeat and twitching nerves. My father paused to give me a look willing me to be strong. My attorney took my shoulder and handed me a tissue.

'I also taught Shaun to play chess, a game at which I believe he has become something of a legend while in jail. I believe that my son has suffered enough. I can tell you that, as a father, if I could step inside his shoes, I would gladly serve the rest of his time in prison. I realise that this is not possible, so all I can do is respectfully ask Your Honour to show mercy in the sentencing of my son today.'

The courtroom was silent for a long time after he'd finished speaking. Even the stenographer wiped tears from her eyes.

It was my turn to speak, so I began to shuffle towards the podium in my leg chains. My eyes met Detective Reid's, who scowled as if trying to psych me out. Our brief eye contact told me we were both thinking the same thing: our personal battle was almost over. Motivated in part by his attitude, I focused all of my willpower on gathering myself back together. I stopped crying and felt embarrassed, ashamed and nauseous. Tremors were running through my body, so I tried to ground myself with yogic breathing. Approaching the judge, conscious of the spasms in my face, I clenched my teeth. I looked up at the judge, who leaned forward, his unblinking eyes studying my face. Up close, his gaze was even more unnerving than Detective Reid's. He had the look of a bird of prey about to swoop on a mouse. My anxiety kept spiking up, forcing me to avert my eyes from his gaze.

'Mr Attwood,' said the judge, 'I know your name is Shaun Patrick

Attwood, and based upon a determination made previously, it is the judgement of the court that you are guilty of money laundering, a Class 3 non-dangerous non-repetitive felony, attempting to commit a dangerous drug violation, a Class 3 non-dangerous non-repetitive felony, and use of wire or electronic communication to facilitate a drug transaction, a Class 4 non-dangerous non-repetitive felony. I read your pre-sentence report and all of the attachments, letters of support, and also the prosecutor's aggravation memorandum. I have also considered the fact that as of today you have done 775 days of pre-sentence incarceration. Does that sound right, Mr Simpson?'

'Yes, Judge.'

'Mr Attwood, is there anything you would like to tell me before I pronounce sentence?'

'Yes, Your Honour. Thanks for the opportunity to address the court.' Trembling, I could only stammer out my words. 'I came to America to be a stockbroker, and America was good to me.' Still congested from crying, I kept sniffing. 'I made lots of money while still young, and after years of hard work and study I stupidly got off track. I ended up throwing wild parties and taking drugs, which led to the commission of these crimes. I have no excuses, Your Honour, and I am deeply sorry for the effects on society my mistakes have caused.

'Despite the hardships of jail, I've made the most of the last two years by studying. I hope the resumé of my achievements shows my sincere desire to return to university in England. While in jail, I've developed writing skills, and my recommendation to buy gold was published in *Investor's Business Daily.*' Hoping my words were having a positive effect, I tried to read his body language, but his fixed look of contempt increased my fear. 'Recidivism is not an option, and in the hundreds of letters of support, my family and friends have expressed their confidence in my future behaviour.

'I invested in drugs out of greed and hedonism. I wish to apologise to the state of Arizona, society and my family for the harm my actions have caused. I am a first-time offender who has sincerely learnt from his mistakes.' I hesitated over whether to use a quote I'd selected, but it just came out. 'Mahatma Gandhi once said that the law should be used to change men's hearts. Well, now that I've gone through this, my heart is in the right place. I humbly ask for your leniency this day.' I figured if the hearing was going to go my way, he'd show some sympathy now. But he didn't. Not even a trace.

'Remain where you are, Mr Attwood. OK, Miss Davis.'

The prosecutor stood to take her turn but seemed at a loss for words. Whether it was part of an act or she had been caught off guard by the emotional atmosphere, I was unsure. The warmth and sincerity of the speeches had surprised everyone. There was an expression of deep thought, and then she began: 'Mr Attwood, you are extremely lucky to have such a loving and caring family. How could you do this to them?' She looked around the court as if expecting everyone to side with her line of attack. 'Your family came here today, some from England even, and spoke so eloquently on your behalf. The only way you could do this to them and the only explanation I can think of for your family's kind words is that you must have a Jekyll and Hyde personality.'

Detective Reid smirked. I felt the goodwill the previous speeches had generated start to diminish.

'It seems you managed to keep your family charmed while you committed a pattern of serious drug crimes over a number of years because your parents live in England and had no clue what was going on here in Arizona. Mr Attwood, have you any idea of the deaths drug dealers cause? Although you were never charged with any violent crimes, isn't it true that your chief enforcer, Mr Peter Mahoney, committed acts of violence?'

Detective Reid was loving this.

'Judge, I filed the submission of the documents for aggravation of Mr Attwood's sentence. In summary, what this all shows is that the information that the state and law enforcement had prior to going up on the wire showed Mr Attwood was the head of a criminal organisation employing hundreds of people over six years, involved in the sale and distribution of millions of dollars of drugs at street value for his own personal gain. That Mr Attwood is an educated man who can make eloquent speeches to the court like you heard today makes his crimes all the more inexcusable. He should have known better. If you look at the volume of drugs dealt, his lead role in the organisation, the state would ask you that this court impose the maximum aggravated sentence, given that the aggravated circumstances far outweigh the mitigating circumstances in this particular case. Thank you.'

Detective Reid was nodding, my nausea rising. With all of the speeches at an end, the judge shuffled his papers around while I exchanged worried glances with my family. Aching with guilt, I prayed the judge would show mercy.

'I have considered all the circumstances presented to me,' the judge said. 'I have considered the mitigating circumstances which are that Mr Attwood avows no prior felony convictions in any jurisdiction, he has a diagnosis of bipolar disorder as indicated in the psychological evaluation, and that, rather than just sitting on his rear in the jail, Mr Attwood took all the classes and his behaviour was exemplary. Also, he has accepted full responsibility for what he did and shown remorse. I have also considered the strong family support that you have in England.'

Hearing this raised my hopes.

'I have also considered the aggravating circumstances, which are your repetitive involvement in the transportation and sales of large quantities of illegal drugs, the negative impact on the community and your lack of moral concern for others in society. As if you were unable to ascertain an ethical difference, you traded drugs like you traded the stock market until you were forced to face the consequences.'

Now I figured it was all going against me and braced for the worst.

'The picture that's painted throughout all this, and also in some of the aggravating-circumstance documents that Miss Davis prepared for me, conflict with your family's view of you. Obviously, they have a lot of love for you, as shown today. But at the same time, they say this is all out of character. Well, it's out of character, but only to the extent this has been going on in the States for over six years.

'I also considered the statutory aggravating factors. The fact that this was committed for personal gain and that there were so many accomplices involved. Based on all that, it is ordered the defendant be sentenced to a term of—'

I felt like I was standing in front of a train about to hit me.

'—9½ years in the Department of Corrections to date from today but with full credit for 775 days of pre-sentence incarceration.'

My relief began immediately – until my attorney sprang up and said, 'I'd just like to seek clarification from the court that, as stipulated in the plea bargain, Mr Attwood is eligible for a half-time release on the balance of the sentence under the terms of Arizona Revised Statutes 41-1604.14: Release of prisoners with detainers; eligibility; revocation of release.' He was referring to the loophole.

'Miss Davis?' the judge said.

'I don't know anything about this,' the prosecutor said. 'Mr Attwood must serve 85 per cent of the sentence in accordance with Arizona's laws.'

As this was not what I'd agreed to in the plea bargain, I was shocked. The half-time release Alan said the prosecutor had previously agreed to would have got me out in 3½ years. Had I signed under false pretences? It would have been better to risk a trial. I felt tricked.

'Here is the plea agreement,' my attorney said, 'specifying that Mr Attwood is eligible to be deported back to England when he has served at least one half of the balance of the sentence imposed by the court.'

'Let me see that.' The judge appeared a little confused, but after reading the paperwork more thoroughly he said, 'Yes, it says here that Mr Attwood is eligible for the half-time release.'

I wondered if Alan had managed to hoodwink the prosecutor by agreeing to a longer sentence knowing he could reduce it through a loophole at the last minute. Or was the prosecutor simply trying it on in front of Detective Reid, who was gunning for a life sentence?

'As far as the Attorney General's Office is concerned,' the prosecutor said, 'Mr Attwood must serve 85 per cent of his sentence. If he is deported back to England, then he would have to serve the balance of his sentence there, too.'

'That's not what the plea says,' my attorney said.

'Then I'm left with no choice but to revoke the plea agreement,' the judge said.

His words were like a punch to the head that hadn't quite knocked me out. I was stunned. I couldn't believe my sentencing was about to be cancelled. I couldn't imagine having to start all over again. Having to spend more months fighting my case from the jail. If the guard had tried to take me away at that moment, I would have yelled at the judge.

'Is the plea agreement you are holding, Judge, the same as the one in Miss Davis's possession?' my attorney asked, urgency in his voice.

The judge didn't reply. After pausing for a few seconds, he said, 'This is most unusual. I'd like to see you both, Miss Davis and Mr Simpson, in my chambers.'

Watching them leave the courtroom and take my future with them, I burned with outrage. It seemed unreal. Maddeningly so. As they hashed it out in private, my family members' faces turned ashen. My dad was holding my mum as if to prevent her from collapsing. Claudia's father, Barry, looked as if he were in the disorientation stage of some tropical illness – unknown to me he'd had a mini-seizure upon entering the building but in spite of that had insisted on staying. Barry was sweating, swaying, unfocused, his mouth moving as if he were trying to garble something that wouldn't quite come out. I was terrified of the sentencing hearing falling through and furious at the whole judicial process. I imagined Alan telling me I just needed to tough the jail out for another year while he continued to fight the case. I could see in the eyes of my parents, sister and aunt Sue they were thinking they'd just flown 5,000 miles for nothing. Detective Reid's eyes were saying, *Gotcha!* On the verge of a nervous breakdown, I waited for the decision. These were the longest, most agonising moments of my life.

The judge, Alan and the prosecutor eventually returned. Had Alan saved the day? I could tell nothing by their faces. Everyone else looked apprehensive. My fingers were tingling, my heart about to pop one of its chambers. But for the handcuffs, I would have clutched my chest.

The judge unsettled me further with his gaze. I swayed as if about to faint. Then he said, 'Based on my conversation with Miss Davis and Mr Simpson, it is the recommendation of this court that the defendant be eligible for the half-time release on the balance of his sentence and be deported back to England at that time.'

His ruling lifted 26 months of uncertainty like a tombstone. It caused Detective Reid to stand and curse. It made my loved ones cheer and throw their hands up in a celebratory fashion. It sent the prosecutor shuffling her paperwork back together as if she wanted to get out of there fast. It moved my attorney to shake my hand, proud of the outcome and no doubt glad to be shot of my case. It even made the escorting guard smile in my direction.

I was surging with relief and smiling bizarrely like a lone survivor emerging from a natural disaster. I had a strange sense of release. My future was no longer up in the air, and that was all that mattered. Even though I'd just received a 9½-year prison sentence, I could see an end to it. I could see the exact day I was getting out. I couldn't wait to get out of Arpaio's jail system to get my prison time started so I could get it finished. Yes!

Acknowledgements

I started writing this book in 2002. The road to publication was a long one and not without its share of steep inclines and hairpin bends. The kindness of many people helped me along the way.

My parents were there from the get-go, posting my entries for 'Jon's Jail Journal' and supporting me unconditionally. My mother spent hours reading my chapters, meticulously writing in comments. The same could be said of my sister, Karen, who attempted to get us both published by working for two years on a separate book. I'd also like to credit my aunt Ann (now deceased) for smuggling my blogs out of the Madison Street jail right under the guards' noses, and my aunt Susan O'Connor and Mick Kelly, who got me started in America.

Also my lifelines at times were Amber Holwegner and her family, Barry, Lori, Josh, Jay, Jazmyne, Diana and Big Dog.

Thank you to everyone who attended my sentencing hearing or wrote letters to the judge, including Lorraine, Jayne, Paula, David, Steven, Christopher, Michelle, Ryan, Duane, Aunty Lily Harrison and her many kids.

Numerous prisoners encouraged me to keep writing. I'd especially like to thank Jack for providing feedback, urging me to write short stories and enter contests. I'd like to thank Otis, whose experiences my short story 'Amazing Grace' is based on. And let's not forget all of the prisoners who've kindly shared their stories with the readers of 'Jon's Jail Journal' over the years: Two Tonys – your horse came in!; Warrior; T-Bone; Mr Frankie – not a man to drop the soap in the shower around!; Iron Man; Weird Al aka Noodles (whose brain I picked many times); the one and only Wild Man – there's plenty more of his madness in the prequel to this book; fellow blogger Shannon C.; the Polish Avenger;

Bran-O; Sarah-Jane of Scotland; Shay; A.R.; Long Island; Slope; Jaime F.; Xavier S.; Red and Bones. These and many other contributors have shown the world that prisoners are human beings too.

Many of the people in this book went over their dialogue and other details with me. Those not mentioned so far include Alan Simpson, Steve J., Joseph B., Joey V., Jimmy H., Gary M., Mickey Blue Eyes and Kinkeroo.

Not all of the staff were big bad rednecks. I'd like to thank Dr Shapiro, a creative writing teacher at Tucson prison, for his feedback, and Dr O, a brilliant prison psychologist who helped my personal development.

I'd like to thank everyone who took the time to write to me, visit or send books to the prisons I went to after Arpaio's jail, especially Zivi and Debbiy, Mike Kelly, Neil and Declan O'Connor, Sue Obaza and Chris Hawthorne (blog commenters extraordinaire), Julie Koningsor (who brought Indian meals to my two food visits), Tony Wimberley, Isabelle Martimbeau, John Senn, Jessicat, Gareth Holmes, Sarah 'The Fair Surrah' Jane-Gray, Nancy Buckland, Pat Hamm, Linda Saville, Andrew Parsons, Tonya Bowman (who also critiqued chapters), Oliver Reed, Larry Florke, Glenda Hill, Alison George, Ed Lieber, Linda Bentley, Pearl Wilson, Gemma Lee, Emily Robinson, Karen Schwartz, Hannah Sassaman, Grace Avarne, Sandra Byrne, Rachel Baker, Denise Brousseau, Rosemarie Dombrowski, James Halliday, Karin Haems, Michal and Luke Jacobs, Georgina Hale, Katerina Kospanova, Alan Payne, Noelle Moeller, Terry Hackett, Misty Matonis, Barbara McDonald, Lorna Prestage, Pippa Ruesink, Sijia, John Williams, Joshua Friedman, Guida Rufino, Mary Wehring, Gavin Reedman, Donald Clark and Puggles, Zen, Lesley Oakes and her family for their generosity, and Rita Abraham for coming up with the title *Hard Time*.

And as for my blog readers – *Wow!* All along this road I could feel you travelling right beside me in spirit. A huge thank-you for being there and for helping me develop as a writer and a person.

Thank you to Barbara Morgan and Caroline Beddie.

For website work, I'd like to thank Paul Kershaw, Ste Wilkinson, Kathi Drafehn (for Facebook and Schmusen), Stephanie Senn (MySpace), Wm. Srite (shaunattwood.com) and Stephen Jones (presentationstoschools.com).

Further down the road, I needed professional help to get published. I'd like to thank Naomi Colvin for spotting my blog and getting me signed up with my first literary agency. Barbara Taylor (now deceased) was my first agent and provided invaluable feedback. After Barbara died, I didn't know what to do until 'Amazing Grace' won first prize in a competition my mum and Stephen Nash of Prisoners Abroad had entered on my behalf. I won a Koestler Award and ended up on their mentor scheme.

I once read in *The New Yorker* that having a mentor was the final thing a would-be author needed to get published. My mentor, Sally Hinchcliffe, embodied that statement for me. For breathing fire on my prose, this little bird-watching lady was labelled 'Dragon Lady' by my blog readers. After six months with Sally, I found a new agent. Sally volunteered her work and travelled to meet me at the British Library from some obscure region of Scotland where she lives away from people and among the wildlife.

A special thank-you to two wonderful teams who help prisoners: Prisoners Abroad, including Stephen Nash, Pauline Crowe and Matthew Pinches, and the Koestler Trust, including Tim Robertson, Ben Monks, Sarah Matheve, and Joyti Waswani. The Koestler team made such a difference to my life that I've added – among the wordplay in this book – an anagram of 'Koestler'. It's a name, and whoever spots it first can email me at attwood.shaun@hotmail.co.uk for a prize.

There are two people whose help came almost at the end of the road but who really made this book possible. Thanks to my literary agent, Robert Kirby, for taking a chance on me and helping restructure the book, and to Bill Campbell for publishing this unknown prison author. Thanks also to Robert's assistant, Charlotte Knee.

A big thank-you to Tony McLellan and Emma Cole for getting me started talking to schools about drugs and prison, and to Mike Richardson for providing the roof over my head that I'm presently writing under. Thank you to Ian Harry and Sue Scam for taking me clothes shopping when I got out, and Sean 'Hammy' Hamilton for getting me drunk.

I guess I should also thank Sheriff Joe Arpaio for creating such an interesting place to write about, and *las cucarachas* for keeping me company throughout many a lonely night.